Pam Bono Designs & June Tailor Present.....

A Quilter's Life In Patchwork

We make every effort to insure that the content of the book and CD-ROM are correct and understandable.

ISBN: 0-615-11210-2
Manufactured in the United States Of America
First Printing

Editor-In-Chief: Pam Bono
Editorial Assistant: Nikki Potter
Executive Producer of CD-ROM: Calvin Cooke
Video Director: Calvin Cooke
Editors: Patricia Rudelic, Nikki Potter, Gigi Thompson and Karen Quinn
Art Director and Book Design: Pam Bono
Illustrator: Pam Bono
Cover & CD-ROM Design: Pam Bono and Nikki Potter
Senior Photographer: Christopher Marona
Photographer: Robert Bono
Photo Stylists: Pam Bono, Robert Bono and Christopher Marona
Marketing and Distribution Directors: June Tailor
Video classroom demonstrations: Jill Repp of June Tailor
Production Managers: Pam Bono and Calvin Cooke

Where to write to us:
Pam Bono Designs, Inc.
P.O. Box 8247 • Durango, CO 81301
June Tailor
2861 Highway 175 • Richfield, WI 53076

Websites:
http://www.pambonodesigns.com
http://www.junetailor.com

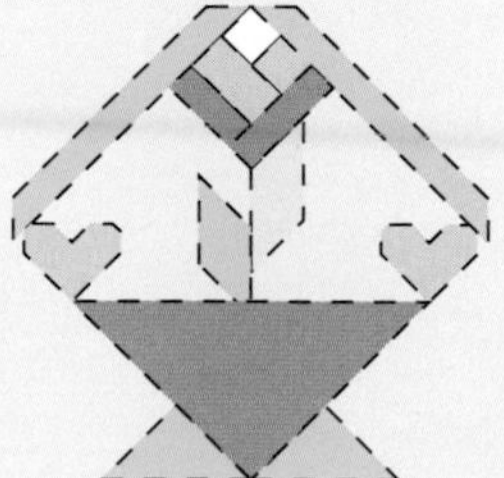

Dedication:

This book is dedicated to our two sons, Dallas and Ryan, and to our daughter-in-law, Cheryl.
To Dallas whose humor and great talent is always an inspiration: Everything good comes to those who don't give up their dreams.
To Ryan and Cheryl: Without your faith in us, and your love, this project would not have been possible. Thank you.

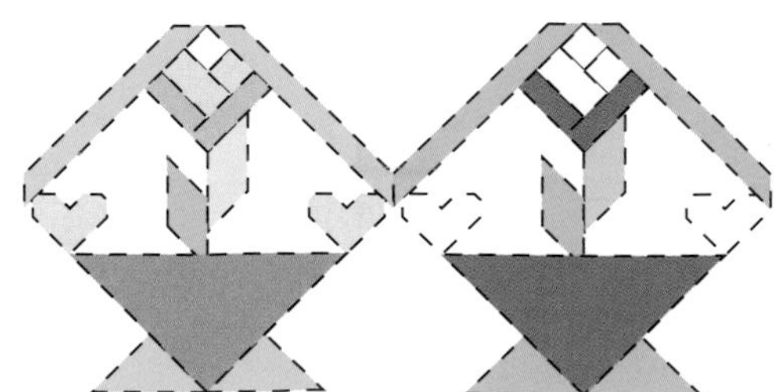

Thanks to.....

Jill Repp and Fran Yogerst at June Tailor for your support and belief in our work, and for being wonderful partners.

Mindy Kettner, our design partner in Canada. What would we do without you!

Calvin Cooke and Josh at Brainstorm Industries for making your part of this project come together on time. And special thanks to Paul at Brainstorm Industries for taking our work and turning it into something special. You are a talented young man.

Faye Gooden for her beautiful quilting, and for caring enough to have everything completed on time for photography.

Special thanks to the owners and staff at Blue Lake Ranch Bed and Breakfast for opening your doors to us for three spectacular days of photography. You have one of the most beautiful places on the face of the earth. Your help was greatly appreciated.

To my brilliant Aussie, quilting friend Patricia Rudelic for editing from "Down Under." The world isn't that big after all.

Suzanne Gamble of Suzanne's Sewing in Durango, CO. Your friendship is never taken for granted, nor is your gorgeous work.

Lisa at Baskin Robbins of Durango for allowing us to shoot in your store, and Joyce at K-Mart of Durango for loaning us a baby crib.

Karen Quinn for allowing us to photograph in your lovely home on top of the world, and Gigi Thompson for work above and beyond the call of duty.

New Home Sewing Machine Company for your wonderful Janome 9000.

Bernina Of America for loaning your great Artista 170.

RJR Fabrics for supplying the beautiful fabrics used in so many of the designs in the book.

P & B Textiles for your supply of lovely fabrics. We have enjoyed using them throughout the book.

Don and Nikki for being here with us. We love you.

Dorothy: I know you were here with me on this one.

Design Credits

1st Day Of School: Mindy Kettner
Bridal Baskets: Pam Bono
Colorado Wedding: Robert Bono
Christmas Colorado Wedding Tablerunner: Robert & Pam Bono
Denim and Daisies: Pam Bono
Don't Fence Me In: Pam Bono and Mindy Kettner
My First Home Quilt: Pam Bono and Mindy Kettner
My First Home Tablecloth: Pam Bono and Mindy Kettner
My First Quilt: Mindy Kettner
My Quilting Friend: Robert Bono
From My Garden Botanical Quilt: Pam Bono
Glorious Morning: Pam Bono
Perennial Pleasures: Pam Bono
Herald Angels: Pam Bono and Mindy Kettner
My Heritage: Pam Bono and Mindy Kettner
Pick Of The Litter: Mindy Kettner
Sherbert: Mindy Kettner and Robert Bono
Snug As A Bug: Pam Bono and Mindy Kettner
Cards, stationery and accessories: Pam Bono

Quilting and Finishing Credits

All quilting by Faye Gooden of All For the Love Of Quilts in Durango, Colorado, with the exception of "Glorious Morning" which was quilted by Julie Tebay of Rochester, Minnesota.
All finishing by: Suzanne's Sewing, Durango, Colorado

Photography Credits

Bridal Baskets, Colorado Wedding Quilt and Tablerunner, Denim & Daisies, My First Home Quilt and Tablecloth, My First Quilt, My Quilting Friend, Glorious Morning, Perennial Pleasures, From My Garden Botanical, Herald Angels Wall Quilt, My Heritage, and Little Quilt by Christopher Marona. Marona Photography, Durango, CO.

All other photography: Robert Bono

Video Filming and Editing

Video filming: Animas Pictures, Durango, Colorado
Editing by: Animas Pictures and Calvin Cooke of Brainstorm Industries, Durango, Colorado.

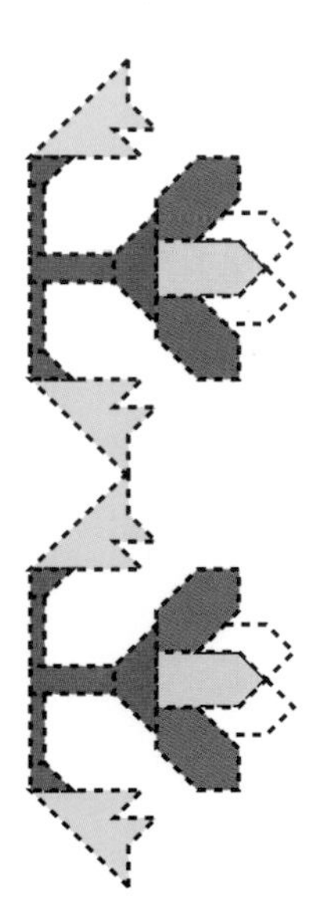

Introduction

Our youngest son, Ryan is a computer expert, and has his own business here in Durango, Colorado. There is not much that Ryan does not know about computers, which prompted a call to me one evening about a year ago.

My husband, Robert and I do the majority of our designing on Macintosh computers, therefore we appreciate and understand their value to the modern world.

Ryan said, "Mom, it's time that you move into the computer generation." Not understanding his meaning, I replied, "I have. You know that we use computers in our work."

Ryan went on to explain that the CD-ROM and software packages have opened up an entire new spectrum to people everywhere, addressing all interests.

We thought about a software package for quilting for several months, realizing that there were wonderful CD-ROM packages available to quilter's, enabling them to design their own quilts. We wanted to do something new and different.

During our participation in several large quilt guild shows, we were able to discuss our ideas with quilter's and get some feedback regarding what they enjoyed the most. Almost every quilter we spoke with said "Oh, don't take away our books! We love our books!"

We had designed a prototype book that was on our computers. We had not done much with it, as no one seemed to understand the concept, nor could they picture the dozens of offshoot projects that accompanied the book designs. It had been frustrating, as we were not

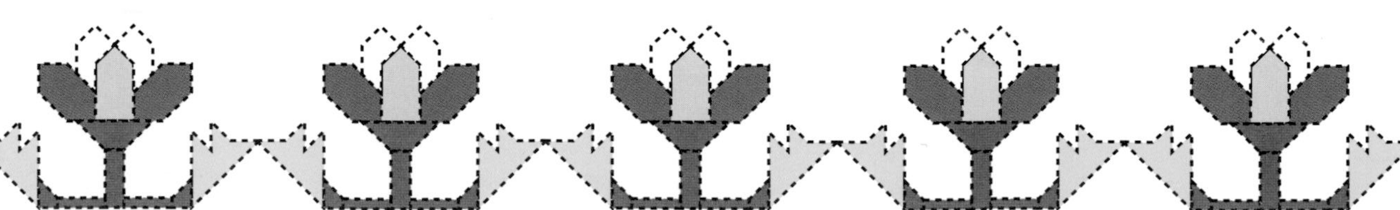

sure how we could give quilter's everywhere the entire package in one book. Now, thanks to Ryan's insight, we have.

While researching our project, I called a friend of mine at June Tailor. I had always felt that they were trendsetters in our industry with their innovative items. For years, Robert and I have used their products constantly. During my discussion with my friend, she introduced me to their new, Colorfast Printer Fabric™ Sheets, which I received the next day. The sample sheets of their incredible fabric opened the door for us to not only bring our book to life, but to expand it into accessory items that everyone who loves quilts could enjoy; even if they do not quilt!

We hope that you will carefully review the "How To Use This Book and CD-ROM" sections, as all of the projects on the CD-ROM coordinate with the book designs.

As we are aware, fabric selection is sometimes difficult for quilter's. Therefore,we have included a special "Color Picker" section in our CD-ROM. Alternate color selections are given for six of the quilts in the book, along with a color selector that gives you the opportunity to choose your own color scheme.

We want quilter's (as well as non quilter's) everywhere to know that this book and CD-ROM come from the heart. They come from a project that we refused to give up on, because we believed in it. May it bring you countless hours of pleasure, as it brought us in preparing it for you.

Happy Quilting!

Pam and Robert Bono

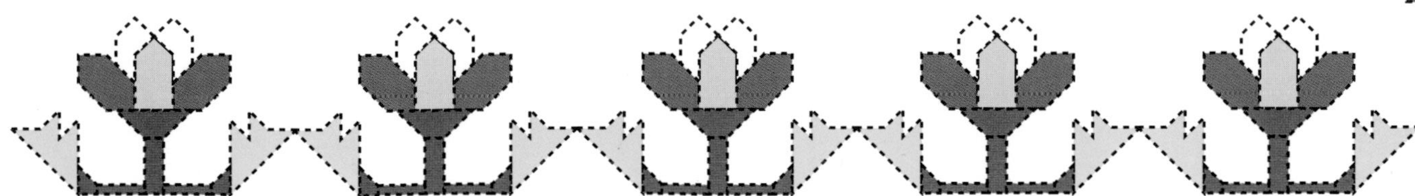

Table Of Contents.....

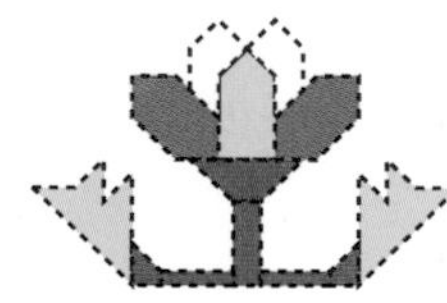

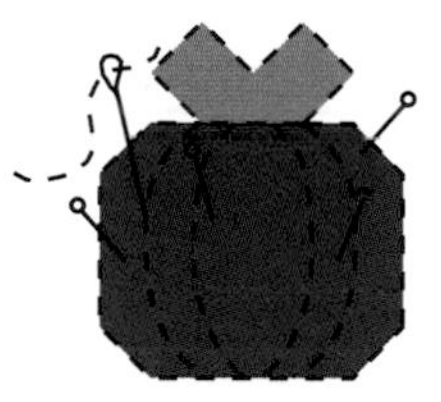

june tailor
RICHFIELD, WISCONSIN

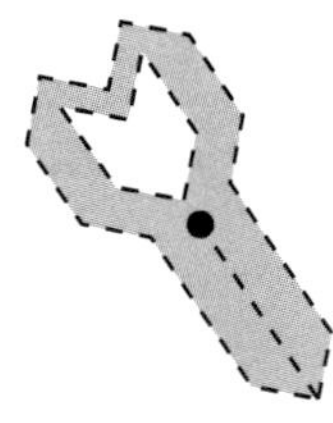

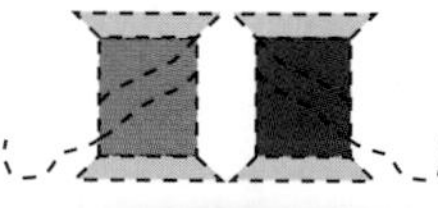

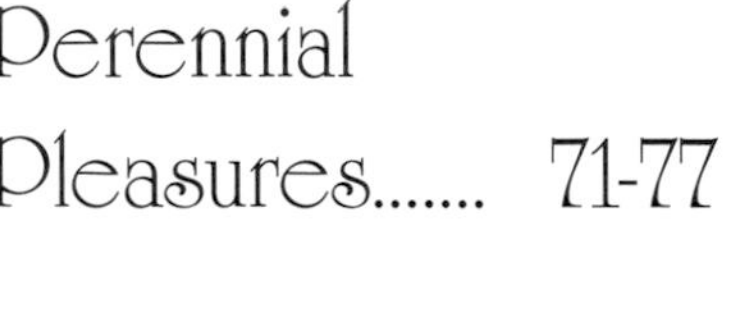
Cheryl Is In

School
MEGAN
9-6-00

The techniques that are shown on the next three pages are used throughout projects in the book and on the CD-ROM in the "S'Mores" section. You may refer to the techniques shown here and also view our classroom demonstrations on the CD-ROM.

STRIP PIECING

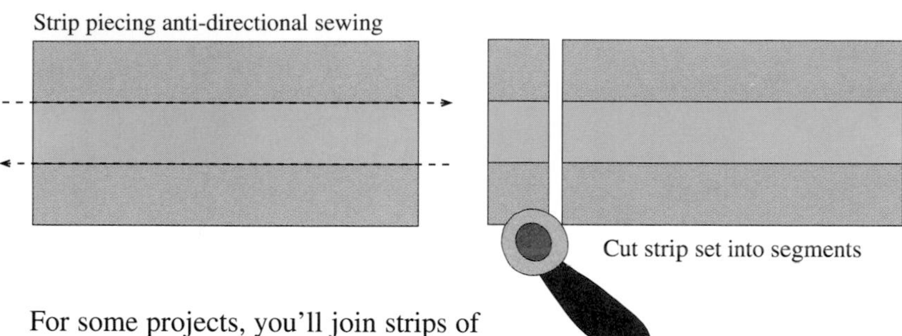

For some projects, you'll join strips of different fabrics to make what is called a Strip Set. Project directions not only show illustrations of each strip set, but specify how many strip sets to make, how many segments are to be cut from each strip set, and the specific size of each segment. To sew a strip set, match each pair of strips with right sides facing. Stitch through both layers along one long edge. When sewing multiple strips in a set, practice "anti-directional" stitching to keep strips straight. As you add strips, sew each new seam in the *opposite* direction from the last one. This distributes tension evenly in both directions, and keeps the strip set from getting warped and wobbly.

DIAGONAL CORNERS

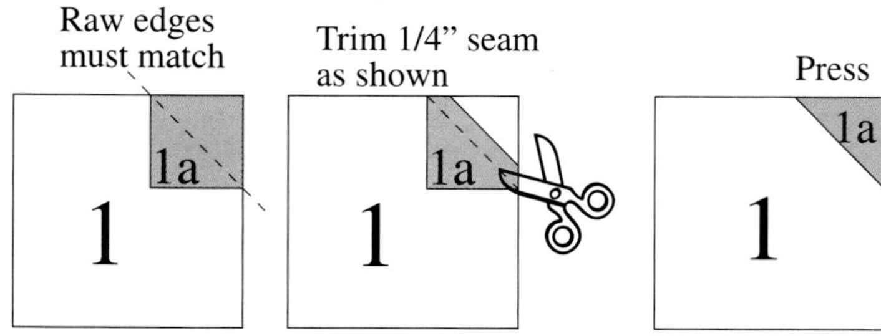

This technique turns squares into sewn triangles. It is especially helpful if the corner triangle is very small, because it's easier to cut and handle a square than a small triangle.

By sewing squares to squares, you don't have to guess where seam allowances meet, which can be difficult with triangles.

Project instructions give the size of the fabric pieces needed. These sizes given in the cutting instructions *include* seam allowance.

The base fabric is either a square or rectangle, but the contrasting corner is always a square.

1. To make a diagonal corner, with right sides facing, match the small square to one corner of the base fabric. It is important that raw edges match perfectly and do not shift.

2. As a seam guide, you may wish to draw or press a diagonal line from corner to corner. For a quick solution to this tedious technique, refer to our instructions on the following pages for The Angler 2™.

3. Stitch the small square diagonally from corner to corner. Trim seam allowance as shown on the diagonal corner square only, leaving the base fabric untrimmed for stability. Press the diagonal corner square over as shown.

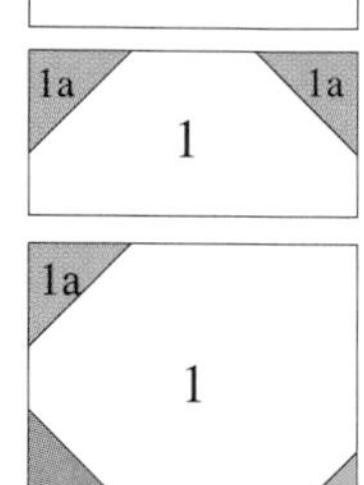

4. Many units in the projects have multiple diagonal corners or ends. When these are the same size, and cut from the same fabric, the identifying letter is the same. But, if the unit has multiple diagonal pieces that are different in size and/or color, the letters are different. These pieces are joined to the main unit in alphabetical order.

5. Many of our projects utilize diagonal corners on diagonal corners as shown above. In this case, diagonal corners are added in alphabetical order. Join first diagonal corner, trim and press out; then add second diagonal corner, trimming and pressing as shown.

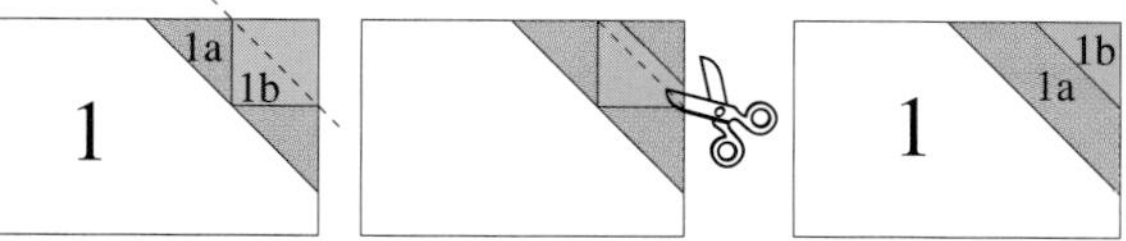

Diagonal corners on diagonal Corners - Join corners in alphabetical order.

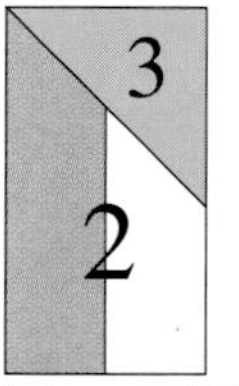

Diagonal Corner on combined, joined units.

6. Our designs also utilize diagonal corners on joined units such as strip sets. In this case the joined unit will have one unit number in the center of the unit as shown at left, with the diagonal corner illustrated with its own unit number.

DIAGONAL ENDS

1. This method joins two rectangles on the diagonal and eliminates the difficulty of measuring and cutting a trapezoid. It is similar to the diagonal corner technqiue, but here you work with two rectangles. Our project instructions specify the size of each rectangle.

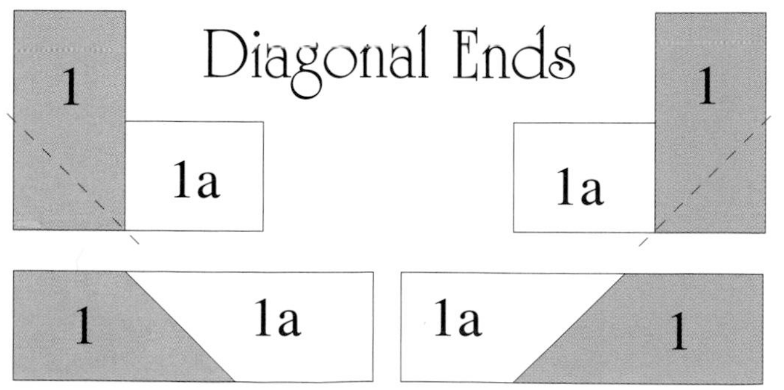

Diagonal End - Left Slant Diagonal End - Right Slant

2. To sew diagonal ends, place rectangles perpendicular to each other with right sides facing, matching corners to be sewn.
3. Before you sew, mark or press the stitching line, and check the right side to see if the line is angled in the desired direction.
4. Position the rectangles under the needle, leading with the top edge. Sew a diagonal seam to the opposite edge.
5. Check the right side to see that the seam is angled correctly. Then press the seam and trim excess fabric from the seam allowance.
6. As noted in Step 2, the direction of the seam makes a difference. Make mirror-image units with this in mind, or you can put different ends on the same strip. This technique is wonderful for making continuous binding strips. Please note on illustration below, diagonal ends are made first; then diagonal corners may be added in alphabetical order.
7. Refer to Step 6 in *Diagonal Corner Section.* Diagonal ends may be added to joined units in the same manner as shown below.

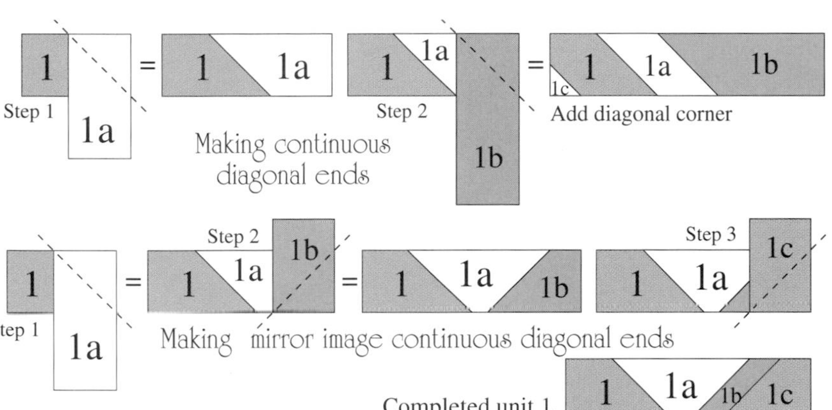

Making mirror image combined unit diagonal ends.

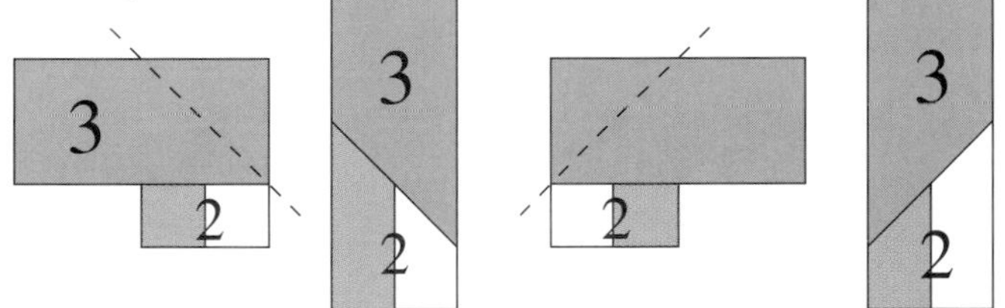

HALF SQUARE TRIANGLES

1. Many patchwork designs are made by joining two contrasting triangles to make a square. Many people use the grid method when dozens of triangles are required in a design. For the designs in this book, we use a simple method to make two or more half square triangles. To do so, draw or press a diagonal line from corner to corner on the back of the lightest colored square. Stitch 1/4" on opposite sides of drawn line. Cut squares apart on drawn line as shown. One such sewn square yields two half square triangles.
2. Press the squares open and trim off the points. As an extra tip, we have found that spraying the fabric with spray starch before cutting the squares to be used keeps them from distorting.
3. Mindy developed a quick little trick for making one half square triangle which we use frequently. A bit more fabric may be used, however it is quick and easy. In this case, draw a line diagonally down

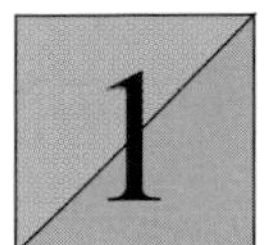

Half Square Triangles

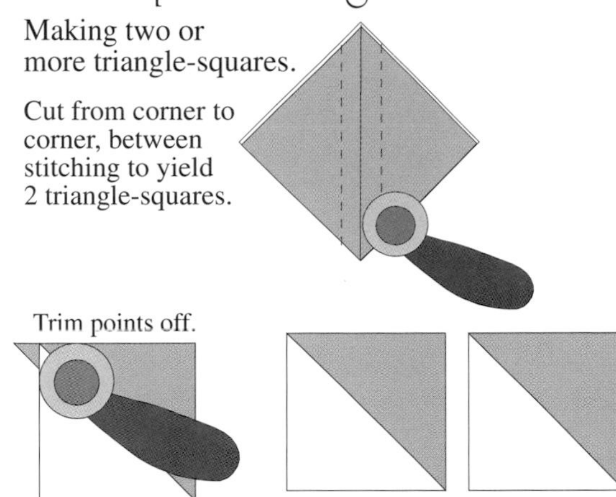

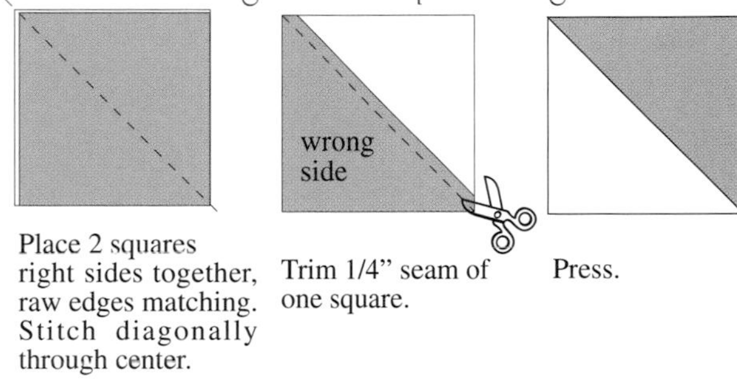

Place 2 squares right sides together, raw edges matching. Stitch diagonally through center.

Trim 1/4" seam of one square.

Press.

the center of the lightest fabric and stitch on the line. Trim the seam as shown and press.

4. The small illustration shows how half square triangle units are marked in the book. A diagonal line is always shown, separating two fabric colors, with the unit number in the center of the diagonal line as shown.

MAKING STRAIGHT-GRAIN FRENCH-FOLD BINDING

1. Each project specifies the number of cross-grain strips to cut for binding. To join two strips end to end, match the ends perpendicular as for Diagonal Ends, Step 2. Join strips end to end in this manner to make one continuous strip that is the length specified in our project instructions.
2. These instructions are for French-Fold straight-grain binding. Doubled binding is stronger than one layer, so it better protects the edges, where a quilt suffers the most wear. We like French-Fold binding because it is easier to make than bias binding, and it requires less fabric.
3. After joining strips, press seam allowances to 1/4", and press them open. Press the binding in half, along the length of the strip.
4. Follow the illustrations on the next page, and begin by aligning and positioning the binding on the front of the quilt top, in the middle of any side. Leave 3" of binding free before the point where you begin.
5. Stitch through all layers with 1/4" seam. Stop stitching 1/4" from the quilt corner and backstitch. (Placing a pin at the 1/4" point beforehand will show you where to stop.) Remove the quilt from the machine.

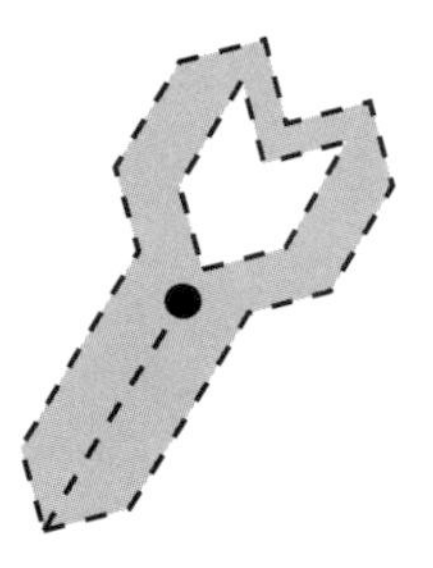

from the corner, and make a 45° angle fold.

7. Bring the binding straight down in line with the next edge, leaving the top fold even with the raw edge of the previously sewn side. Begin stitching at the top edge, sewing through all layers. Stitch all corners in this manner.

8. Stop stitching as you approach the beginning point. Fold the 3" tail of binding over on itself and pin. The end of the binding will overlap this folded section. Continue stitching through all layers to 1" beyond the folded tail. Trim any extra binding.

9. Trim the batting and backing nearly even with the seam allowance, leaving a little extra to fill out the binding.

10. Fold the binding over the seam allowance to the back. When turned, the beginning fold conceals the raw end of the binding.

11. Blind stitch the folded edge of the binding to the backing fabric. Fold a miter into the binding at back corners.

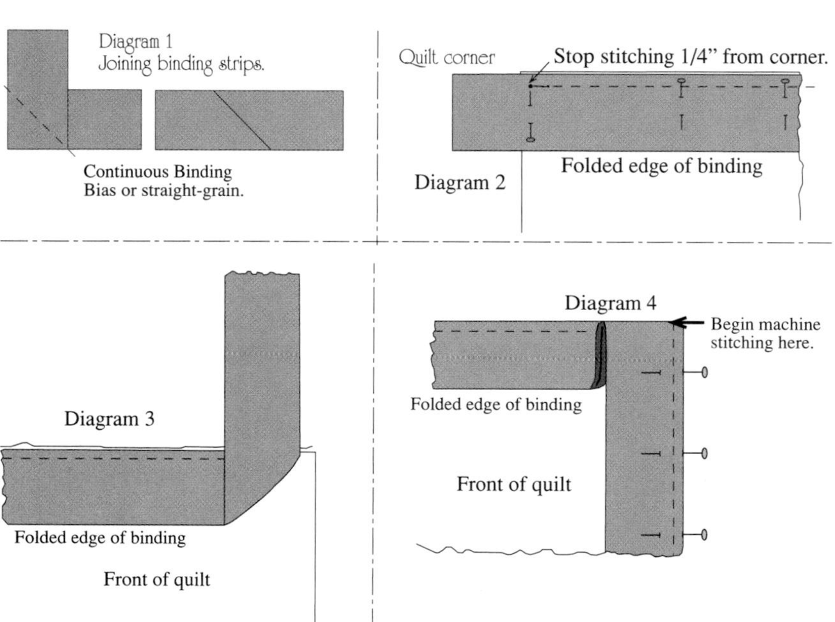

Robert invented the first Angler between our first and second books for Oxmoor House. He watched me drawing diagonal line seam guides that took forever! I recall him saying "There has got to be a better way!" He found a better way. This little tool is now used by millions of quilter's all over the world with results that cut piecing time in half. The instructions are included below for the new upgrade. It may be purchased in fabric and quilt shops everywhere.

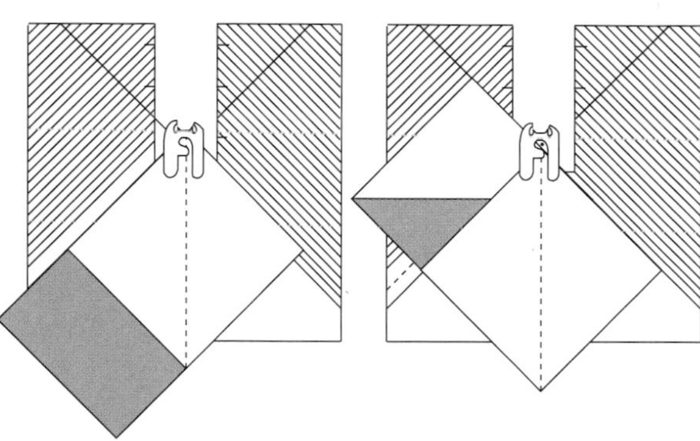

DIAGONAL CORNERS AND FLYING GEESE

1. Align diagonal corners with raw edges matching. Line fabric up so that right side of square is aligned with first 45° line on right as shown, with the tip of the fabric under needle. No seam guide lines will need to be drawn unless the square is larger than 7 3/4". As feed dogs pull fabric through machine, keep fabric aligned with the diagonal lines on the right until center line of "Angler 2™" bottom is visible.

2. Keep the tip of the square on this line as the diagonal corner is fed through the machine. Trim seam as shown and press.

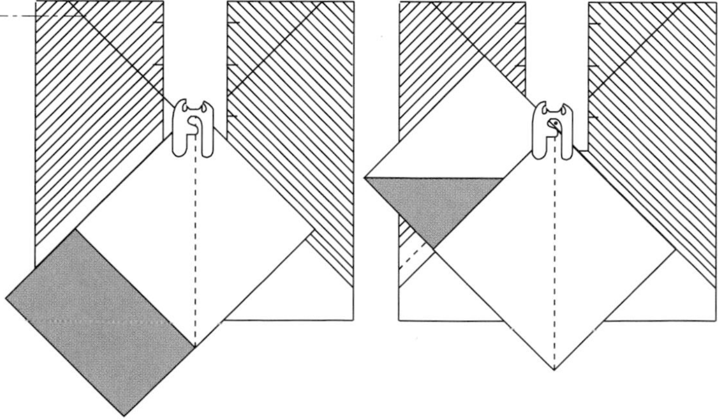

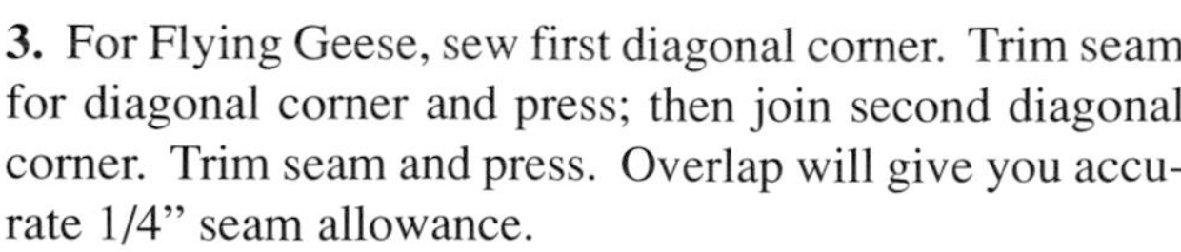

3. For Flying Geese, sew first diagonal corner. Trim seam for diagonal corner and press; then join second diagonal corner. Trim seam and press. Overlap will give you accurate 1/4" seam allowance.

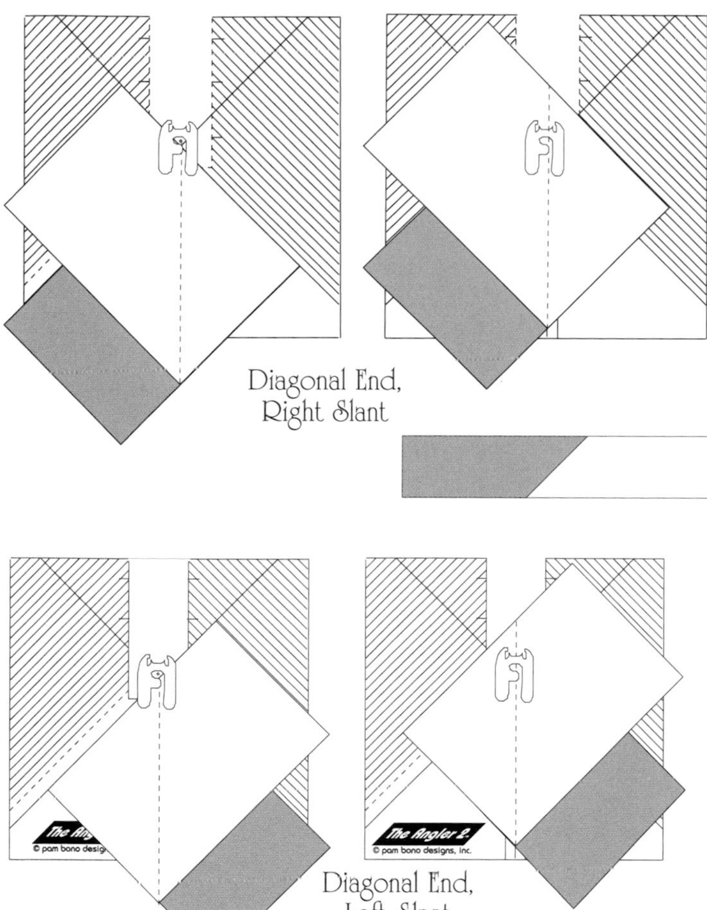

Diagonal End, Right Slant

Diagonal End, Left Slant

DIAGONAL END RIGHT AND LEFT SLANTS

1. For both slants, prepare rectangles with raw edges matching. For right slant, align top rectangle with first 45° line on right side of "Angler 2™."

2. Bottom rectangle should align on first 45° left line as shown. As feed dogs pull fabric through machine, keep fabric aligned with the diagonal lines on the right until center line on "Angler 2™" bottom is visible. Keep the top of the rectangle on this line as it is fed through the machine. Trim seam and press.

3. For left slant, line top rectangle up with first 45° line on left side of "Angler 2™" as shown. As rectangles are fed through machine, keep top rectangle aligned with left diagonal lines on "Angler 2™" until center bottom line is visible. **THIS TECHNIQUE IS GREAT FOR JOINING BINDING STRIPS!

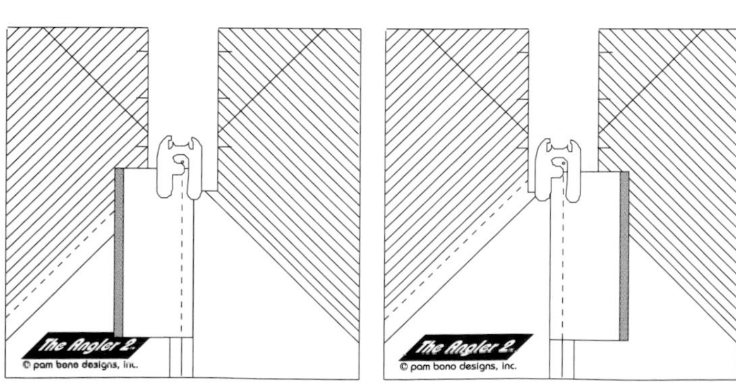

Accurate 1/4" Seams

ACCURATE 1/4" SEAMS

1. Referring to illustration of 1/4" seam line, note that fabric is lined up on 1/4" seam line, and that stitching is along center guide line. To take a full 1/4" seam, line fabric up on 1/4" seam line as shown. If you want a "scant" 1/4" seam, line fabric up so that the seam guide line shows.

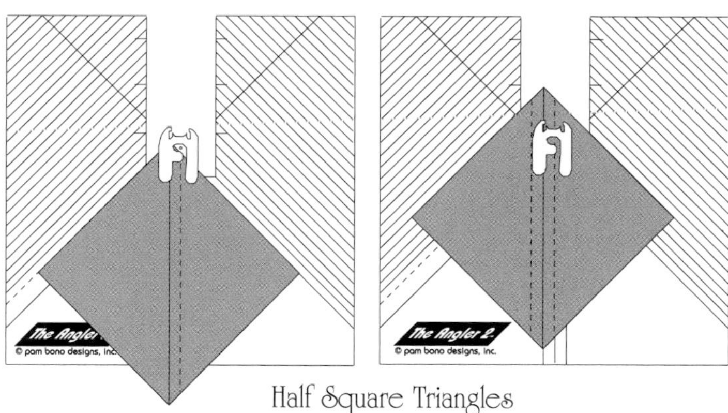

Half Square Triangles

HALF SQUARE TRIANGLES

1. For half square triangles, prepare squares with right sides together and raw edges matching. Line up the right side of the squares on line one on the right side of "Angler 2™" as shown. Left side of square needs to be aligned with *dashed* diagonal line on "Angler 2™."

2. As feed dogs pull square through machine, keep top part of square aligned with the diagonal lines on the "Angler 2™" until left seam line is visible as shown.

3. Keep point on this line until seam is sewn. Turn square around and repeat for other seam. Seams will be 1/4" from center as shown. Cut half square triangles apart on center line. Trim off tips and press.

For a complete tutorial of patchwork and quilting basics, please refer to the following books:
"Quick Rotary Cutter Quilts"
Pam Bono Designs - Oxmoor House
"More Quick Rotary Cutter Quilts"
Pam Bono Designs - Oxmoor House

USING THE BOOK AND CD-ROM TOGETHER

The book and CD-ROM are designed to work in conjunction with one another. The "S'Mores" section of the CD-ROM is a collection of additional accessories that coordinate with the book projects. To open each feature, simply click on the icon with your mouse, thus opening that particular section for you to enjoy and make further choices for additional or complimentary projects. Each "S'More" project may be printed out for your convenience. The icon below is a good example, as the "S'More" section for "Bridal Basket" offers a ring bearer's pillow and a lovely tablerunner.

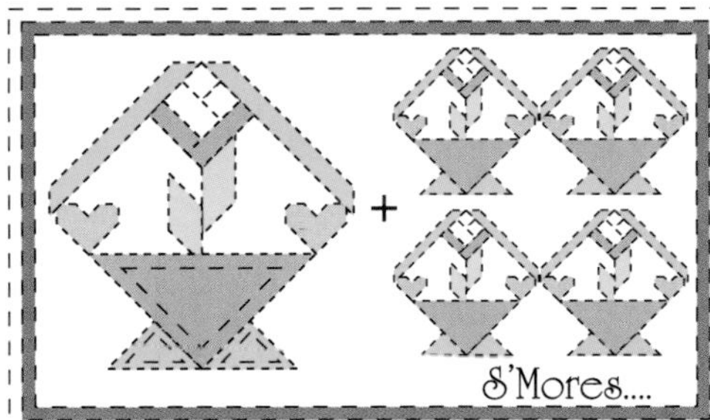

A "color picker" is in place on your CD-ROM to help you personalize your color choices for six of the quilt designs in our book. Each design offers three alternate color schemes for that particular motif. A page showing the outline illustration of the quilt you select, gives you the creative freedom to fill in your own colors. Your color selections may then be printed out to take along to the fabric store of your choice to select your fabrics. Below is an example of the "Color Picker" icon.

Interactive Color Change Board

A special video "classroom" is included, with demonstrations for the techniques used throughout our book and CD-ROM. The icon for this section is shown below.

This icon will appear on the first page of each project in the book. The icon will have a graphic pertaining to that particular design motif. The video demonstrations that apply to the techniques used within the project will be listed next to the icon. These demonstrations may be easily accessed by clicking on the icon. A list of the videos will then appear for you to view. Select your choice and enter your personal classroom.

Click on this icon to access coordinating stationery, cards, gift tags, envelope decorations, and quilt labels that you can not only personalize, but that you can make into fabric letters.

Washable

Colorfast Printer Fabric™ Sheets

Instructions For Use With Color Inkjet Copier Or Printer

- *COPYING ON A COLOR INKJET COPIER:*
  1) Load one sheet of ***Colorfast Printer Fabric***™ into paper tray so copying occurs on fabric side of sheet.
  2) Place photos, graphics or text into copier and copy.
- *PRINTING WITH A COLOR INKJET PRINTER:*
  1) Use one of our stationery, card, gift tag, quilt label, or envelope decorations on your computer screen.
  2) Load one sheet of ***Colorfast Printer Fabric***™ *into paper tray. Print on fabric side of sheet.*
- *AFTER COPYING OR PRINTING:*
  1) Remove back from fabric and allow ink to dry.
- *COLORFAST TREATMENT:*
  1) Rinse gently in cold water. Do not wring. Lay flat to dry.
- *LAUNDERING:*
  1) **Do not use detergent.**
  2) ***Colorfast Printer Fabric***™ can be washed by hand or machine in cold water. If machine washing, use gentle cycle. ***Remove promptly.*** Lay flat to dry.
  3) If soiled, add liquid fabric softener to cold water wash. Lay flat to dry.

To purchase extra Colorfast Printer Fabric™ Sheets, contact us at: http://www.pambonodesigns.com.

Instructions For Use With Our Stationery, Cards & Labels

1. Print cards, gift tags, stationery, quilt labels and envelope decorations on your inkjet printer or copier using June Tailor ***Colorfast Printer Fabric***™ Sheets. These gift items may be personalized by following our instructions for personalizing your projects on our CD-ROM. After printing, peal away the plastic film sheet on the back side of the fabric,and follow the instuctions above for colorfast treatment.
2. Cut a large enough piece of Steam-A-Seam 2® to cover the back of the project you are making. Steam-A-Seam 2® must be used with a hot steam iron for best results. This is a wonderful product for bonding fabric together for this type of project, as it adds body.
3. Remove paper from one side of the Steam-A-Seam 2®. Place the sticky side of the Steam-A-Seam 2® on the back side of the project. Press in place, keeping iron on the Steam-A-Seam 2® for 10 seconds. Move iron to any other place that has not been pressed so that all of the Steam-A-Seam 2® is pressed in place. Remove the remaining paper. **To keep the Steam-A-Seam 2® from possibly sticking to your iron, use a press cloth.*
4. Cut out your project. We suggest cutting card fronts with a pinking shears for a cute effect. Card stock may be purchased at most print shops or office supply stores. Some come packaged with envelopes.
5. For the 5" x 7" cards, use a 7" x 10" piece of card stock. Lightly draw a line 5" up from short end of card (which will be in the center). Use an X-acto knife and ***gently*** score the card to make folding it in half easier. Fold the card in half.
6. Place the card front (with Steam-A-Seam 2® pressed on back) on top of card stock front. Press in place with a steam iron.
7. Gift tags are designed to fit a 2" x 3" piece of card stock. Personalize your gift tag before printing. Press gift tags in place on card stock. Punch a hole in top left hand corner. Cut off a 9" piece of thin gold cord. Form a loop in the center and push loop through the punched hole. Pull ends of cord through loop and tie raw ends in a knot.
8. Our envelope designs may be pressed onto the front of any envelope using Steam-A-Seam 2®. Try to position them in the bottom left corner so as not to interfere with address.
9. Personalize all quilt labels with name and date. Follow instructions for using Steam-A-Seam 2® and press quilt labels on quilt back in bottom corner.
10. It's fun to write a "fabric letter". Use our stationery designs for your letters. Print on ***Colorfast Printer Fabric***™ ***Sheets.*** Trim excess fabric to stationery outer lines. You may use June Tailor Fray Block™ around outer edges before folding for mailing.

Using Our Instructions....

The following points explain how the instructions in our book, and on our CD-ROM "S'More" section are orgainzed. You'll find all projects are made easier if you **read this section thoroughly** and follow each tip.

* At the beginning of each project, techniques used are shown with the video icon. Click your mouse and view them before beginning, or refer to them on pages 8-11.

* The materials list provides you with yardage requirements for the project. We have included the exact number of inches needed to make the project, with yardages given to the nearest 1/8 yard. By doing this, we are giving you the option to purchase extra yardage if you feel that you may need more.

* A color key accompanies each materials list, matching each fabric with the color-coded illustrations given with the project directions.

* Cutting instructions are given for each fabric, the first cut, indicated by an •, is usually a specified number of crossgrain strips.

* Second cuts, indicated by a *, specify how to cut those strips into smaller pieces. The identification of each piece follows in parenthesis, consisting of the block letter and unit number that correspond to the assembly diagrams. For pieces used in more than one unit, several unit numbers may be given.

* Organize all cut pieces in zip-top bags and label each bag with the appropriate unit numbers. This avoids confusion and keeps a lot of pieces stored safely until they're needed.

*** In order to conserve fabric, we have carefully calculated the number of units that can be cut from specified strips. In doing this, units may be cut in two or three different places from a variety of strips. So that cut units may be organized efficiently, the units that appear in more than one strip are shown in red on the cutting list. This immediately tells you that there will be more of that specific unit. Additional cuts are not only show in red, but the words "add to" are shown within the parenthesis so that you may keep that zip top bag open, knowing in advance that there will be more units to add.**

* Large pieces such as sashings and borders are generally cut first to be sure you have enough fabric.

* To reduce further waste of fabric, you may be instructed to cut some pieces from a first-cut strip, and then cut that strip down to a narrower width to cut additional pieces.

* Cutting instructions are given for the whole quilt as shown. If you want to make just one block, see information under "Making One Block."

* Cutting and piecing instructions are given in a logical step-by-step progression. Follow this order in all cases to avoid confusion.

* Every project has one or more block designs. Instructions include block illustrations that show the fabric colors and the numbered units.

* Individual units are assembled first, use one or more of the quick-piecing techniques described on pages 8-11 and shown on our CD-ROM video section.

* Strip-set illustrations show the size of the segments to be cut from that strip set. The illustrations also designate how many strip sets are to be made. The strip set segments are then labeled as units as shown in the block illustrations. Keep strip set segments in a labeled zip-top bag as for other units.

* Assembly diagrams are given for each block and an exact description of how to assemble the block is written. Follow the instructions to join units in the proper sequence. Some blocks are further divided into sections, which are joined according to instructions.

* Each unit in the assembly diagrams are numbered. The main part of the unit is indicated with a number only. A diagonal line represents a seam where a diagonal corner or end is attached. Each diagonal piece is numbered with the main unit number plus a letter (such as 1a).

* Some units have multiple diagonal corners or ends. When these are the same size and are cut from the same fabric, the identifying letter is the same. But if the unit has multiple diagonal pieces (as many do), that are different in size and/or color, the letters are different. These pieces are joined to the main unit in alphabetical order.

* Half square triangles are shown as assembled, with the unit number in the center of the square.

* Practice the techniques used in the book and CD-ROM with scraps before beginning the project. Refer to assembly diagrams frequently, following the unit identification system carefully. Organizing your work as suggested will save time and avoid confusion.

* Many extra illustrations are given throughout the projects for assembly of unusual or multiple units for your convenience.

* Piecing instructions are given for making one block. Make the number of blocks stated in the project instructions to complete the project as shown.

* A diary page is provided for you after the main book projects. Record your projects on these special pages and keep the book as a diary to be passed through your family.

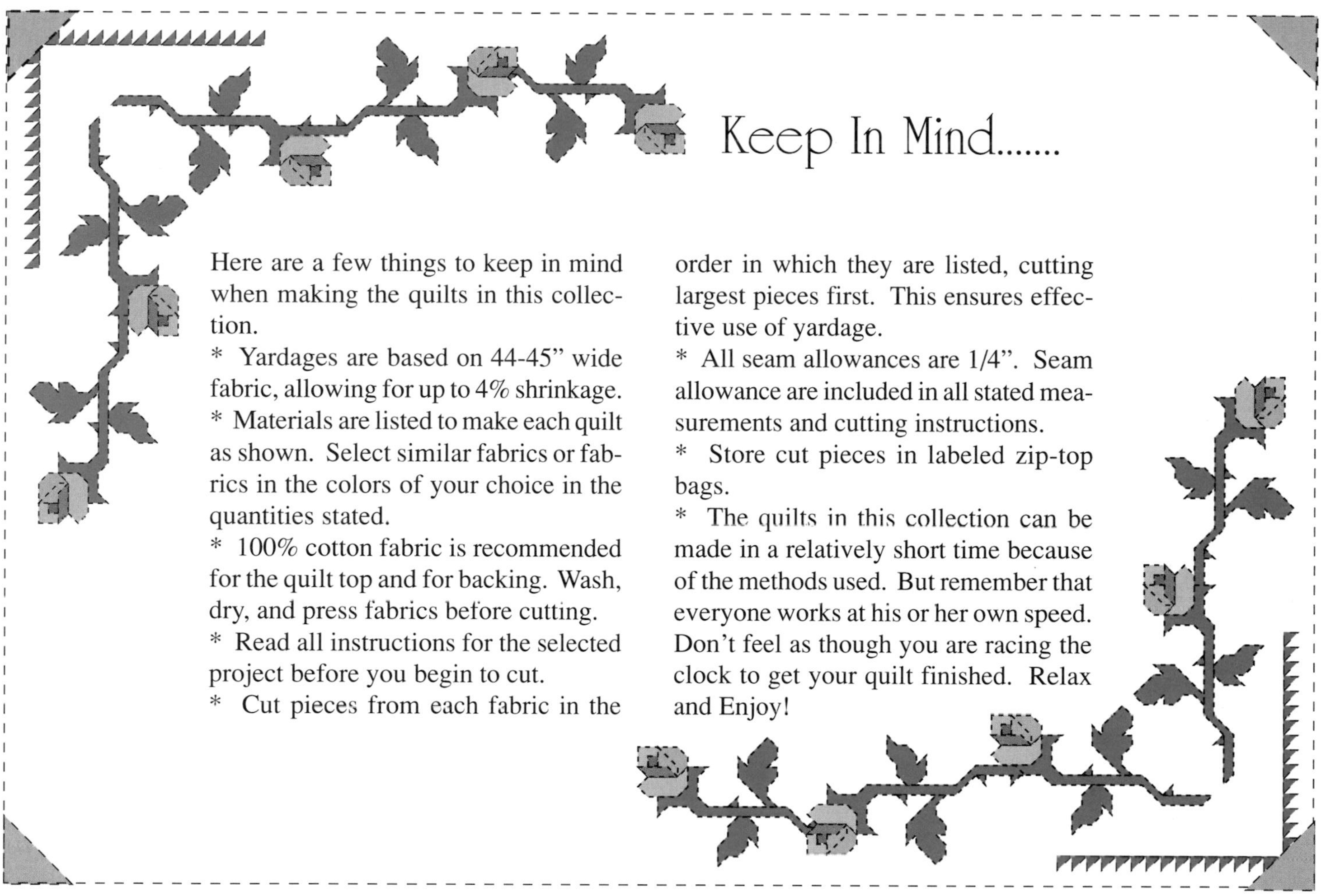

Keep In Mind.......

Here are a few things to keep in mind when making the quilts in this collection.

* Yardages are based on 44-45" wide fabric, allowing for up to 4% shrinkage.
* Materials are listed to make each quilt as shown. Select similar fabrics or fabrics in the colors of your choice in the quantities stated.
* 100% cotton fabric is recommended for the quilt top and for backing. Wash, dry, and press fabrics before cutting.
* Read all instructions for the selected project before you begin to cut.
* Cut pieces from each fabric in the order in which they are listed, cutting largest pieces first. This ensures effective use of yardage.
* All seam allowances are 1/4". Seam allowance are included in all stated measurements and cutting instructions.
* Store cut pieces in labeled zip-top bags.
* The quilts in this collection can be made in a relatively short time because of the methods used. But remember that everyone works at his or her own speed. Don't feel as though you are racing the clock to get your quilt finished. Relax and Enjoy!

How To Make One Block

Cutting instructions are given for making the quilt as shown. But there may be times that you want to make just one block for a project of your own design.

All you have to do is count. Or divide, if preferred.

With each cutting list is an illustration for the block(s). Unit numbers in the cutting list correspond to the units in the illustrations. Count how many of each unit are in the block illustration. Instead of cutting the number shown in the cutting list, cut the number you need for one block.

Should you wish to make two or more blocks, multiply the number of units X the number of blocks you wish to make.

If you prefer, you can figure it out just from the cutting list. If the quilt shown has twenty blocks, for example, then divide each quantity by twenty to determine how many pieces are needed for one block.

Robert's Checklist Of Supplies To Make the Job Quick and Easy!

* Rotary Cutter. There are several different rotary cutters on the market. They are available in different shapes and sizes. Choose the one that is the most comfortable in your hand, remembering that the larger the blade, the longer it will last.

* Replacement Cutter Blades. Be sure to get the blade that matches your cutter.

* Cutting Mat. The size of the mat is based (of course), on the size of your cutting area. I use the 23" x 35" June Tailor Cutting Mat. I also use June Tailor's "Cut 'N Press Plus™ as I can use one side to cut strip set segments, and the other side to press during the sewing process.

* Acrylic Ruler. I use several sizes. My favorites are an 8" x 24", a 6" x 18", and the most used is my 3 1/2" x 12".

* Sewing Thread. Use a good quality thread.

* Seam Ripper. We all use them frequently - no matter how good we think we are!

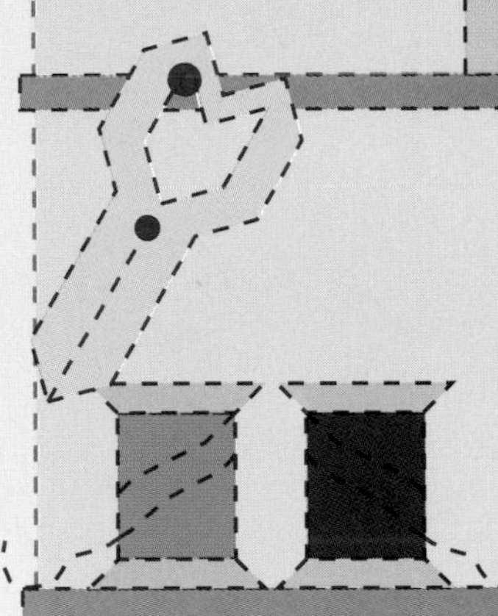

* Pins and Pincushion. We especially like the long, thin, fine pins for quilting.

* Scissors. Here again, I use two or three different sizes to do different jobs.

* The Angler 2™. Once you have used it, you wonder how you got along without it!

* Iron and Ironing Board. June Tailor, in my opinion makes the best ironing board covers as they are ruled so that blocks may be adjusted a bit during the pressing process.

* Zip-top plastic bags to store cut pieces, and masking tape to label them.

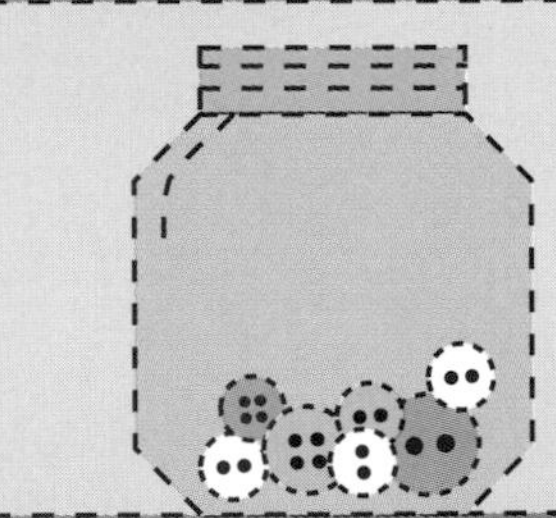

* Marking Pens. I keep water erasable pens handy for marking quilt designs, and also fine tipped felt fabric marking pens.

* Quilting needles for hand quilting.

* Quilting thread.

* Thimbles.

* Quilting hoop and frame.

* Walking Foot (for machine quilting).

* Bicycle Clips (for machine quilting).

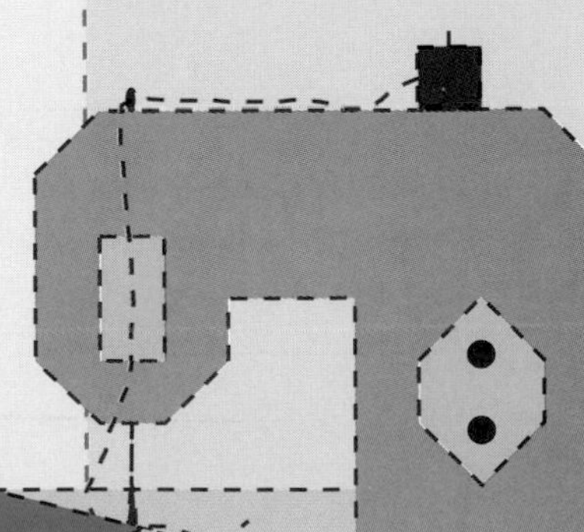

"S'Mores" On Our CD-ROM.

Bonus Stationery Design

My First Quilt

QUILT TOP EXPRESS™

Making Diagonal Corners

Using The Grid Marker

Video Demonstration
Take 1

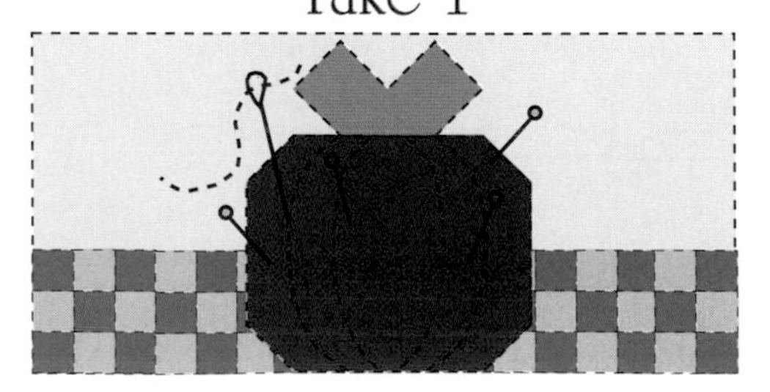

Quilt finished size: 77 3/4" x 100 1/4"
Sewing maching Block A: 22 1/2" square
Blocks B, C, E, and F: 11 1/4" square
Scissors Block D: 7 1/2" x 15"
Checkerboard blocks G, H and I: 11 1/4" square

Materials

All QUILT TOP EXPRESS instructions and yardages are shown in red.

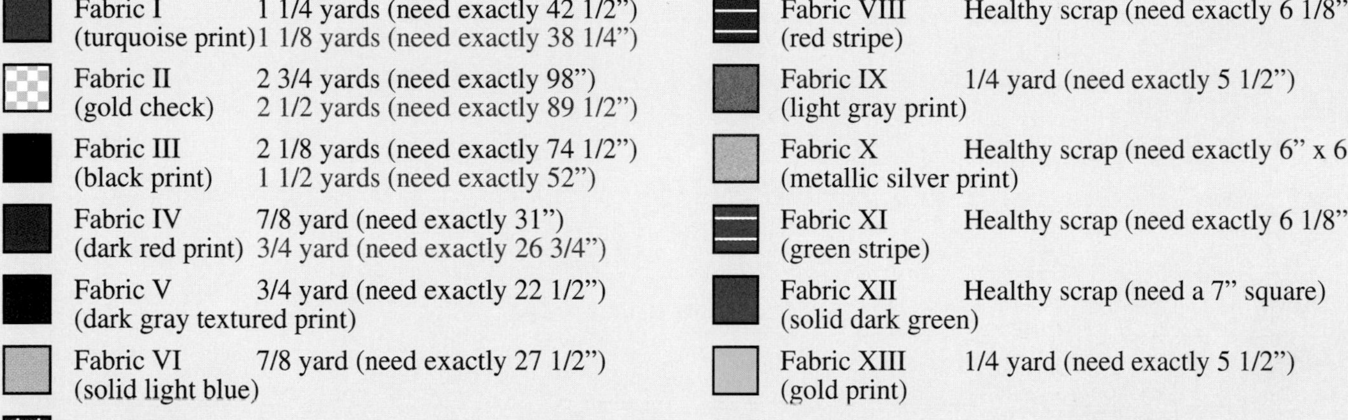

Fabric I (turquoise print)	1 1/4 yards (need exactly 42 1/2") 1 1/8 yards (need exactly 38 1/4")
Fabric II (gold check)	2 3/4 yards (need exactly 98") 2 1/2 yards (need exactly 89 1/2")
Fabric III (black print)	2 1/8 yards (need exactly 74 1/2") 1 1/2 yards (need exactly 52")
Fabric IV (dark red print)	7/8 yard (need exactly 31") 3/4 yard (need exactly 26 3/4")
Fabric V (dark gray textured print)	3/4 yard (need exactly 22 1/2")
Fabric VI (solid light blue)	7/8 yard (need exactly 27 1/2")
Fabric VII (bright red print)	Healthy scrap (need exactly 8" x 19")
Fabric VIII (red stripe)	Healthy scrap (need exactly 6 1/8" x 8")
Fabric IX (light gray print)	1/4 yard (need exactly 5 1/2")
Fabric X (metallic silver print)	Healthy scrap (need exactly 6" x 6 1/2")
Fabric XI (green stripe)	Healthy scrap (need exactly 6 1/8" x 10")
Fabric XII (solid dark green)	Healthy scrap (need a 7" square)
Fabric XIII (gold print)	1/4 yard (need exactly 5 1/2")
Backing:	6 yards
QUILT TOP EXPRESS™	2 packages

On A Personal Note:

I believe that everyone has special memories about their first quilt. Our diary page is provided for you to record yours. Somehow, that first quilt just does not seem "good enough" in comparison to those that follow with gained experience. However, it is a wonderful triumph regardless, and something special that gives us a true sense of accomplishment.

I have never recorded my thoughts regarding my first quilt, which was a baby quilt, but there IS a certain quilt that will always stand out from all of the rest, as it is filled with memories of an experience that Robert and I will not forget. My third quilt, but my first full-sized one, was designed for our son, Dallas' bed. It was never used for his bed, however. I thought it would be fun and appropriate to share our experience with fellow quilter's.

The quilt was designed in 1977, and was called "Transportation Quilt". Dallas loved garbage trucks and there were few designs available at that time for boys. Therefore, I just had to include a garbage truck in the 20 transportation blocks. The quilt took me FOREVER to complete, or so it seemed.

We were attempting to build our business, and had little money to spare. About this time, we had written to Better Homes & Gardens requesting an appointment. A few months after the Transportation Quilt was completed, along with several other new designs, we received a call from Better Homes & Gardens. They wanted to review our work. We were ecstatic!

We were packing for our trip to Des Moines, and the Transportation Quilt was folded in a corner, awaiting Dallas' new bed. Robert asked, "You are going to take the Transportation Quilt aren't you?" My reply: "Robert, that quilt took forever! No one in their right mind would want to make it!" He insisted that the quilt be included in our repertoire. At the last minute, in a rush, the quilt was added to the "quilt trunk".

When we reached Des Moines and unpacked, the quilts were brought into the hotel room first! Going back to the car, we stood in amazement, discovering in the excitement, we had forgotten our clothes! Taking a good portion of our allotted travel money, we desperately searched for appropriate clothing. Stores were closing, and we were asked to leave! Robert ended up with what he calls "high water" pants, and I forgot to purchase stockings. During the presentation, the Transportation Quilt was still folded. The buyer had reviewed our line and she asked, "What is that quilt?" I unfolded it cautiously. She stared at it, and promptly swept it up to show to the Editor In Chief.

It first appeared in Better Homes & Gardens magazine in July of 1981. To date, we have sold over 200,000 patterns. The quilt is reserved for Dallas' children.

Two morals to this story: Robert is generally right, and you just never know!

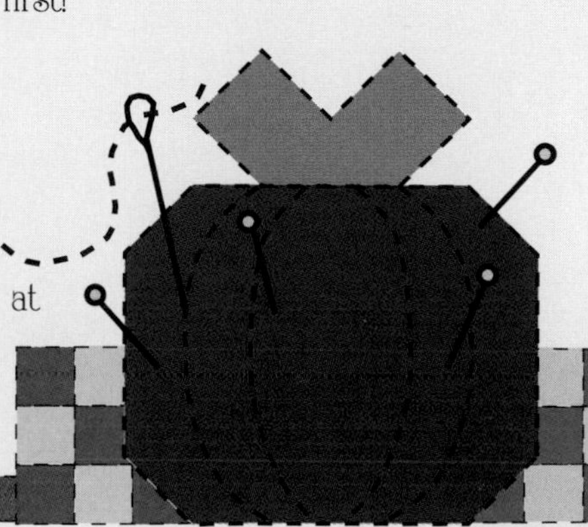

This quilt has been designed using one of two methods. The first method is as follows: Nine patches made with strip sets. The second method as follows: Nine patches made with QUILT TOP EXPRESS™. This method is shown below so that you may decide which method will be best for you. This is a beginner quilt, and QUILT TOP EXPRESS™ helps to insure accuracy.

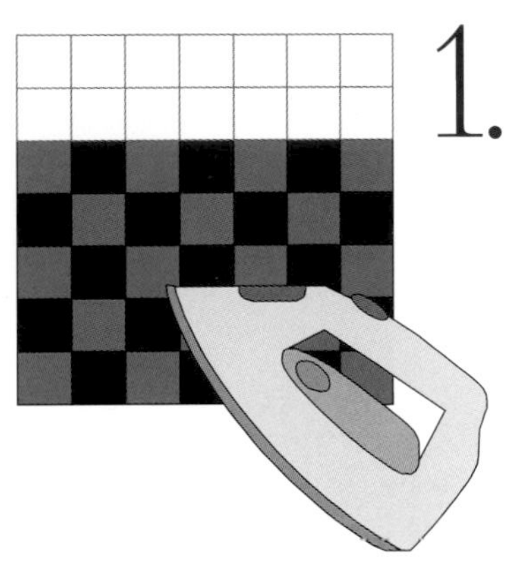

1\.
** Place cut quilt squares onto grid with the fusible (rough) side up.*
** Trim away any excess interfacing.*
** Fuse shapes in place using a dry iron, medium heat setting. Hold the iron in one place for 10-12 seconds, then reposition.*
** Continue in this manner until entire quilt top has been fused.*

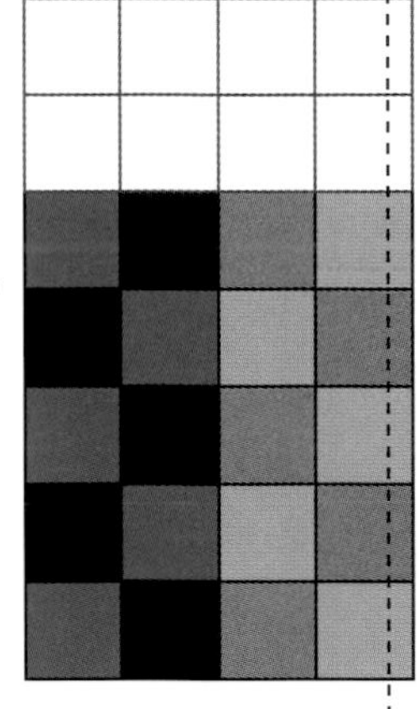

2\.
** Starting with the rows on the longer side of your design, fold the first two rows right sides together and sew in 1/4" seam allowance.*
** Repeat for remaining rows.*

SNIPS

3\.
** Make a 1/4" snip in the seam allowances where your squares intersect or where vertical and horizontal rows will meet.*

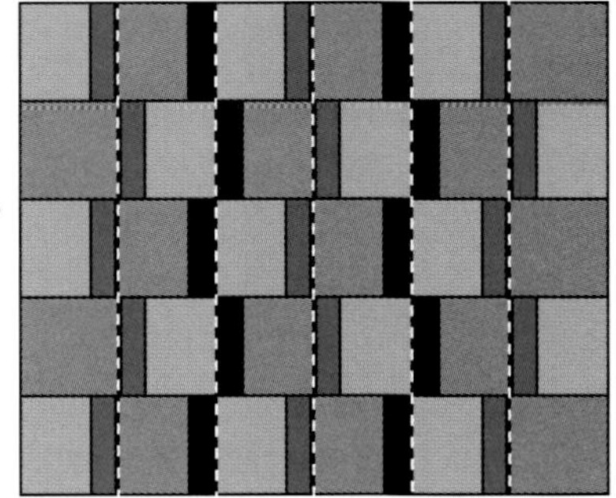

4\.
** Press seam allowances in alternate directions.*
** Sew opposing set of rows in same manner.*
Press seam allowances.

NOTE: In order to see the lines on QUILT TOP EXPRESS properly, it is best to place a large piece of white fabric under it on your ironing pad. ALWAYS PRESS QUILT TOP EXPRESS WITH A DRY IRON. TRIM QUILT TOP EXPRESS AWAY FROM BLOCK EDGES AFTER BLOCK IS PIECED AND PRESS ON FABRIC SIDE.

CUTTING

NOTE: All "Q" units in cutting instructions stand for "quilt top". These are units that are not incorporated into blocks. **Cutting instructions shown in blue indicate that the quantity of units are combined and cut in 2 or more different places to conserve fabric.**

From Fabric I cut: (turquoise print)

- Ten 4 1/4" wide strips for Strip Sets 1, 2, 5, & 6.
- For QUILT TOP EXPRESS method, cut:
- Nine 4 1/4" wide strips. From these, cut:
  - * Eighty – 4 1/4" squares (Block G and I and units A21, A22, A24, A30, A33, A35, A37)

From Fabric II, cut: (gold check)

- Eight 8" wide strips. From these, cut:
  - * Two – 8" x 41 3/8" (Q3 border) Piece two together to = 82 1/4" length
  - * Two – 8" x 34 1/8" (Q4 border) Piece two together to = 67 3/4" length
  - * Two – 8" x 30 1/8" (Q5 border). Piece two together to = 59 3/4" length.
  - * Two – 8" x 22 7/8" (Q6 border) Piece two together to = 45 1/4" length.
  - * One – 8" square (Q8)
- Eight 4 1/4" wide strips for Strip Sets 1, 2, 3, and 4.

- For QUILT TOP EXPRESS method, cut:
- Six 4 1/4" wide strips. From these, cut:
  - * Fifty-four – 4 1/4" squares (Block G and H, and units A18, A25, A27, A36)

From Fabric III, cut: (black print)

- Eight 4 1/4" wide strips for Strip Sets 5 and 6.
- For QUILT TOP EXPRESS method, cut:
- Eight 4 1/4" wide strips. From these, cut:
  - * Sixty–six - 4 1/4" squares (Block I and units A20, A23, A29, A31, A32, A34)
- Nine 2 1/2" wide strips for straight grain binding
- Nine 2" wide strips for Q9 and Q10 borders. Piece together end to end for borders.

From Fabric IV, cut: (dark red print)

- Four 4 1/4" wide strips for Strip Sets 3 and 4.
- For QUILT TOP EXPRESS method, cut:
- Three 4 1/4" wide strips. From these, cut:
  - * Twenty-seven – 4 1/4" squares (Block H and units A19, A26, A27)
- Seven 2" wide strips for Q1 and Q2 borders. Piece together end to end for borders.

From Fabric V, cut: (dark gray textured print)

- One 8" wide strip. From this, cut:
  - * Three – 8" squares (Q7)
  - * One – 3 1/2" x 8" (A11)
  - * Two – 1 5/8" x 8" (D8)
  - * Two – 1 1/4" x 8" (D7)
  - * Four – 2" x 7 5/8" (D5)
- One 6 1/2" wide strip. From this, cut:
  - * One – 5" x 6 1/2" (A1)
  - * One – 2" x 6 1/2" (A4)
  - * Three – 2" x 5" (A2, A7)
  - * Three – 2" x 3 1/2" (A6, A9)
  - * Thirty-six – 2" squares (A3a, B1a, B2, D1a, D3a, D4a)
- One 3 1/2" wide strip. From this, cut:
  - * Two – 3 1/2" square (D2)
  - * Four – 1 1/4" x 13 5/8" (D6)
  - * Three – 2" squares (add to A3a, B1a, B2, D1a, D3a, D4a)
- One 3 1/4" wide strip. From this, cut:
- Cut strip into three 3 1/4" x 11 3/4" segments. Cut these in half lengthwise so that you have six - 1 5/8" x 11 3/4" (B5)
- From remainder of 3 1/4" strip, cut:
  - * Three – 2" squares (add to A3a, B1a, B2, D1a, D3a, D4a)
- One 1 1/4" wide strip. From this, cut:
  - * Three – 1 1/4" x 9 1/2" (B4)

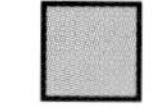

From Fabric VI, cut: (solid light blue)

- One 9 1/2" wide strip. From this, cut:
  - * Three – 9 1/2" squares (B1)
  - * One – 2" x 9 1/2" (A12)
  - * Two – 1 1/4" x 9 1/2" (C4)
  - * Four – 2" x 8" (E2, F2)
- One 3 1/2" wide strip. From this, cut:
  - * One – 3 1/2" x 6 1/2" (A10)
  - * One – 3 1/2" x 5" (A8)
  - * Five – 2" x 3 1/2" (A14, C3)
  - * One – 1 5/8" x 15 1/2" (A16)
  - * One – 1 1/4" x 12 1/2" (A15)
- One 2 3/8" wide strip. From this, cut:
  - * One – 2 3/8" x 15 1/2" (A17)
  - * Two – 2" x 8" (add to E2, F2)
  - * Five – 2" squares (A1a, A7a, A11a, C1a, C2a, E3a, F3a)
- Three 2" wide strips. From these, cut:
  - * Three – 2" x 11" (E5, F5)
  - * Thirty-one – 2" squares (add to A1a, A7a, A11a, C1a, C2a, E3a, F3a)
  - * One – 1 1/4" x 12 1/2" (add to A15)
- Three 1 5/8" wide strip. From this, cut:
  - * Four – 1 5/8" x 11 3/4" (C5)
  - * Three – 1 5/8" x 11" (E4, F4)
- One 1 1/4 " wide strip. From this, cut:
  - * Three – 1 1/4" x 11 3/4" (E6, F6)

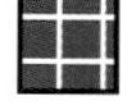

From Fabric VII, cut: (bright red print)

- Two – 8" x 9 1/2" (C1)

From Fabric VIII, cut: (red stripe)

- One – 6 1/8" x 8" (F1)

From Fabric IX, cut: (light gray print)

- One 3 1/2" wide strip. From this, cut:
  - * Two – 3 1/2" x 8" (D1)
  - * Four – 2" x 3 1/8" (D3)
  - * Four – 2" squares (D2a)
- One 2" wide strip. From this, cut:
  - * Four – 2" x 6 1/2" (D4)

From Fabric X, cut: (metallic silver print)

- Three – 2" x 6 1/2" (B3)

From Fabric XI, cut: (green stripe)

- Two – 6 1/8" x 8" (E1)
- One – 2" square (A13)

From Fabric XII, cut: (solid dark green)

- Four – 3 1/2" squares (C2)

From Fabric XIII, cut: (gold print)

- One 3 1/2" wide strip. From this, cut:
  - * One – 3 1/2" x 5" (A3)
  - * One – 2" x 3 1/2" (A5)
  - * Three – 2" x 9 1/8" (E3, F3)
- One 2" wide strip. From this, cut:
  - * Three – 2" x 9 1/8" (add to E3, F3)

ASSEMBLY

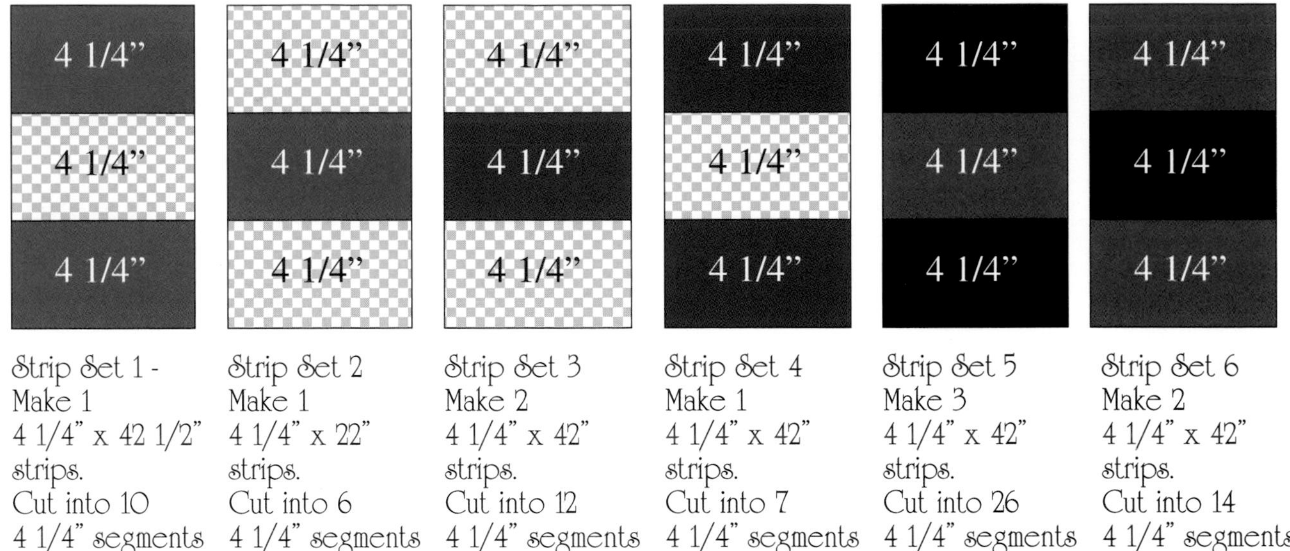

Strip Set 1 - Make 1 4 1/4” x 42 1/2” strips. Cut into 10 4 1/4” segments

Strip Set 2 Make 1 4 1/4” x 22” strips. Cut into 6 4 1/4” segments

Strip Set 3 Make 2 4 1/4” x 42” strips. Cut into 12 4 1/4” segments

Strip Set 4 Make 1 4 1/4” x 42” strips. Cut into 7 4 1/4” segments

Strip Set 5 Make 3 4 1/4” x 42” strips. Cut into 26 4 1/4” segments

Strip Set 6 Make 2 4 1/4” x 42” strips. Cut into 14 4 1/4” segments

1. If you are using the strip set method for your quilt top, refer to the illustrations above and make each strip set as directed under the illustrations. Cut into the required number of segments.
2. At this time, refer to the illustration above and make the required number of checkerboard, 9 patch blocks, by joining the strip set rows. Press seams on each row in opposite directions so that locking seams when assembling the quilt will make for easy seam matching. Take care to match your seams when joining rows.

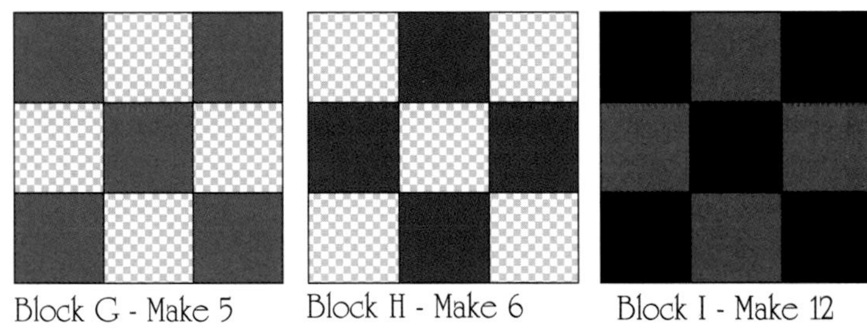

Block G - Make 5 Block H - Make 6 Block I - Make 12

NOTE: If you are a beginner, and want a good exercise for making strip sets and 9 patch blocks, this is for you. Many teachers do not believe in pinning. I am all for it when you are a beginner, and even if you are experienced - once in a while pins DO HELP! I like to match my seams, and place a pin close to each side of the matched seam. Works for me!
3. If you are using QUILT TOP EXPRESS™ to make the checkerboard blocks, refer to the illustrations and instructions given for this method. Lay each square on grid lines for each block. Squares should be directly next to each other. Stitch as shown in QUILT TOP EXPRESS™ illustrations. Clip seams and trim QUILT TOP EXPRESS™ away from block edges after block is pieced, and press on *fabric* side.

BLOCK A

1. Use diagonal corner technique to make one each of units 1, 3, 7, and 11.
2. To assemble Block A, begin by joining units 2-3-2 in a row. Add Unit 1 to top of these combined units, and Unit 4 to bottom as shown.
3. Join units 6-5-6 in a row. Join units 7 and 8 as illustrated; then add these combined units to combined units 6-5-6. Join units 9 and 10. Add combined unit 9-10 to right side of combined units 5-8; then join Unit 11 to top of these combined units.
4. Join the two sewing machine sections together referring to Block A diagram.
5. Join units 12-13-14. Join these combined units to top of sewing machine. Join Unit 15 to opposite sides; then add Unit 16 to bottom and Unit 17 to top to complete sewing machine.
6. For border, use 4 1/4” squares of Fabrics II and II, III and IV for units 18, 19, 20, and 21. These may be ripped out of a strip set if necessary. Join these squares together in a horizontal row and add this row to sewing machine top.
7. Join one segment of Strip Set 6 with one 4 1/4” square of Fabric II for units 22, 23, 24 and 25. Add to sewing machine block bottom.
8. Join one segment of Strip Set 4 with one segment of Strip Set 5 in a vertical row as shown for units 26-31. Add to left side of Block A.
9. Join one segment of Strip Set 5 with 4 1/4” squares of Fabrics I and II as shown. Join in a vertical row. Add to right side of sewing machine block to complete piecing for Block A.
10. For QUILT TOP EXPRESS™ method, lay squares of each color shown for units 18-21 on QUILT TOP EXPRESS™ and join seams. Trim away QUILT TOP EXPRESS™ and press seams. Join this row to top of block. Repeat this procedure for bottom and side squares as shown.

11. To complete the block, place tear-away pellon behind the sewing machine. Using a fusible pellon, cut a small square with pinking shears to place under the "needle." Draw a straight line down from the sewing machine with a pencil for placement of needle. Draw thread as it would look threaded on the machine.

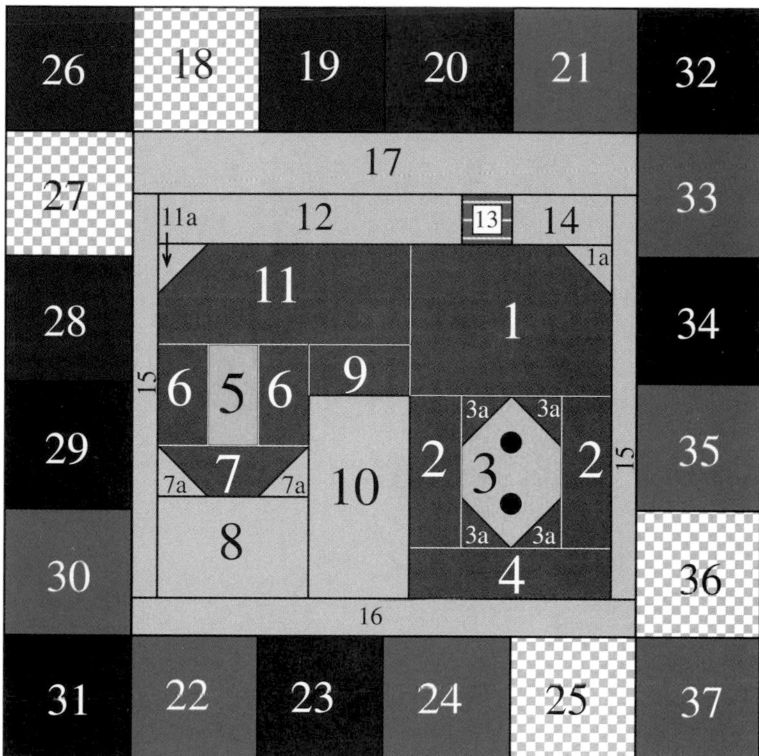

Block A. Make 1.

12. We used a metallic silver thread for the needle, and also accentuated the circles in Unit 3 by stitching inside of them with silver metallic thread. Use a close, medium wide satin stitch and stitch the needle, and green thread. Tear pellon away on back side of block.

NOTE: For the needle, we used a wider stitch close to the machine and tapered it down to a fine point at the end of the needle.

BLOCK B

1. Use diagonal corner technique to make one of Unit 1. 2. To assemble Block B, begin by joining units 2-3-2 in a row as shown; then add Unit 4 to top of combined units, and Unit 1 to bottom. Add Unit 5 to opposite sides to complete Block B.

BLOCK C

1. Use diagonal corner technique to make one of Unit 1 and two of mirror image Unit 2. Check illustration for correct placement of diagonal corners on the mirror image unit.
2. To assemble, join units 3-mirror image units 2-and 3 in a row as shown. Add Unit 4 to top of combined units, and Unit 1 to bottom. Join Unit 5 to opposite sides to complete piecing.
3. This is where we had fun with this little block. Refer to our illustration of the pincushion on the first page of these instructions. Using a pen or chalk, mark curved lines on pincushion to show that it is "plump".
Draw a needle with a bit of thread in it, and draw pins in various places on the pincushion. Again using tear-away pellon behind the block, use a dark red or gray thread for "plump" lines and silver metallic for needles and pins. We used green thread to stitch the thread going through the needle. Satin stitch as in Block A, Step 11. Make 2.

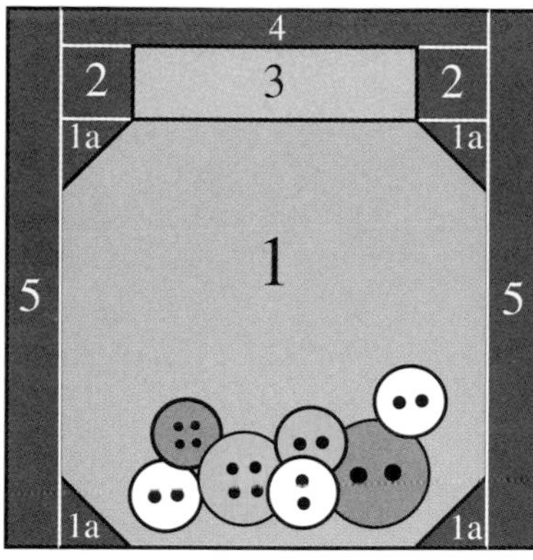

Block B - Make 3

BLOCK D

1. For scissors Block D, use diagonal corner technique to make one each of units 1 and 2. Use this technique to make two each of mirror image Unit 3, checking illustration for correct placement of diagonal corners. Make two of Unit 4.
3. To assemble, begin by joining the two mirror image units 3 as shown; then add Unit 2 to bottom of these combined units. Join Unit 1 to bottom of combined units 3-2 as shown in a vertical row.
4. Join units 4 and 5 in a vertical row as illustrated, turning Unit 4 correctly for mirror image. Add these two units to opposite sides of scissors. Join Unit 6 to opposite sides; then add Unit 8 to top of scissors and Unit 7 to bottom.
5. Draw a line as indicated on our illustration with a dashed line. Again, using tear-away pellon behind your applique, stitch the line in black thread. We also stitched a metallic silver circle at the top of the line.

Block C - Make 2

BLOCKS E AND F

1. These two blocks are exactly the same except for the stripe which is the thread. Follow these instructions for both blocks.
2. Use diagonal corner technique to make two each of Unit 3.
3. To assemble blocks, join units 2-1-2 in a vertical row as shown; then add Unit 3 to top and bottom. Join units 4 and 5 to sides. Refer to illustration for correct placement of these units, as they are placed differently in each block. Add Unit 6 to top to finish the piecing of each block.
4. We satin stitched thread coming off of the spool for a cute effect.

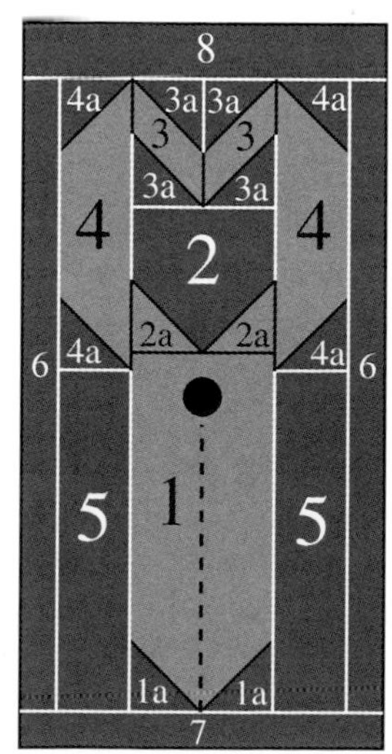

Block D. Make 2

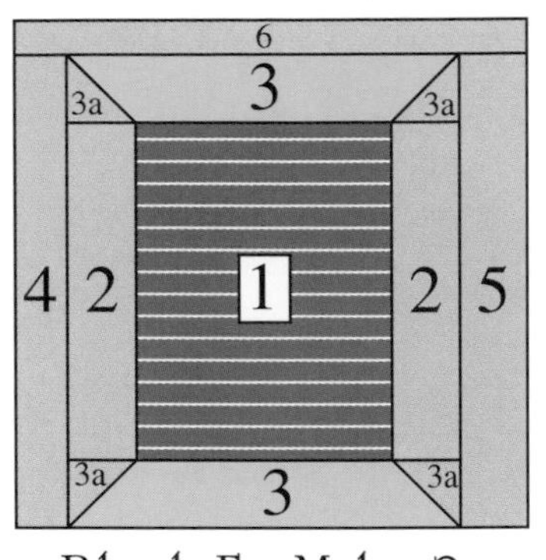

Block E - Make 2

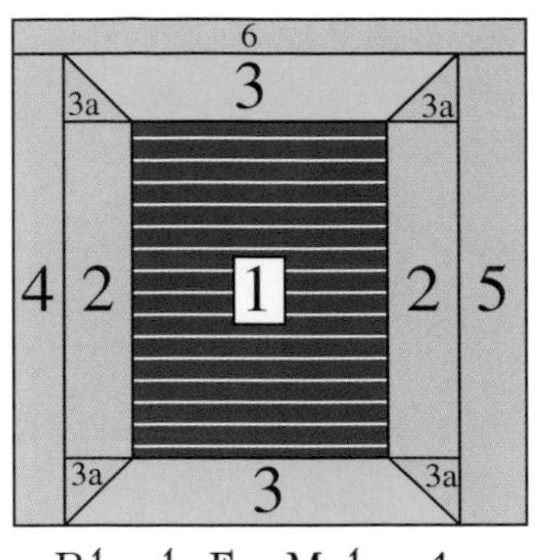

Block F - Make 1

QUILT ASSEMBLY

1. To assemble your quilt top, refer to our quilt top diagram and begin with the top row of your quilt. From left to right, join blocks I-G-I-G- and B in a row.
2. For second row, join blocks E-I-C-H- and I in a row as shown.
3. For row three, join blocks I-H-I-B and G in a row.
4. Row four is made my joining blocks H-I-F-I- and H in a row.
5. For row 5, join blocks B-G-I-C- and I in a vertical row.
6. For remaining two rows, begin by joining blocks H-I-H in a row. Join blocks I-G- and E in a row. Join the two rows together as shown; then add Block A to left side, matching seams.
7. Join all rows together, referring to quilt diagram frequently for correct placement.
8. Join pieced 2" wide strips of Fabric IV to top and bottom of quilt top for Border 1. Trim off ends even with quilt top. Repeat for sides of quilt top for Border 2.
9. Join the pieced 8" x 82 1/4" strip of Fabric II to left side of quilt top for Border 3. Join the pieced 8" x 64 3/4" strip of Fabric II and one of scissors Block D together as shown and add to right side of quilt top as shown.
10. For top and bottom borders, join the pieced 8" x 59 3/4" strip of Fabric II with two 8" squares of Fabric V on opposite short ends as shown. Add to quilt top for Border 5, matching seams. For bottom border, join the pieced 8" x 45 1/4" strip of Fabric II to one scissors block D as shown. Join corner Unit Q7 to left side, and corner Unit Q8 to right side. Add to quilt bottom, matching seams.
11. Join the 2" wide strips of Fabric III to top and bottom of quilt top, trimming even with quilt top for Border 9. Join side borders 10 to opposite sides of quilt in same manner to complete quilt top.

QUILTING & FINISHING

1. The quilting for this piece was kept relatively simple. We "stitched in the ditch" on the 9-patch blocks and the other blocks in the center section of the quilt. A few wavy lines were added to the button jar to give the effect of glass.
2. June Tailor's Grid Marker was used to make a 60° grid on the large outer borders. See our video on the CD-ROM for a demonstration of this great tool.
3. Make 370" of straight-grain french fold binding from Fabric III, and bind your quilt.
4. The finishing was fun. All of those extra buttons in *your* button jar can now be used and sewn into the button jars on the quilt and into each corner.

QUILT TOP ASSEMBLY DIAGRAM

My First Quilt:

Bridal Basket Quilt

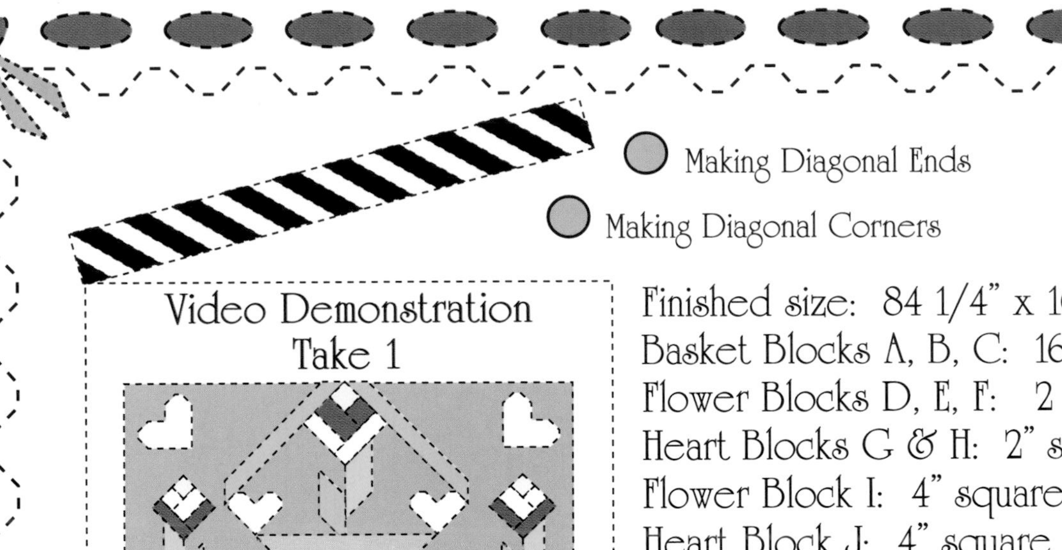

Finished size: 84 1/4" x 106 1/2"
Basket Blocks A, B, C: 16" square
Flower Blocks D, E, F: 2 3/4" sq.
Heart Blocks G & H: 2" squares
Flower Block I: 4" square
Heart Block J: 4" square
Border Block K: 19" square
Border Block L: 19 1/4" x 22"

MATERIALS

Fabric I (lilac print)	2 3/8 yards (need exactly 83 1/8")
Fabric II (white on ivory print)	3 3/4 yards (need exactly 134 1/8")
Fabric III (solid medium lilac sateen)	2 1/8 yards (need exactly 76 1/8")
Fabric IV (solid light pink sateen)	3/4 yard (need exactly 24")
Fabric V (solid medium green sateen)	1/2 yard (need exactly 12 3/8")
Fabric VI (light green print)	7/8 yard (need exactly 31 1/4")
Fabric VII (light yellow print)	1/2 yard (need exactly 13 3/8")
Backing	7 1/2 yards

CUTTING

Cutting instructions shown in red indicate that the quantity of units are combined and cut in 2 or more different places to conserve fabric. *NOTE: All "Q" units in cutting instructions stand for "quilt top". These are units that are not incorporated into blocks.*

From Fabric I, cut: (lilac print)

- One yard to cut 2" wide bias strips.
- Two 8 7/8" wide strips. From these, cut:
  - * Eight – 8 7/8" squares (C15) cut in half diagonally to = 16 triangles
  - * Eight – 3" x 3 1/2" (C10)
  - * Twenty-four – 7/8" squares (H1a, H3a)
- One 6 7/8" wide strip. From this, cut:
  - * Three – 6 7/8" squares (B8) cut in half diagonally to = 6 triangles
  - * Three – 5 5/8" squares (C14) cut in half diagonally to = 6 triangles
  - * Nine – 1 1/2" squares (D2, H2)
- One 5 5/8" wide strip. From this, cut:
  - * One – 5 5/8" square (add to C14) cut in half diagonally to = 2 triangles
  - * Four – 1 1/2" x 5" (C3)
  - * Four – 2" x 4" (C4)
  - * Four – 3 1/4" x 3 3/4" (C1)
  - * Five – 1 1/2" x 2 1/2" (D3)
- From scrap, cut:
  - * Four – 1 1/2" squares (add to D2, H2)
  - * Nine – 1 1/4" x 2 1/2" (C2, C6, E4)
  - * Eight – 7/8" squares (add to H1a, H3a)
- Three 4 1/2" wide strips. From these, cut:
  - * Sixty-eight – 1 1/2" x 4 1/2" (I5)
  - * Sixteen – 1 1/2" x 3 1/2" (I4)
- Two 3 1/2" wide strips. From these, cut:
  - * Fifty-two – 1 1/2" x 3 1/2" (add to I4)
- One 3 3/8" wide strip. From this, cut:

* Four – 3 3/8" squares (C9) cut in half diagonally to = 8 triangles
* Four – 3 1/4" squares (C7)
* Four – 3 1/8" squares (C12) cut in half diagonally to = 8 triangles

• One 3" wide strip. From this, cut:
* Four – 3" x 3 1/4" (C5)
* Six – 1 1/4" x 3 1/4" (E5)
* Five – 1 1/4" x 2 1/2" (add to C2, C6, E4)

From Fabric II, cut: (white on ivory print)

• One 14 3/8" wide strip. From this, cut:
* Two – 14 3/8" squares (L1) cut in half diagonally to = 4 triangles
* One – 11 5/8" square (K1) cut in half diagonally to = 2 triangles

• From scrap, cut:
* Four – 1 1/2" x 2 1/2" (F3)
* Forty-seven – 7/8" squares (G1a, G3a)

• Two 11 5/8" wide strips. From these, cut:
* Four – 11 5/8" squares (add to K1) cut in half diagonally to = 8 triangles
* Three – 8 7/8" squares (A15, B15) cut in half diagagonally to = 6 triangles

• From scrap, cut:
* Eleven – 1 1/2" x 5" (A3, B3)
* Fourteen – 1 1/4" x 2 1/2" (A2, A6, B2, B6)
* Forty-one – 7/8" squares (add to G1a, G3a)

• Five 8 7/8" wide strips. From these, cut:
* Nineteen – 8 7/8" squares (add to A15, B15) cut in half diagonally to = 38 triangles
* Two – 6 7/8" squares (C8) cut in half diagonally to = 4 triangles
* Four – 5 5/8" squares (A14, B14) cut in half diagonally to = 8 triangles

• From scrap, cut:
* Eight – 1 1/4" x 2 1/2" (add to A2, A6, B2, B6)
* Twenty-six – 1 1/2" squares (F2, G2)

• One 5 5/8" wide strip. From this, cut:
* Seven – 5 5/8" squares (add to A14, B14) cut in half diagonally to = 14 triangles

• One 3 3/8" wide strip. From this, cut:
* Eleven – 3 3/8" squares (A9, B9) cut in half diagonally to = 22 triangles
* One – 2 1/2" x 4 1/2" (J1)

• Two 3 1/4" wide strips. From these, cut:
* Eleven – 3 1/4" x 3 3/4" (A1, B1)
* Eleven – 3 1/4" squares (A7, B7)
* Two – 3 1/8" squares (A12, B12) cut in half diagonally to = 4 triangles

• One 3 1/8" wide strip. From this, cut:
* Nine – 3 1/8" squares (add to A12, B12) cut in half diagonally to = 18 triangles
* Four – 3" x 3 1/4" (A5, B5)

• Three 3" wide strips. From these, cut:
* Twenty-two – 3" x 3 1/2" (A10, B10)
* Seven – 3" x 3 1/4" (add to A5, B5)
* Five – 2 1/2" x 4 1/2" (add to J1)

• Nine 2 1/2" wide strips. From these, cut:
* Forty-eight – 2 1/2" x 4 1/2" (add to J1)
* Fifty-four – 2 1/2" squares (J2)
* Three – 2" x 4" (A4, B4)

• One 2" wide strip. From this, cut:
* Eight – 2" x 4" (add to A4, B4)

From Fabric III, cut: (solid medium lilac sateen)

• One 6 7/8" strip. From this, cut:
* Three – 6 7/8" squares (A8) cut in half diagonally to = 6 triangles
* Four – 4 1/8" squares (L2) cut in half diagonally to = 8 triangles
* Six – 1 1/4" x 4 1/2" (Q7)

• Four 2 1/2" wide strips. From these, cut:
* Fifty-four – 2 1/2" squares (J3)
* Six – 1 1/2" x 2 1/2" (E3)
* Nine – 1 1/4" x 2 1/2" (D4, F4)
* Two – 1 1/4" x 4 1/2" (add to Q7)

• Twelve 2 1/4" wide strips. From these, cut:
* Four – 2 1/4" x 22 1/2" (L5)
* Ten – 2 1/4" x 19 1/2" (K6)
* Ten – 2 1/4" x 17 3/4" (K7)
* Six – 1 1/2" squares (E2)
* Nine – 1 1/4" x 3 1/4" (D5, F5)

• Twelve 1 3/4" strips. From these, cut:
* Two – 1 3/4" x 32 1/2" (Q6)
* Two – 1 3/4" x 30" (Q5)
* Two – 1 3/4" x 19" (Q2)
* Two – 1 3/4" X 16 1/2" (Q1)
* Ten – 1 3/4" x 12 1/2" (K3)
* Ten – 1 3/4" x 11 1/4" (K2)

• From scrap, cut:
* Fifty – 1 1/4" squares (J1a, J2a)

• Nine 1 1/4" wide strips. From these, cut:
* Four – 1 1/4" x 16 3/4" (L3)
* Four – 1 1/4" x 17 1/2" (L3a)
* 166 – 1 1/4" squares (add to J1a, J2a)

From Fabric IV, cut: (solid light pink sateen)

• Nine 2" wide strips. From these, cut:
* Sixty-eight – 2" x 3 1/2" (I3)
* Sixty-eight – 2" squares (I2)

• Four 1 1/2" wide strips. From these, cut:
* Thirty – 1 1/2" x 2 1/2" (G3, H3)
* Thirty-four – 1 1/2" squares (F1, G1, H1)

From Fabric V, cut: (solid medium green sateen)

• One 9" wide strip. From this, cut:
* Twenty-two – 1 1/4" x 9" (A13, B13)
* Fifteen – 2" x 3" (A4a, B4a, C4a)

• From scrap, cut:
* Fourteen – 1 1/4" squares (A5a, B5a, C5a)

• One 3 3/8" wide strip. From this, cut:
* Eleven – 3 3/8" sqaures (A11, B11) cut in half diagonally to = 22 triangles
* One – 1 1/4" square (add to A5a, B5a, C5a)

From Fabric VI, cut: (light green print)

• One 22 1/2" wide strip. From this, cut:
* Four – 1 3/4" x 22 1/2" (L4)
* Two – 2" x 22" (Q4)

* Two – 2" x 19" (Q3)
* Ten – 1 3/4" x 17 3/4" (K5)
* Thirty – 2 1/4" squares (A1a, A4b, B1a, B4b, C1a, C4b)

• Five 1 3/4" wide strips. From these, cut:
* Ten – 1 3/4" x 16 1/2" (K4)

From Fabric VII, cut: (light yellow print)

• One 3 3/8" wide strip. From this, cut:
* Four – 3 3/8" squares (C11) cut in half diagonally to = 8 triangles
* Six – 1 1/4" x 9" (C13)

• Five 2" wide strips. From these, cut:
* Sixty-eight – 2" squares (I1)
* Eleven – 1 1/2" squares (D1, E1)
* Two – 1 1/4" x 9" (add to C13)

BLOCK ASSEMBLY

BASKET BLOCKS A, B, & C

1. Illustrations are shown for all three basket blocks. Assembly is the same for each of the basket blocks. The only difference in the blocks is the change of color. Please refer to block diagrams frequently for correct color identification. Assembly instructions are given for Block A.

2. Assembly instructions for smaller flower and heart blocks D, E, F, G, and H are given first as they are incorporated into the larger basket blocks shown.

Block D - Make 5

3. Refer to illustrations of flower head blocks D, E and F. The construction is the same for each. Join units 1 and 2; then add Unit 3. Join Unit 4 to the combined units; then add Unit 5 to right side to complete each block.

Block E - Make 6

4. Block D is the flower head in Block B. Block E is the flower head in Block A, and Block F is the flower head in Block C. Construct the flower head blocks prior to beginning the large basket blocks.

5. Small heart blocks G and H are also constructed in the same way. Use diagonal corner technique to make one each of units 1 and 3.

Block F - Make 4

6. To assemble, join units 1 and 2; then add Unit 3 to right side to complete block. Block G hearts are used in basket blocks A and B. Block F hearts are used in basket Block C.

7. Refer to large drawings of each basket block for correct placement of color.

8. We have used Block A as our assembly example. Refer to the assembly illustrations. Begin by using diagonal corner technique to make one each of units 1, and 5.

9. For combined units 3-4 refer to diagram of Row 2 and use diagonal end technique to make one of Unit 4.

Join units 3 and 4; then add diagonal corner 4b to top right corner as shown.

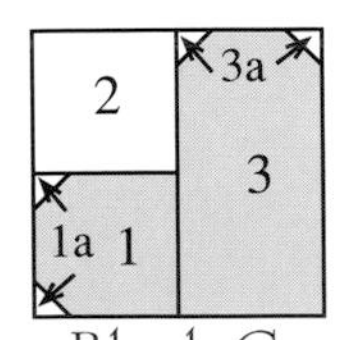

Block G
Make 22

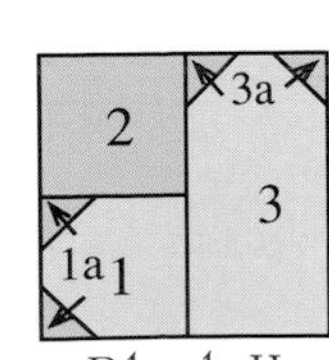

Block H
Make 8

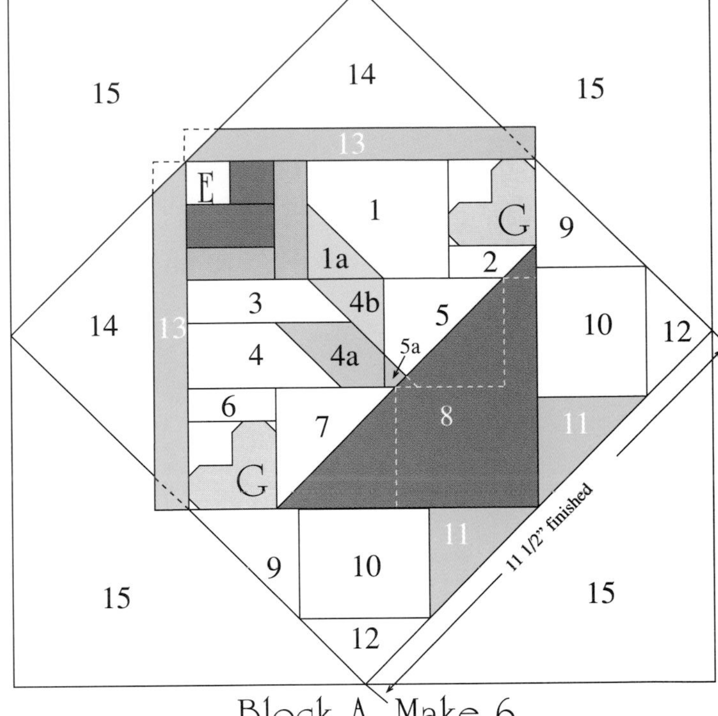

Block A. Make 6.

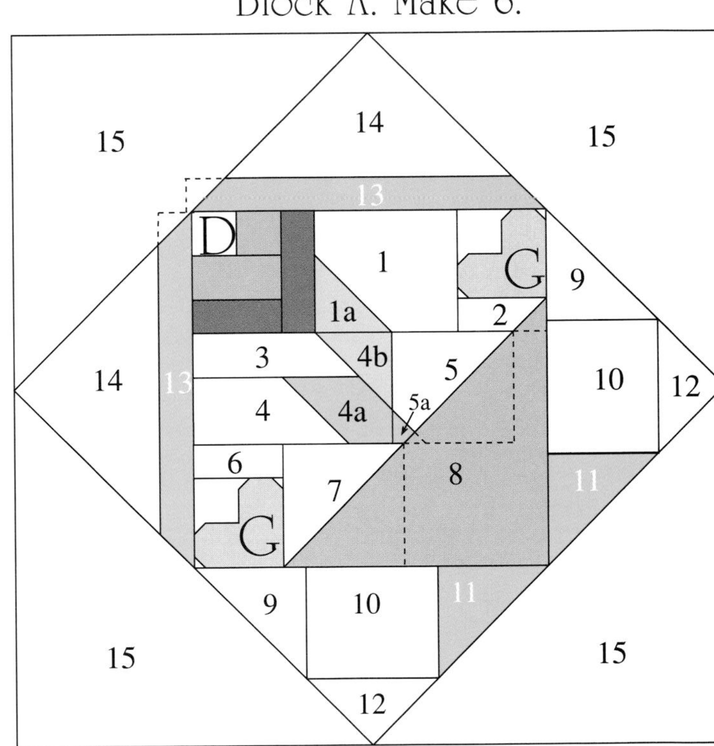

Block B. Make 5.

10. After preparing the units in steps 8 and 9, begin assembly by referring to Row 1 diagram. Join completed Block E with Unit 1. Join Block G with Unit 2 as shown. Join combined Block G-Unit 2 section to Block E-Unit 1 to complete Row 1.

11. For Row 2, join combined units 3-4 to Unit 5 for Row 2.

12. For Row 3, join Unit 6 and Block G as shown, checking illustration for correct placement of Block G. Add Unit 7 to right side to complete Row 3.

13. Refer to Illustration 1 at top right corner of this page. Assemble the three rows as shown in the diagram, joining them at the

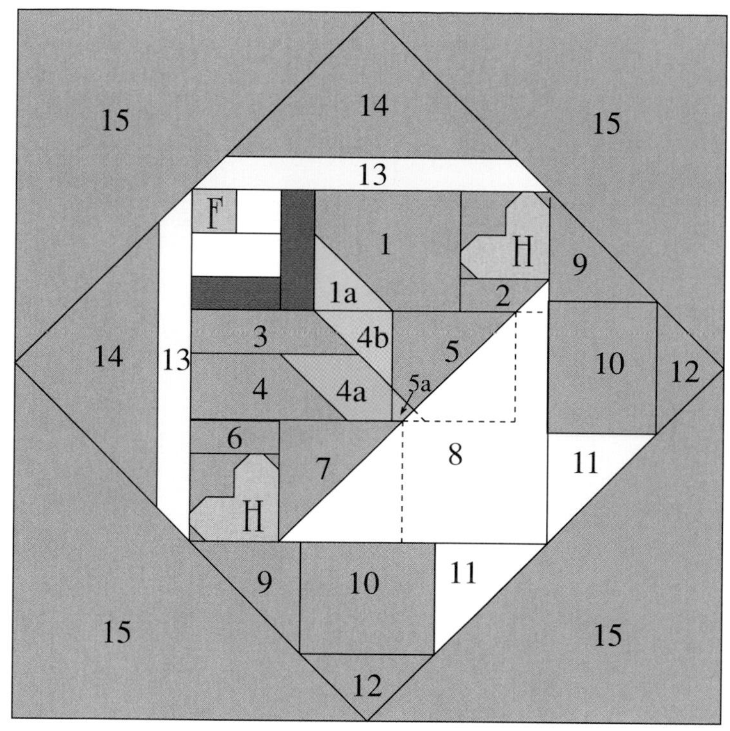

Block C. Make 4.

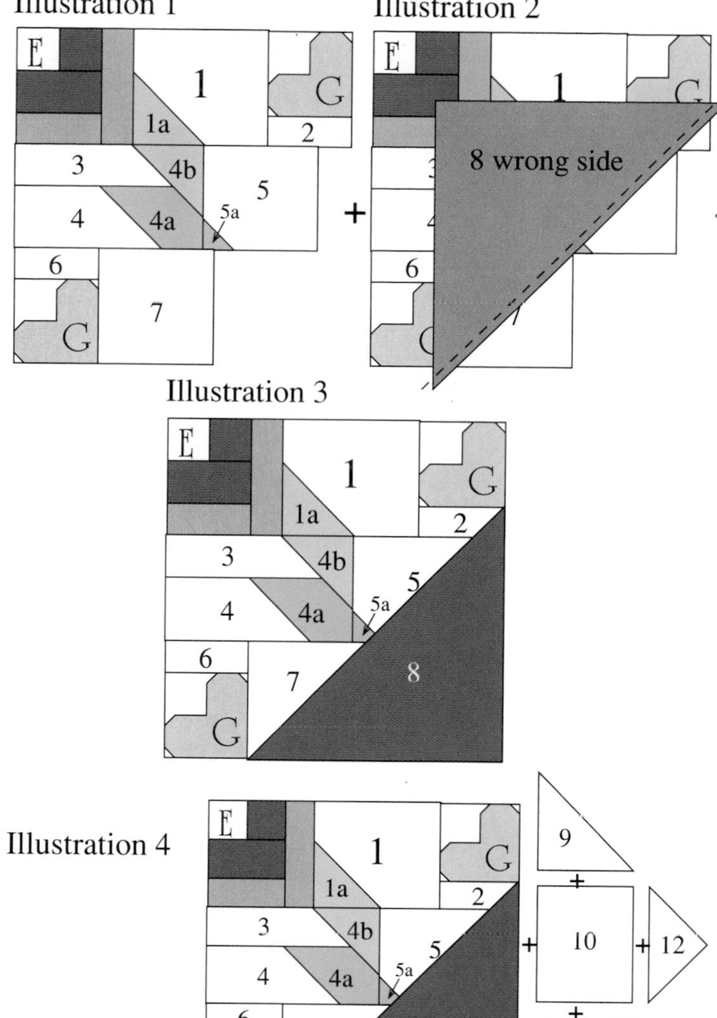

left with the right side being ragged.

14. Refer to Illustration 2, and place triangle Unit 8 right sides together across jagged edge of flower basket top. Triangle edge will be placed 1/4" below Block G points. Stitch an accurate 1/4" seam. Press Unit 8 down. The flower and basket should form an 11 3/4" square.

15. Refer to Illustration 4. Units 9-10-and 11 are joined in a row on both bottom sides of the basket; then triangle Unit 12 is added. Refer to illustration for correct placement of units. Join these combined units to basket sides as shown in Illustration 5 on following page.

16. Join one Unit 13 to top edge of basket as shown. Dashed lines indicate where to trim the rectangle. Add second Unit 13 to left side of basket, again trimming as shown.

17. Join long side of triangle Unit 14 to both sides of Unit 13 as shown. Join the four long sides of Unit 15 triangles all the way around block to complete all basket blocks. Blocks should measure (with seam allowance), 16 1/2" square. Complete all basket blocks.

CENTER MEDALLION AND BORDER BLOCKS

1. Flower Block I and Heart Block J are used in the center medallion and also in border blocks K and L.

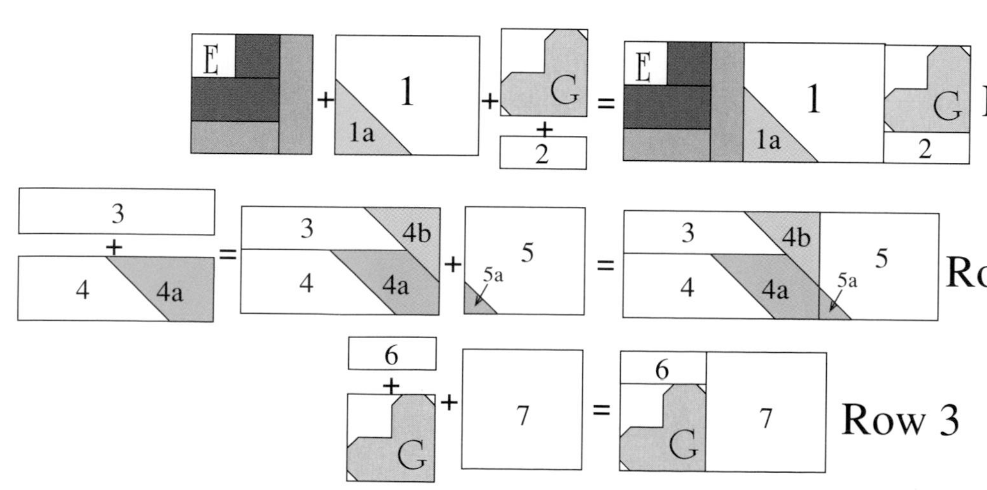

2. For Block I, assemble as for blocks D, E, and F. Make sixty-eight. For medallion and border blocks.

3. Heart Block J is assembled as for blocks G and H. Make fifty-four.

4. For center medallion, begin with one Block B. Join Border Q1 to opposite sides of Block B as shown in medallion diagram. Join Border Q2 to top and bottom; then add Border Q3 to opposite sides. Join Border Q4 to top and bottom.

5. For top and bottom heart/flower borders,

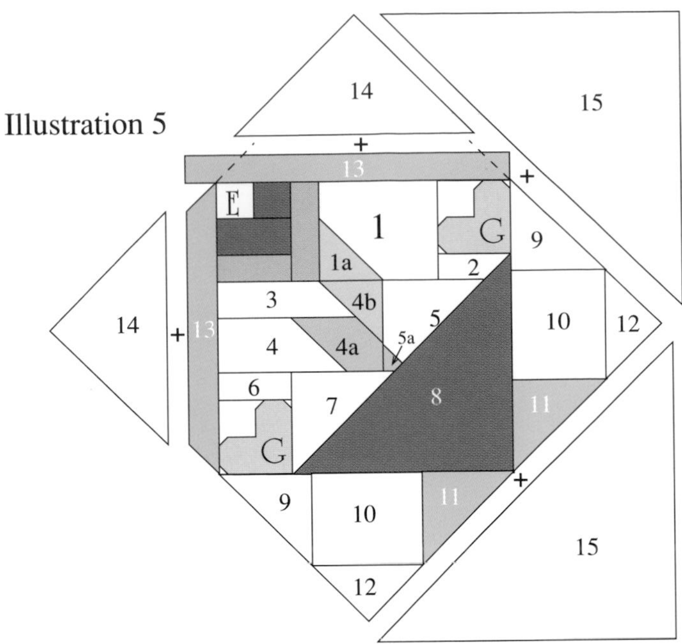

join Block J-Block I-Unit Q7-Block J-Unit Q7-Block I- and Block J in a horizontal row as shown. Make two of these rows and join to top and bottom of basket center.

6. For side heart/flower border rows, make two vertical rows as follows: Block I-Block J-Block I-Unit 7-Block J-Unit 7-Block I-Block J- and Block I. Join to opposite sides as shown.

7. Join Unit Q5 to opposite sides of medallion; then join Unit Q6 to top and bottom to complete medallion.

8. To make Border Block K, begin by joining Unit K2 to right side of one short end of triangle K1. Trim any excess. Join Unit K3 to remaining short side of triangle as shown.

9. Join Block I-Block J- and Block I in a row. Add to side of triangle with flower head facing upwards. For remaining side of triangle, join Block I-Block J-Block I-and Block J in a row as shown.

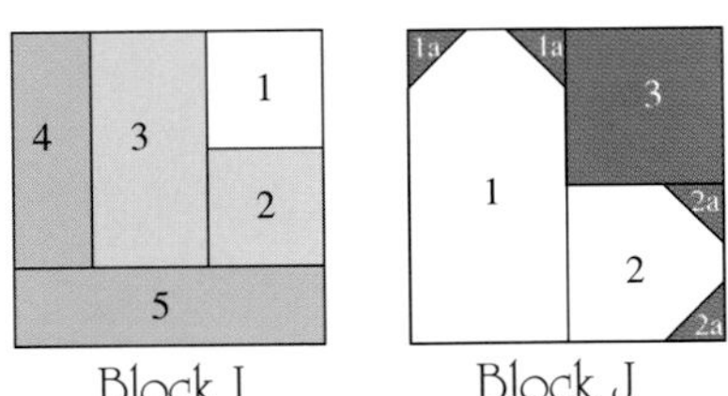

Block I Block J

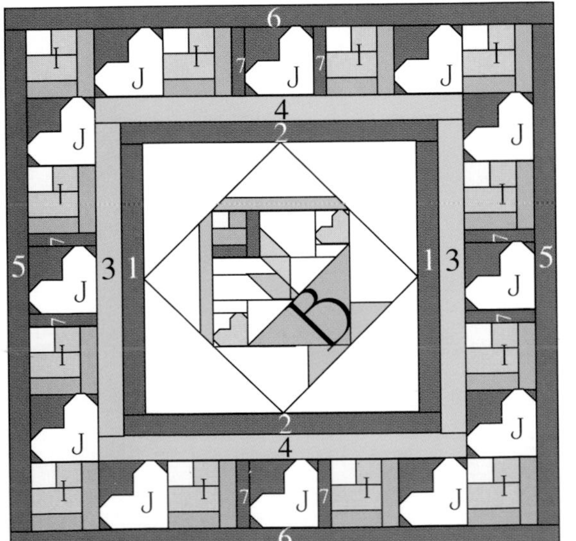

Join to remaining side of triangle as shown, matching seams.

10. Join Unit K4 to one side of triangle, and trim the short end next to the flower head at a 45° angle. Join Unit K5 as shown and trim.

11. Join Unit K7 to one side of triangle block and trim as shown at a 45° angle. Add remaining Unit K6, trimming the short end as shown to complete Block K.

12. For Border Block L, begin by joining triangle Unit L2-Block I-Block J- and Block I. Refer to illustration for correct placement of row. Flower head needs to line up at tip of short side of triangle as shown. Refer to illustration and trim triangle L2 even with bottom of L1 triangle as shown.

13. Join Block J-Block I-BLock J-Block I- and L2 triangle in a row. Add to remaining side of triangle as shown, matching seams. Trim L2 triangle even with bottom of L1 triangle.

14. Join units 4 and 5; then add to long side of L1 triangle. Trim off at a 45° angle as shown in diagram. Join Unit L3 to flower/heart side of triangle, lining up at tip of heart Block J. Trim short end even with triangle Unit 2, trimming any portion of Block I that is extending. Repeat for remaining L3 strip to complete corner Block L.

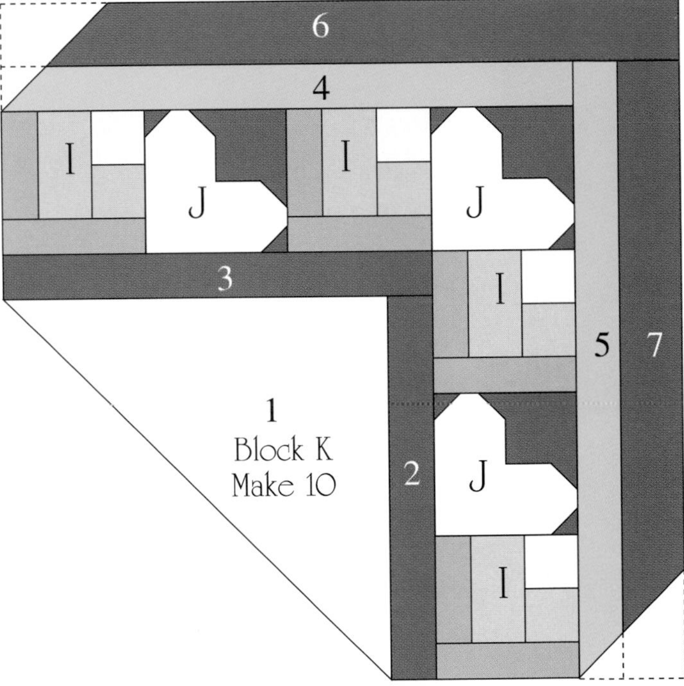

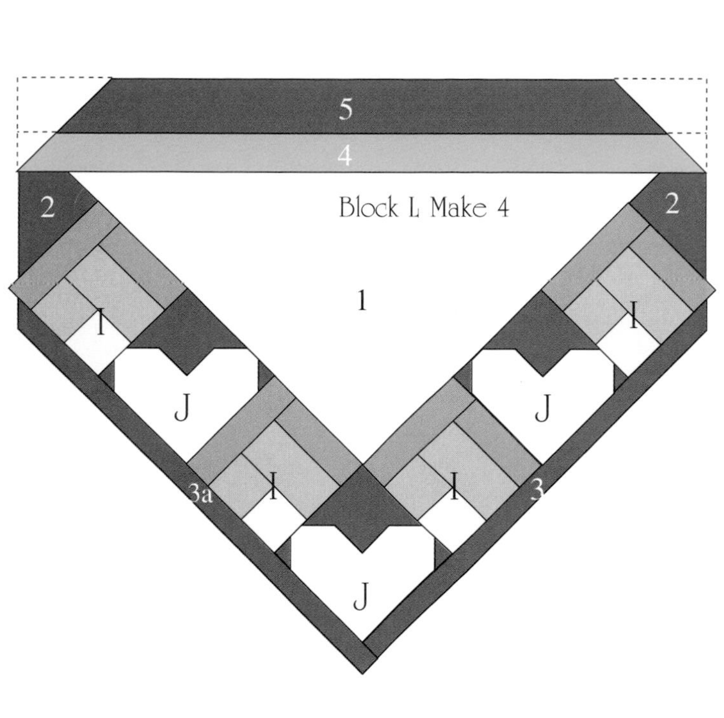

QUILT TOP ASSEMBLY

1. Refer to Illustration 1, and join blocks A and B together . Please note that the position of the blocks change according to the side of the medallion they are on. Join the combined blocks to opposite sides of medallion as shown in Illustration 2.
2. Refer to illustration 2 and lay out two rows of alternate blocks A and B with Border Block K. Check illustration for correct placement. Join the blocks together. Block K corner will jut out as shown. This small area will be "set in" with other blocks later.
3. Join the two rows to opposite sides of center section. Match your seams. The point of Block K should line up exactly with point of medallion center. Refer to Illustration 3 for exact placement.

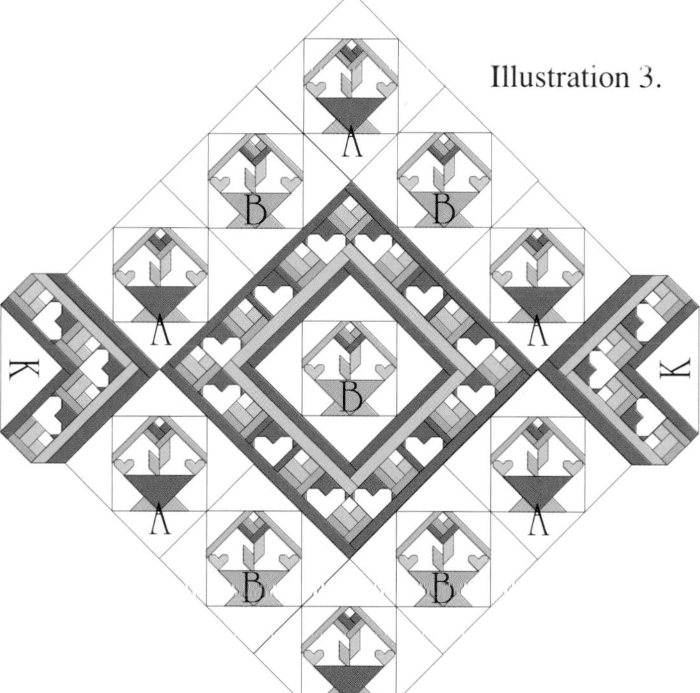

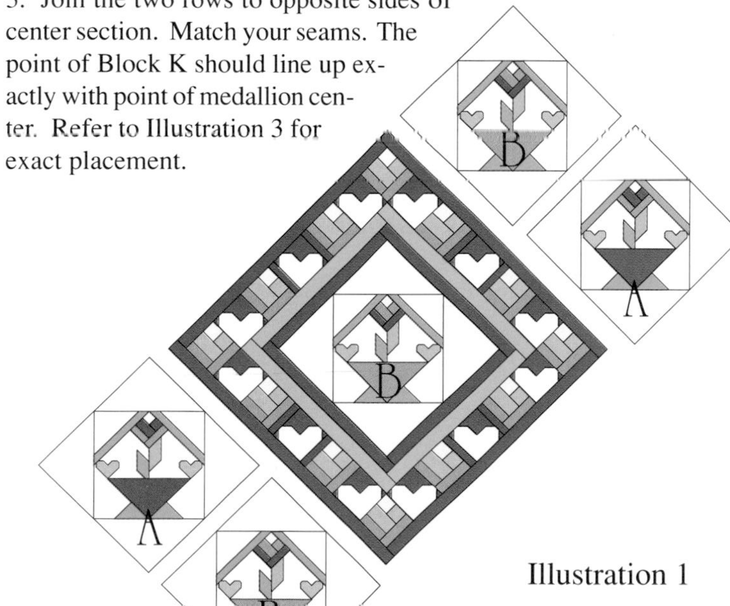

Illustration 1

Joined units. Join to quilt top. Join units together

4. Refer to Quilt Assembly Diagram on left, and begin by joining Blocks C, K and corner Block L together. Join the K-C-K blocks together first; then add corner block L.

5. To set in corner block L, match corners of both K blocks, and L block, right sides together and pin. Stitch from edge to 1/4" away from next edge. Clip to stitching, turn and stitch again to 1/4" from next corner. Clip to stitching, turn once more and complete stitching. Reinforce your stitching at end.

6. Complete each corner section as shown; then add to quilt top, one corner section at a time, setting in the Block K's where they meet. Complete all four corners in this manner.

QUILTING AND FINISHING

1. We used the design below for the border blocks and the bow only at the top of all of the baskets. Hearts were quilted on the sides of the basket blocks and the bottom. Enlarge the design on a copy machine in a vertical format to fit your blocks. Stitch in the ditch around all patchwork.

2. Make 420" of 2" wide bias binding from Fabric I, and bind your quilt.

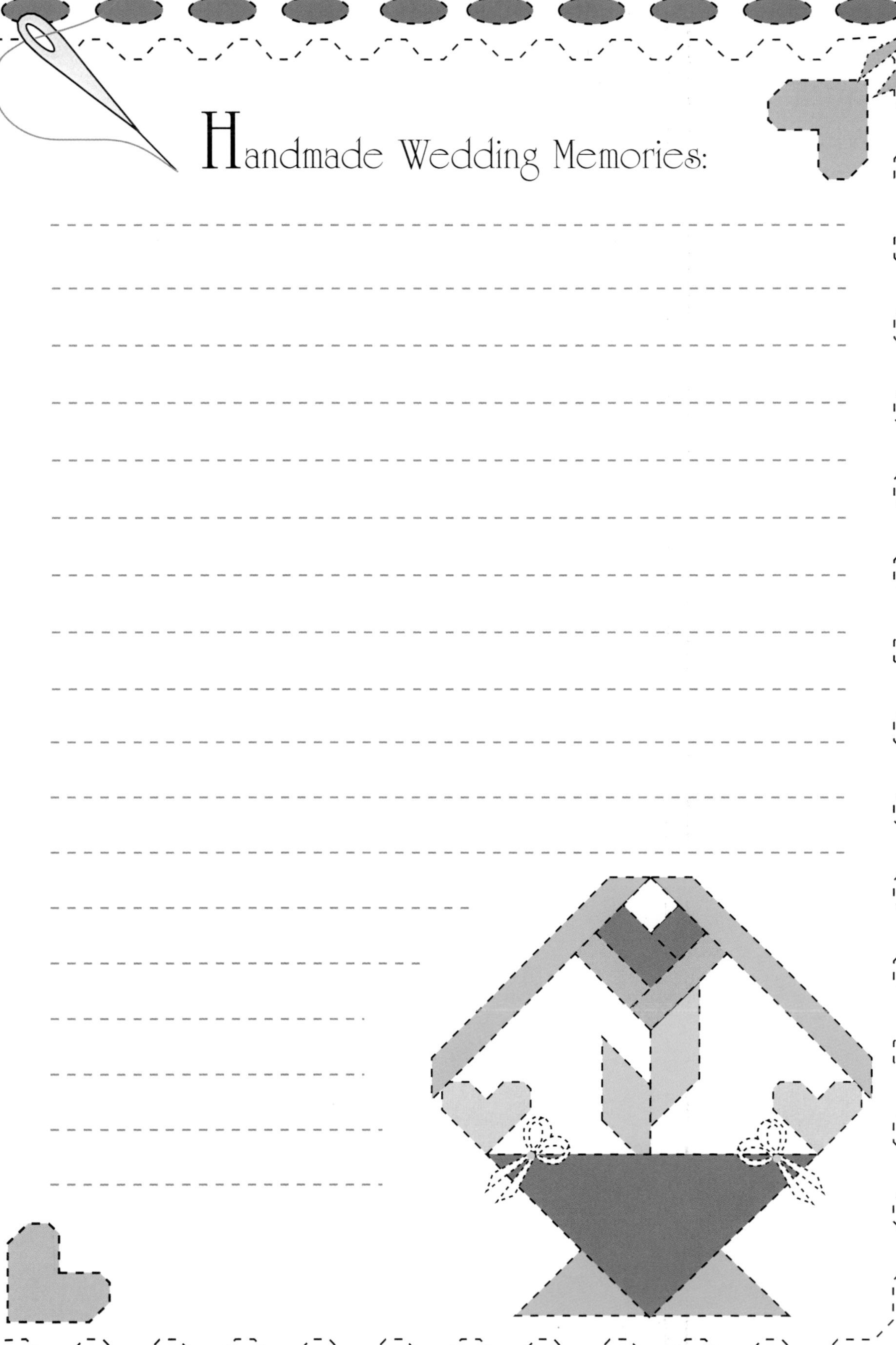

Handmade Wedding Memories:

My First Home

First Home Quilt

Video Demonstration
Take 1

* Making diagonal corners
* Double diagonal corner on corner
* Diagonal ends
* Making one half square triangle
* How to use the grid marker

Finished Size:
93" x 116 1/2"

On A Personal Note:

No matter the size or shape, everyone relates to that special place called "Home." Although our first home was small and in a different state, we still recall that special feeling of finally owning a place we could call our own. When Robert and I selected fabrics for this quilt, traditional colors were chosen to give a warm and cozy feeling. The great thing about this project is its versatility. Not only does it give us many side projects, but it gives us a place to personalize it. In our case, the 1985 date stitched onto our quilt signifies our move to Colorado and our first home in Durango. What a monumental task - but well worth the effort!

MATERIALS

Fabric I (beige print)	7 3/4 yards (need exactly 276")
Fabric II (med. olive print)	1 5/8 yards (need exactly 90 7/8")
Fabric III (med. green print)	7/8 yard (need exactly 28")
Fabric IV (light blue print)	3/8 yard (need exactly 11 1/2")
Fabric V (med. gray/blue print)	1/2 yard (need exactly 14 1/2")
Fabric VI (dark blue print)	3/8 yard (need exactly 12 1/2")
Fabric VII (tan check)	3/8 yard (need exactly 11")
Fabric VIII (dark green print)	1/4 yard (need exactly 7 1/2")
Backing	8 1/4 yards
Fabric IX (dark brown print)	1/4 yard (need exactly 6 1/2")
Fabric X (solid rust)	1/8 yard (need exactly 2 1/2")
Fabric XI (med. brown print)	1/8 yard (need exactly 3 1/2")
Fabric XII (dark gold print)	1/4 yard (need exactly 6")
Fabric XIII (light gold print)	3/8 yard (need exactly 12")
Fabric XIV (dark red print)	1/4 yard (need exactly 6 1/2")
Fabric XV (dark brown check)	1/8 yard (need exactly 4 1/2")
Fabric XVI (solid flesh)	1/8 yard (need exactly 3 1/2")

Cutting instructions shown in red indicate that the quantity of units are combined and cut in 2 or more different places to conserve fabric. *NOTE: All "Q" units in cutting instructions stand for "quilt top". These are units that are not incorporated into blocks.*

CUTTING

From Fabric I, cut: (beige print)

- One 10 1/2" wide strip. From this, cut:
  - * Two – 10" x 10 1/2" (Q22)
  - * One – 6 1/2" x 10 1/2" (Q25)
  - * Two – 4 1/2" x 10" (Q23)
  - * One – 4 1/2" x 8 1/2" (G17)
- One 8 1/2" wide strip. From this, cut:
  - * Four – 4 1/2" x 8 1/2" (Q6)
  - * Four – 4" x 8 1/2" (Q16, Q28)
  - * One – 3 1/2" x 8 1/2" (E16)
  - * Two – 2 1/2" x 8 1/2" (Q5)
- Two 7 1/2" wide strips. From this and scrap, cut:
  - * Four – 4" x 7 1/2" (Q29)
  - * Seventeen – 2 1/2" x 7 1/2" (D2, G13)
  - * Eighteen – 1 1/2" x 7 1/2" (B1, D3)
- One 6 1/2" wide strip. From this, cut:
  - * One – 5 1/2" x 6 1/2" (G3)
  - * One – 4 1/2" x 6 1/2" (Q24)
  - * Three – 3 1/2" x 6 1/2" (Q1, G4)
  - * Two – 2 1/2" x 6 1/2" (E5a)
  - * Two – 6" squares (Q17a)
- Three 6" wide strips. From these, cut:
  - * Two – 6" x 31 1/2" (Q18)
  - * Six – 6" squares (add to Q17a)
  - * Two – 3" x 6" (E4a)
  - * Two – 5 1/2" squares (Q32)
  - * Two – 3 1/2" x 5 1/2" (H6)
- Two 5 1/2" wide strips. From these, cut:
  - * Two – 5 1/2" x 18 1/2" (B13)
  - * Two – 4 1/2" x 5 1/2" (Q2)
  - * Two – 3" x 5 1/2" (E3a)
  - * Six – 2 1/2" x 5 1/2" (B7, E5b, Q21)
  - * Two – 2" x 5 1/2" (Q20)
  - * Two – 1 1/2" x 5 1/2" (Q Spacer 1)
  - * Two – 5" squares (E13a)
  - * Two – 3" x 5" (E4b)
- One 5" wide strip. From this, cut:
  - * Four – 3 1/2" x 5" (E2a)
  - * Four – 2 1/2" x 5" (E6a)
  - * Two – 2 1/2" x 16 1/2" (Q8)
- Two 4 1/2" wide strips. From these, cut:
  - * Ten – 4 1/2" squares (E1a, F7a)
  - * One – 3 1/2" x 4 1/2" (G14)
  - * Two – 3" x 4 1/2" (E3b)
  - * Six – 2 1/2" x 4 1/2" (Q7b, B9a)
  - * Two – 1 1/2" x 4 1/2" (F2)
  - * One – 4" x 13" (Q15, Q26)
- Sixteen 4" wide strips. From these, cut:
  - * Two – 4" x 41 1/2" strips (Q10) Piece together to equal one 4" x 82 1/2" strip.
  - * Two – 4" x 35 1/2" (Q12)
  - * Four – 4" x 22 1/2" (Q13)
  - * Four – 4" x 16" (Q27)
  - * Seven – 4" x 13" (add to Q15, Q26)
  - * Four – 4" x 12 1/2" (Q14)
  - * Forty – 4" squares (C1a)
  - * Two – 3 1/2" x 14 1/2" (B4)
- Five 3 1/2" wide strips. From these, cut:
  - * Two – 3 1/2" x 16" (E14)
  - * Forty-two – 3 1/2" squares (A1b)
  - * Two – 2 1/2" x 3 1/2" (F16)
  - * Nine – 2 1/2" x 3" (D1a)
- Fifteen 3" wide strips. From these, cut:
  - * Two – 3" x 42" (Q34)
  - * Four – 3" x 36" (Q34)

* Join the 36" long strips on opposite short sides of the 42" long strips to yield two 3" x 113" long borders.

  - * Four – 3" x 41" (Q30) piece short ends together to yield two 3" x 81 1/2" borders
  - * Two– 3" x 41 1/2" (Q33) piece short ends together to yield one 3" x 82 1/2" border.
  - * Two – 3" x 36 1/2" (Q31) piece short ends together to yield one 3" x 72 1/2" border.
  - * Two – 3" x 16 1/2" (Q9)
- Twenty-one 2 1/2" wide strips. Ten for Strip Set 1. From remainder and scrap, cut:
  - * One – 2 1/2" x 14 1/2" (Q3)
  - * Two – 2 1/2" x 12 1/2" (Spacer 2)
  - * Twenty-three – 2 1/2" x 3" (add to D1a)
  - * 130 – 2 1/2" squares (B5a, B6c, B10, F4a, F8, G6a, G16, H3, I1a, I2a, J1a, K1a, K2a, Q7a)
  - * One – 2" x 12 1/2" (Q11)
  - * Eight – 2" x 2 1/2" (H2)
- Two 2" wide strips. From these, cut:
  - * Two – 2" x 25 1/2" (Q4) piece short ends together to yield one 2" x 50 1/2"
  - * One – 1 1/2" x 11 1/2" (F17)
  - * Four – 1 1/2" x 3 1/2" (F10, G10a)
  - * Five – 1 1/2" squares (A1a, B2, B3a, B9d, B11a, F14, G15a, H5a)
- Seven 1 1/2" wide strips. From these, cut:
  - * Two – 1 1/2" x 33 1/2" (H7)
  - * Two – 1 1/2" x 24" (Q19) Piece together to = one 47 1/2" long strip.
  - * Two - 1 1/2" x 12 1/2" (QSpacer 3)
  - * Two – 1 1/2" x 2 1/2" (B12)
  - * Ninety-eight – 1 1/2" squares (add to A1a, B2, B3a, B9d, B11a, F14, G15a, H5a)

From Fabric II, cut: (medium olive print)

- 1 yard for bias binding
- One 7" wide strip. From this, cut:
  - * Four – 7" squares (Q17)
  - * Eight – 3 1/2" squares (J1, Q37)
- One 5 1/2" wide strip. From this, cut:
  - * One – 5 1/2" x 11 1/2" (F4)
- From scrap, cut:
  - * Sixteen – 1 1/2" x 2 1/2" (Q35)
- Six 3 1/2" wide strips. From these, cut:
  - * Seventy – 3 1/2" squares (add to J1, Q37)
  - * One – 2 1/2" x 3 1/2" (F5)
  - * Two – 2 1/2" squares (F7b)
  - * One – 2 7/8" square (Q38) cut in half diagonally to yield 2 triangles.
- One 1 7/8" wide strip. From this, cut:
  - * Twenty-two – 1 7/8" squares (Q35a, Q36a) cut in half diagonally to yield 44 triangles.

• Thirteen 1 1/2" wide strips. Ten for Strip Set 1. From remainder, cut:

* One – 1 1/2" x 42" (Q39)
* Two – 1 1/2" x 26 1/4" (Q39)
* Join the 26 1/4" strips on opposite short ends of the 42" long strip for one 1 1/2" x 93 1/2" strip.
* Six – 1 1/2" x 4" (Q36)

From Fabric III, cut: (medium green print)

• Two 7 1/2" wide strips. From these, cut:
  * Twenty- 4" x 7 1/2" (C1)

• Two 6 1/2" wide strips. From these, cut:
  * Twenty-six – 2 1/2" x 6 1/2" (D1,Q7)

From Fabric IV, cut: (light blue print)

• One 9" wide strip. From this, cut:
  * Two – 3 1/2" x 9" (E7)
  * Two – 3 1/2" x 8 1/2" (B6)
  * Two – 2" x 8 1/2" (E9)
  * Two – 1 1/2" x 8 1/2" (E10)
  * Six – 2 1/2" squares (E8a, E11a)

• One 2 1/2" wide strip. From this, cut:
  * One – 2 1/2" x 23 1/2" (E12)

From Fabric V, cut: (medium gray/blue print)

• Two 5 1/2" wide strips. From these, cut:
  * One – 5 1/2" x 6 1/2" (G5)
  * Twenty-two – 3 1/2" x 5 1/2" (A1)

• One 3 1/2" wide strip. From this, cut:
  * Two – 3 1/2" x 5 1/2" (add to A1)
  * One – 3 1/2" square (F6)
  * Two – 1 1/2" x 3 1/2" (G10)
  * Two – 1 1/2" x 2 1/2" (G8)
  * One – 2 1/2" x 11 1/2" (F3)

From Fabric VI, cut: (dark blue print)

• One 6 1/2" wide strip. From this, cut:
  * Two – 4 1/2" x 6 1/2" (K2)
  * Four – 2 1/2" x 6 1/2" (K1)
  * Four – 4 1/2" x 6" (I2)
  * Two – 2 1/2" x 6" (I1)

• One 6" wide strip. From this, cut:
  * Six – 2 1/2" x 6" (add to I1)
  * Two – 4 1/2" x 5 1/2" (F7)
  * Six – 1 1/2" x 7 1/2" (H1)

• From scrap, cut:
  * Eight – 1 1/2" x 2 1/2" (H4)

From Fabric VII, cut: (tan check)

• One 7 1/2" wide strip. From this, cut:
  * One – 7 1/2" x 25 1/2" (E13)
  * Six – 3 1/2" x 5 1/2" (A1)

• One 3 1/2" wide strip. From this, cut:
  * Six – 3 1/2" x 5 1/2" (add to A1)

From Fabric VIII, cut: (dark green print)

• One 4 1/2" wide strip. From this, cut:
  * Four – 4 1/2" x 12 1/2" (E1)
  * Two – 3 1/2" x 9 1/2" (E2)
  * Two – 3" x 7 1/2" (E3)
  * One – 3" x 6 1/2" (E4)

• One 3" wide strip. From this, cut:
  * One – 3" x 6 1/2" (add to E4)
  * Two - 2 1/2" x 4 1/2" (E5)

From Fabric IX, cut: (dark brown print)

• One 6 1/2" wide strip. From this, cut:
  * One – 6 1/2" x 11 1/2" (E11)
  * Two – 3 1/2" x 4 1/2" (E15)
  * One – 3 1/2" squares (G1)
  * One – 1 1/2" x 3 1/2" (F1)

From Fabric X, cut: (solid rust)

• One 2 1/2" wide strip. From this, cut:
  * Two – 2 1/2" x 3 1/2" (E6)
  * Two – 2 1/2" squares (F9)
  * Two – 1 1/2" x 5 1/2" (G11, F15)
  * One – 1 1/2" x 3 1/2" (F13)
  * Two – 1 1/2" squares (F11)

From Fabric XI, cut: (medium brown print)

• One 3 1/2" wide strip. From this, cut:
  * One – 3 1/2" square (G14a)
  * Two – 1 1/2" squares (B1a)
  * Two – 2 1/2" x 8 1/2" (B9b)
  * One – 2 1/2" x 5 1/2" (G6)
  * Three – 2 1/2" squares (B6c, G16)

From Fabric XII, cut: (dark gold print)

• One 3 1/2" wide strip. From this, cut:
  * One – 3 1/2" x 5 1/2" (G12)
  * Four – 3 1/2" squares (B3, B6c)
  * Four – 2 1/2" x 5 1/2" (B5, B9)

• One 2 1/2" wide strip. From this, cut:
  * Four – 2 1/2" squares (B6b, B11)
  * Two – 1 1/2" x 5 1/2" (B8)
  * Five – 1 1/2" squares (B6a, B9c, G9)

From Fabric XIII, cut: (light gold print)

• One 6 1/2" wide strip. From this, cut:
  * Two – 6 1/2" x 8 1/2" (E8)

• One 5 1/2" wide strip. From this, cut:
  * One – 5 1/2" x 27 1/2" (I15)

From Fabric XIV, cut: (dark red print)

• One 6 1/2" wide strip. From this, cut:
  * One – 4 1/2" x 6 1/2" (K2)
  * Two – 2 1/2" x 6 1/2" (K1)
  * Six – 3 1/2" x 5 1/2" (A1)

From Fabric XV, cut: (dark brown check)

• One 4 1/2" wide strip. From this, cut:
  * Two – 4 1/2" x 7 1/2" (flower boxes)

From Fabric XVI, cut: (solid flesh)

• One 3 1/2" wide strip. From this, cut:
  * Two – 3 1/2" squares (F12, G2)
  * One – 2 1/2" square (G15)
  * One – 1 1/2" x 2 1/2" (G7)

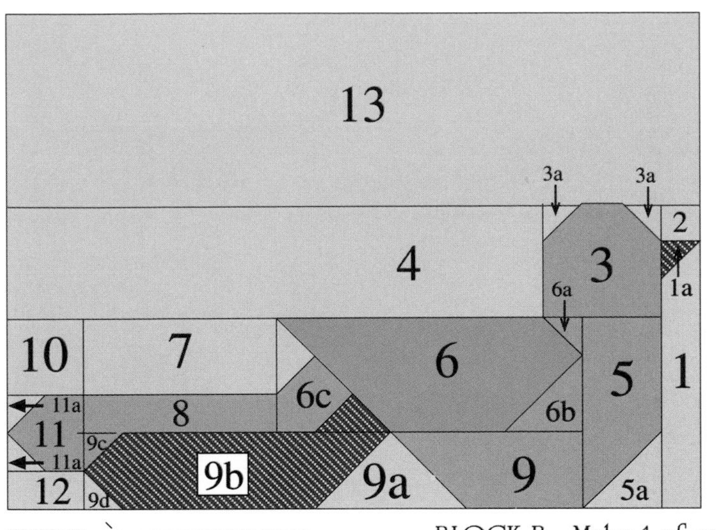

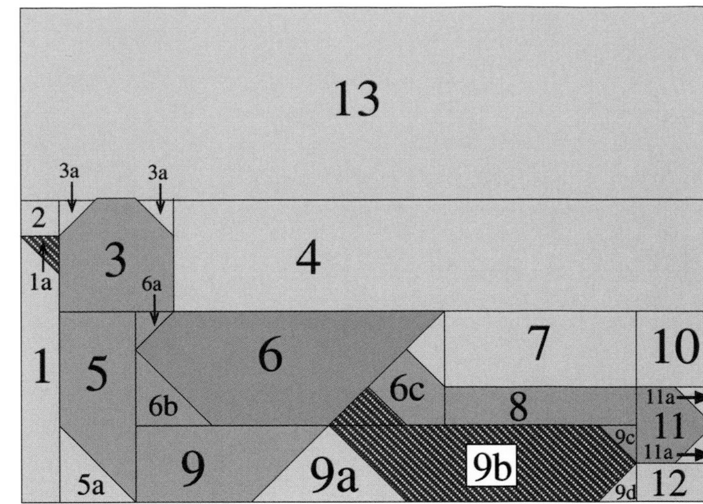

BLOCK B - Make 1 of each. - Finishes to: 13" x 18"

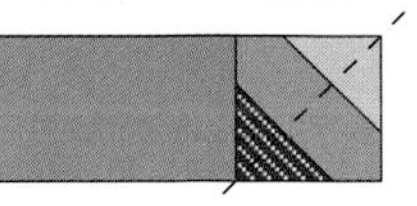

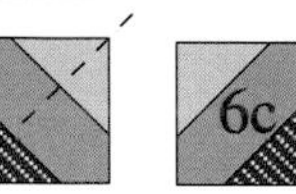

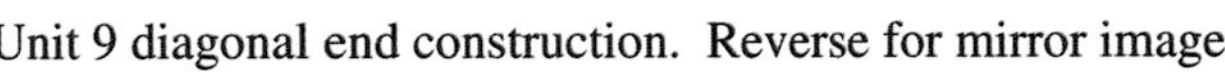
Unit 9 diagonal end construction. Reverse for mirror image.

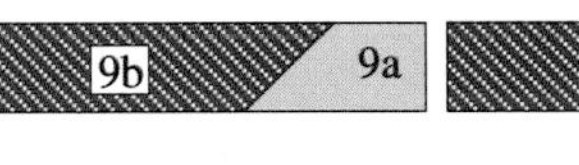

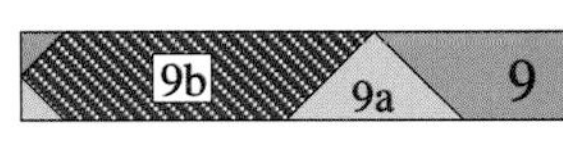

ASSEMBLY

STRIP SETS

1. Refer to illustration below and make Strip Set 1 as shown, using fabrics I and II. Cut segments as directed. Repeat this procedure for all three strip sets.

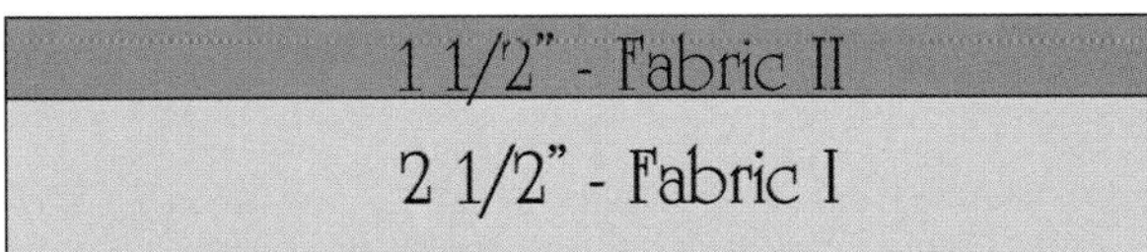

Strip Set 1. Make 10

Cut two - 14 1/2" segments (Unit 1c)
Cut nineteen - 11 1/2" segments (Unit 1d)
Cut four - 6" segments (Unit 1e)
Cut eight - 5" segments (Unit 1a)
Cut twenty-four - 4 1/2" segments (Unit 1b)

BLOCK A

1. Use diagonal corner technique to make two each of mirror image units 1. Join together as shown. Make a total of twenty-one Block A hearts from the fabrics given in the block illustration.

Block A - Make 21
Finishes to: 5" x 6"
Make 3 from Fabric XIV
Make 6 from Fabric VII
Make 12 from Fabric V

BLOCK B

1. Please note that there are two of Block B, and that they are mirror images. Both drawings are furnished for easy reference.
2. For each block, use diagonal corner technique to make one each of units 1, 3, 5, 6, and 11.
3. For Unit 6, refer to illustration above showing multiple diagonal corner Unit 6c. Make this unit for the two mirror image blocks. Join diagonal corners 6a and 6b first; then add Unit 6c as shown. Correct placement and accuracy of stitching is essential to make this section work.
4. Use diagonal end technique to make one of Unit 9. Join continuous diagonal corners 9a and 9b first; then add diagonal corners 9c and 9d as shown.
5. To assemble Block B, begin by joining units 1 and 2. Join units 3 and 4. Join units 7 and 8; then add Unit 6 to these combined units as shown. Please refer to mirror image drawing frequently for correct placement of units.
6. Join units 10, 11, and 12 in a vertical row as shown. Join completed Unit 9 to bottom of combined units 6-8. Join units 5 and combined units 10-12 to opposite ends of Peacock as shown. Add combined units 3-4 to top of wing section; then join combined units 1-2 to head section.
7. Join Unit 13 to top of bird to complete Block B.
8. For Peacock top feather, refer to drawing of quilt for correct placement, and draw feathers in place. Place tear-away pellon behind each applique section. Use close, medium wide satin stitch in brown thread and stitch feathers. Tear pellon away on back and satin stitch circular feather design by hand with 2 strands of brown embroidery thread.

BLOCK C

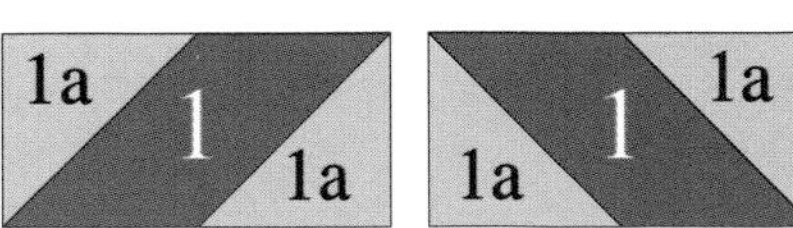

BLOCK C - Make 10 of each
Finishes to: 3 1/2" x 7"

1. Please note that Block C is a mirror image. Both illustrations are shown for easy reference.
2. Use diagonal corner technique to make Unit 1 of Block C. Make ten of each as directed above.

BLOCK D

1. Please note that Block D is a mirror image. Both illustrations are shown for easy reference.
2. Use diagonal corner technique to make one of Unit 1 as shown.

3. To assemble block, join Unit 2 to top of leaf and Unit 3 to bottom of leaf to complete Block D.

BLOCK E

1. Use diagonal corner technique to make one each of units 11 and 13.
2. Use diagonal corner technique to make two each of Unit 8 and four each of Unit 1.
3. Use diagonal end technique to make two each of units 2, 3, 4, and 5. Refer often to illustration for correct placement of units, as trees are mirror images.
4. To assemble Block E, begin by joining units 10-8 and 9 in a

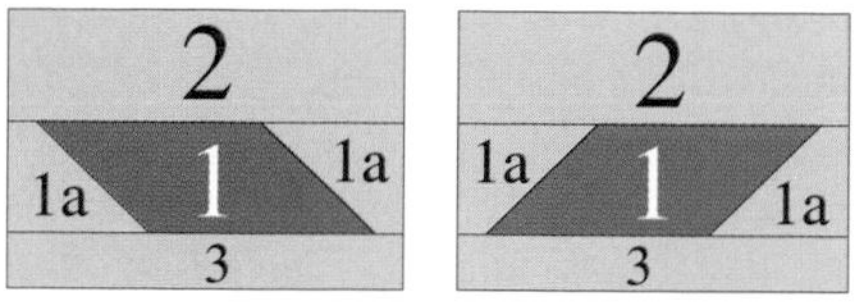

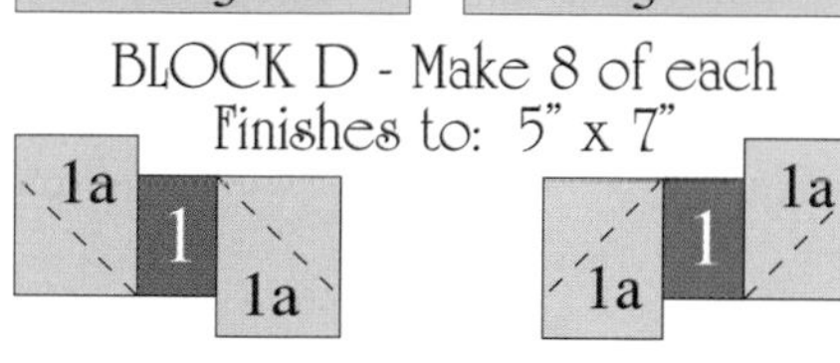

BLOCK D - Make 8 of each
Finishes to: 5" x 7"

BLOCK F

1. Use diagonal corner technique to make one of Unit 4, and two of mirror image Unit 7.
2. To assemble Block F, begin by joining units 2-1-2 in a horizontal row. Add units 3 and 4 as shown.
3. Join units 5 and 6 in a row; then add mirror image units 7 to opposite sides of these combined units, checking correct placement of arm units 7. Add this completed section to skirt section.
4. For head section, join units 14-13-14 in a row as shown; then join Unit 15 to bottom. Add Unit 16 to opposite sides of combined hair units; then add Unit 17 to top as shown.
5. Join mirror image units 8 and 9. Join units 10 and 11. Join these two combined units together and add to opposite sides of head Unit 12. Join combined units 13-17 to top of head section.
6. Join head and body sections together as shown to complete Block F.

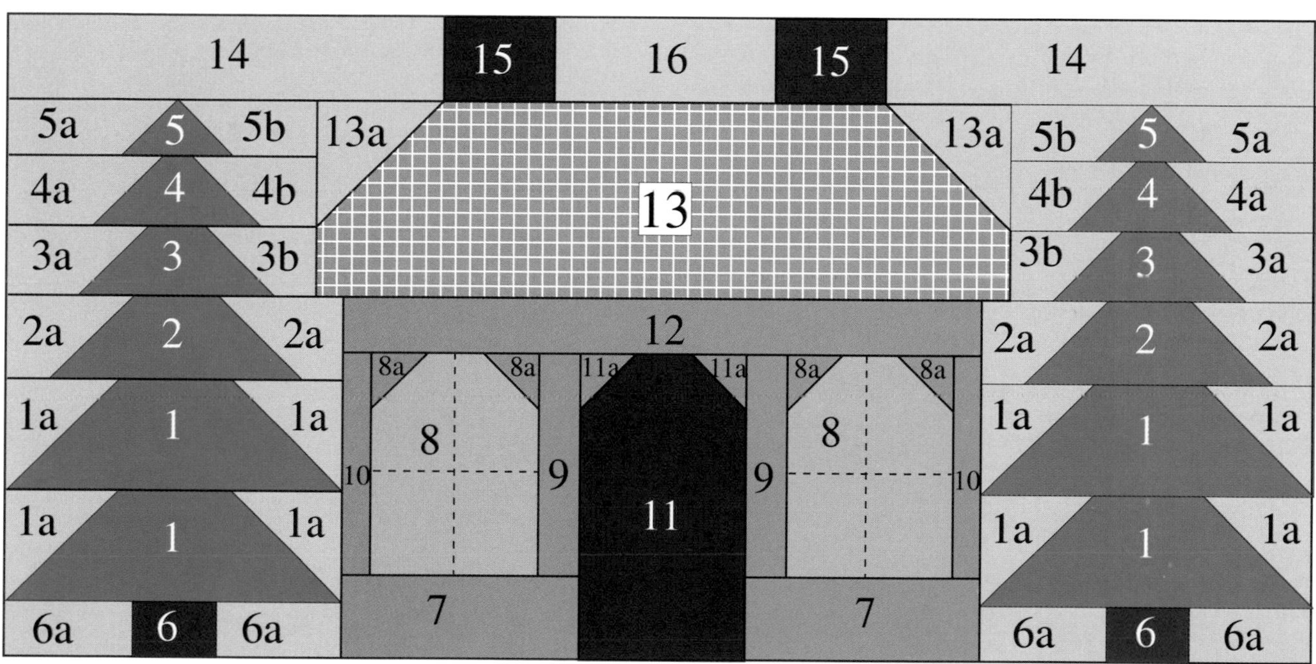

BLOCK E - Make 1 - Finishes to: 23" x 47"

row. Refer to illustration for correct placement of mirror image units 9 and 10 for right window.

5. Join Unit 7 to bottom of 8-10 combined units. Join the window sections to opposite sides of door Unit 11 as shown; then add Unit 12 to top. Set aside.
6. Join units 6a-6-6a in a row as shown. Join the two Unit 1 sections for each tree together; then add completed Unit 6 to bottom and Unit 2 to the top. Join these tree sections to opposite sides of house bottom, checking for correct placement of mirror image Unit 2.
7. Join mirror image units 3, 4, and 5 in a row as shown; then join to opposite sides of roof Unit 13. Add these combined tree/roof units to house bottom.
8. Referring to illustration, join units 14-15-16-15 and 14 in a horizontal row as shown; then join to top of house to complete Block E.
9. Refer to complete quilt diagram and draw cross sections in windows. Use tear-away pellon behind windows, and using a close, medium-wide satin stitch in brown thread, stitch window cross sections. Tear pellon away from back.

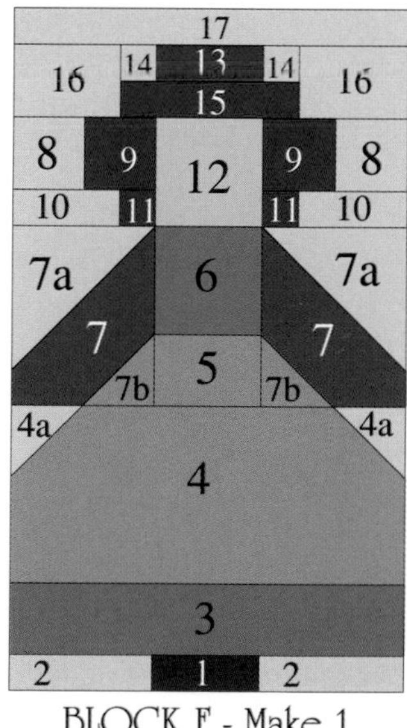

BLOCK F - Make 1
Finishes to: 11" x 19"

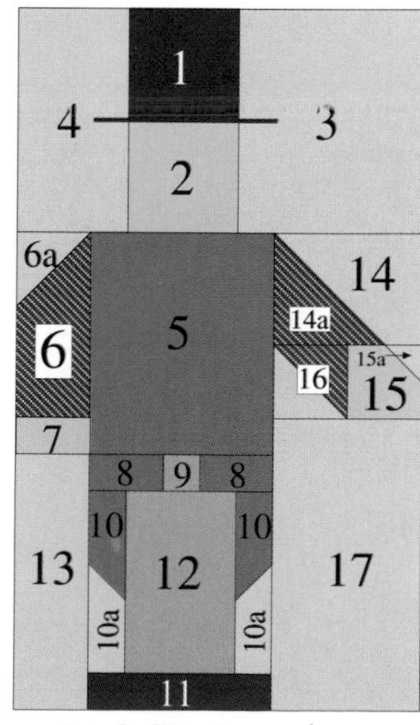

BLOCK G - Make 1
Finishes to: 11" x 19"

BLOCK G

1. Use diagonal corner technique to make one each of units 6, 14, and 15.
2. Use diagonal end technique to make two mirror image units 10.
3. To make Unit 16, place 2 1/2" squares of fabrics I and XI right sides together. Draw a diagonal line down center, and stitch on line. Trim seam and press.
4. To assemble Block G, join units 1 and 2; then add Unit 3 to right side of combined units, and Unit 4 to left side.
5. Join units 6 and 7; then add to body Unit 5 as shown.
6. Join units 15 and 16; then add Unit 14 to top of combined units, matching arm seam as shown. Join Unit 17 to bottom of combined units.
7. Join units 8-9-8 in a horizontal row. Join units 10-12-10 in a row; then add combined units 8-9-8 to top and Unit 11 to bottom. Join Unit 13 to left side of these combined units.
8. Join suit section to extended arm section, then join head section to top of all combined units to complete Block G.
9. Draw a line that extends 2" beyond bottom of hat on each side. Draw a line down center of Unit 12, forming two legs. Place tear-away pellon behind hat and leg line and satin stitch lines with dark brown thread. Tear pellon away.

BLOCK H

1. Use diagonal corner technique to make one of Unit 5.
2. To assemble block, refer to illustration and make four vertical rows of units 2-4-3-4 and 2 as shown. Join units 1 to each side of combined units to make the fences.
3. For center section, join units 6 to opposite sides of Unit 5; then add units 7 to top and bottom as shown. Join fences on opposite sides of center section.
4. Print your own personalization, using water erasable pen in plaque Unit 5. Place tear-away pellon behind printed area, and satin stitch in the color of your choice. Tear pellon away.

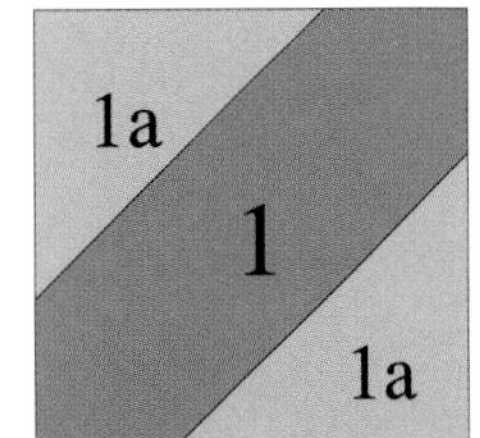

BLOCK I - Make 4
Finishes to: 5 1/2" x 8"

BLOCK I

1. Use diagonal corner technique to make one of Unit 2, and one each of mirror image units 1.
2. Join units 1-2-1 together in a row as shown, matching seams to complete Block I.

BLOCK J - Make 28
Finishes to: 3" square

BLOCK J

1. Use diagonal corner technique to make Block J as shown.

BLOCK K

1. Use diagonal corner technique to make one of Unit 2. Make one each of mirror image units 1.
2. Join units 1-2-1 together in a row as shown, matching seams to complete Block K.

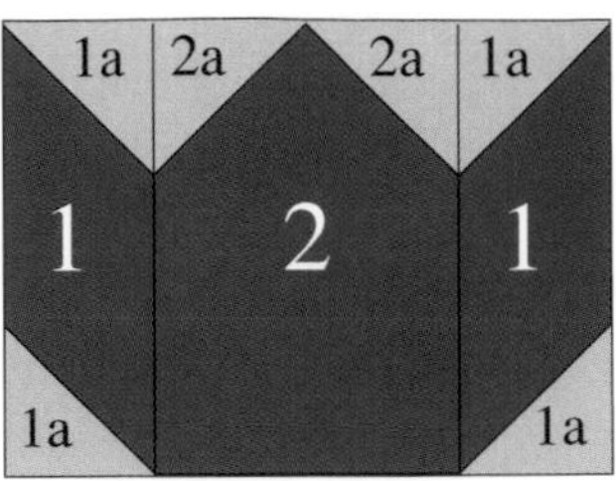

BLOCK K - Make 3
Finishes to: 6" x 8"
Make 2 Fabric VI
Make 1 Fabric XIV

UNIT 7

1. Leaf units 7 are made by using the diagonal corner and diagonal end techniques as shown. Refer to illustrations for correct placement of mirror image units.

Unit 7

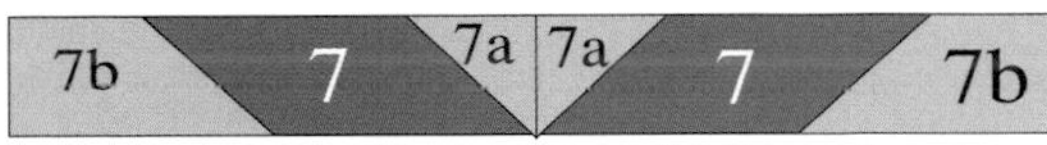

Make 3 - Finishes to: 2" x 12"
(diagonal corners)

Make 2 - Finishes to: 2" x 16" (diagonal ends)

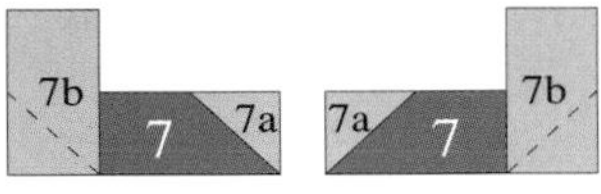

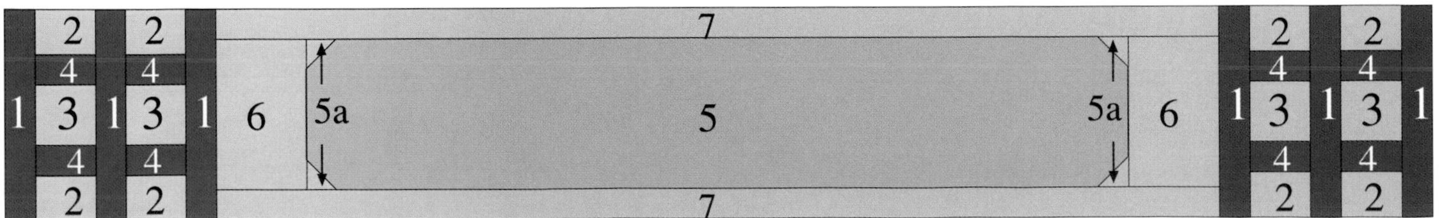

BLOCK H - Make 1 - Finishes to: 7" x 47"

QUILT ASSEMBLY

QUILT TOP SECTION

1. Join Unit Q1 to opposite sides of Fabric XIV tulip K; then add Unit Q3 to bottom of this tulip section.
2. Join Unit Q2 to opposite sides of Fabric V heart Block A as shown. Join heart to bottom of tulip.
3. Join mirror image peacock blocks B to opposite sides of assembled tulip/heart; then add Unit Q4 across bottom of combined blocks.
4. Join Unit Q5 to top of remaining Block K tulips; then join Unit Q6 to opposite sides and Unit Q8 across bottom. Join Unit Q9 to bottom of diagonal end leaf Unit Q7. Add these combined units to bottom of Unit Q8. Make two of these combined tulip/leaf sections. Add these sections to opposite sides of peacock blocks; then join pieced Unit Q10 across top.
5. Join Unit Q11 to bottom of one diagonal corner Unit Q7 as shown; then join units 12 to opposite sides of leaf Q7 unit.
6. To make a template for the large cross stitches, draw a 2" square box and mark an "X" diagonally from corner to corner. Trace the "X" onto template plastic and cut out with X-acto knife. Trace first "X" 10 1/2" from edge of leaf Unit Q7 with water erasable pen. Center the "X" on Unit Q12. Draw two more "X's" 1" apart as shown in large quilt diagram. Using rust thread, satin stitch large cross stitches with tear-away pellon behind them. *If you have an embroidery machine, you may wish to stitch out the X's using your machine/software.*
7. Join combined leaf Unit Q7 and large cross stitches to bottom of tulip/peacock section. Draw legs and top knots on peacocks, and stamens on tulips as shown. Satin stitch as before. Using two strands of embroidery floss, satin stitch by hand the 1/4" top knot circle tips on peacocks and tulips.
8. For center section of quilt top and bottom, begin by joining two Block I tulips on opposite sides of Unit Q18. Make two. For top and bottom of center section Refer to quilt diagram and find center of bottom Unit Q18. Draw series of "X's" as shown and satin stitch.
9. Join pieced Unit Q19 to bottom of Block E house; then add Block H as shown.
10. Join Unit Q24, one Fabric XIV "A" Block and Unit Q25 in a vertical row. Join Blocks F & G to opposite sides as shown. Keeping in mind that these are mirror image units, join units Q20 and Q21 to opposite sides of remaining Fabric XIV heart blocks A. Join these heart sections to opposite sides of F & G blocks. Add to bottom of Block H.
11. Join Unit Q18 with tulip Block I corners to top and bottom of center section, making certain that Q18 tulip unit with "X's" is at the bottom as shown.
12. Join units Q13 and Q14 with two mirror image C blocks as shown in illustration. Make 2.
13. For vine top and bottom row, refer to quilt diagram and join Strip Set Unit 1a with Block J matching seams. Check diagram for correct placement and make 2 mirror image units for ends of rows. For center of row, alternate five Strip Set Unit 1b segments with four J blocks, checking correct position of strip set segment and J blocks. Make 2 of these rows.
14. Join units Q15 and Q16 with two mirror image C blocks as shown in illustration. Make 2.
15. Refer to illustration and join vine row with combined units Q15-Q16- and Block C rows. Add these rows as shown to top and bottom of quilt center section.
16. For vine side rows, refer to quilt diagram and join Strip Set Unit 1a with Block J matching seams. Check diagram for correct placement and make 2 mirror image units for ends of rows. For center of row, alternate seven Strip Set Unit 1b segments with six J blocks, checking correct position of strip set segment and J blocks. Make 2 of these rows.
17. Join Unit Q13 with two mirror image C blocks and two Unit Q26 as shown. Make two of these rows.
18. Join the vine and leaf rows together; then add Unit Q17 to opposite ends, matching vine seams. Join these rows to sides of center section matching vine seams at top and bottom.
19. Join units Q27, Q28 and Q29 with four mirror image C blocks as shown in illustration. Add these rows to sides of quilt top, matching seams where leaf "C" blocks match to vines.
20. Join pieced border Unit Q30 to opposite sides of center section; then join pieced border Unit Q31 to bottom.
21. Referring to illustration for correct placement of mirror image leaf blocks D, make a row of D blocks and A blocks, alternating Fabric V and VII hearts. Add this row to bottom of quilt.
22. For side heart/leaf rows, begin with Spacer 1 joined to one Fabric V "A" block as shown. Join Spacers 1 and 3 to top and bottom of leaf Unit Q7 as shown. Complete row by alternating five mirror image D blocks with three Fabric V "A" blocks and two Fabric VII "A" blocks as shown. Join Unit Q32 to bottom of each row. Add rows to sides of quilt.
23. Join the top peacock section to the house section of the quilt top; then join pieced border Unit Q33 to the bottom of the quilt. Join pieced border Unit Q34 to opposite sides of quilt top as shown.

MAKING SCALLOPED BORDER

1. To make any scalloped unit, use the correct Strip Set 1 segment shown in the illustration below, and add diagonal corner Q37 to opposite ends of the unit as shown.
2. For the bottom scalloped border, triangle units Q36a are added to bottom of Unit Q36. This unit is then added to Unit S/S/ 1d. Diagram shows dashed line where Unit 37 is trimmed even with small triangle on Unit 36. Trim all scalloped units in this manner except for segment S/S 1c. For Unit S/S 1c, refer to diagram showing that one side is trimmed and the other is not trimmed so that it is even with the top border.
3. Use diagonal corner technique and make all of Strip Set 1 units 1c, 1d, and 1e as shown.
4. For quilt bottom scallop, join two of S/S 1e, six of Unit Q36 and five of S/S 1d in a row as shown; then join to quilt bottom.

5. For side scallops, each row begins with S/S 1c. Eight Unit Q35 are alternated between S/S 1d and S/S 1e as shown. Finish each row off at bottom edge with one Unit Q38 triangle. Make two of these rows, referring to diagram for proper order of units; then join to quilt sides.
6. To complete scallops, trim each Unit Q37 as directed above.

QUILTING

1. Refer to our illustratioin and the CD-ROM under "My First Home Pillows," for stitching patterns for quilt.
2. Cut 540" of 2" wide bias binding and bind your quilt.

FINISHING

Making Flower Box & Flowers

1. For flower boxes, fold 4 1/2" x 7 1/2" piece of Fabric XV in half widthwise, right sides together. Stitch around three sides, leaving opening to turn. Clip corners and turn right side out. Slip stitch opening closed.
2. Pin flower box so that it lays approximately 1" up from bottom of window and is centered. Top stitch in place around 3 sides, leaving the top open.
3. Cut 1" wide strips of bias from scraps of Fabrics II and III for flower stems. Using 1/4" seams, stitch bias strips right sides together along lengthwise edge. Trim seams to 1/8".
4. Place raw seam at back side of bias, and press bias on right side. Trim to desired lengths and pin one or two along fence and 3-4 in each flower box. Curve the bias for the flower stems. Hand whip in place, turning under short raw edges.
5. To make the yo yo flowers, determine the size that you want your completed flower to be. As an example, if you want a 1 1/2" in circumference circle, you will need to draw a 3 1/2" in circumference circle. Turn under 1/4" seam allowance. We finger press the seam under.
6. Run a gathering stitch by hand around outside top edge of circle using two strands of thread. Be sure to catch in your turned under seam allowance. Gather tightly and tie off your gathering threads. Turn over and hand tack around the center circle so that it stays in place.
7. Secure the flower to the quilt top with a button in the center hole. Make desired number of flowers in different sizes and colors.

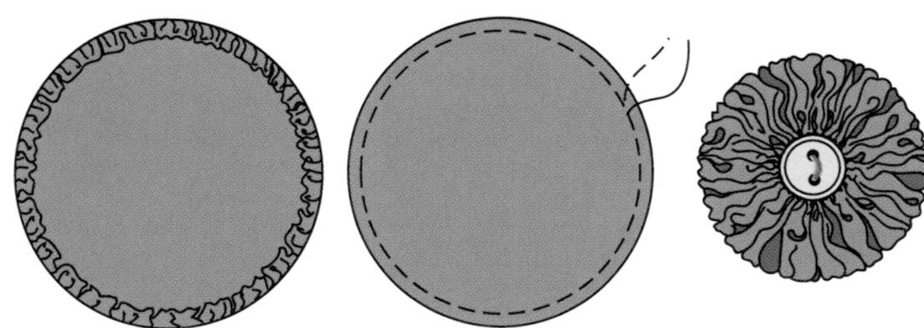

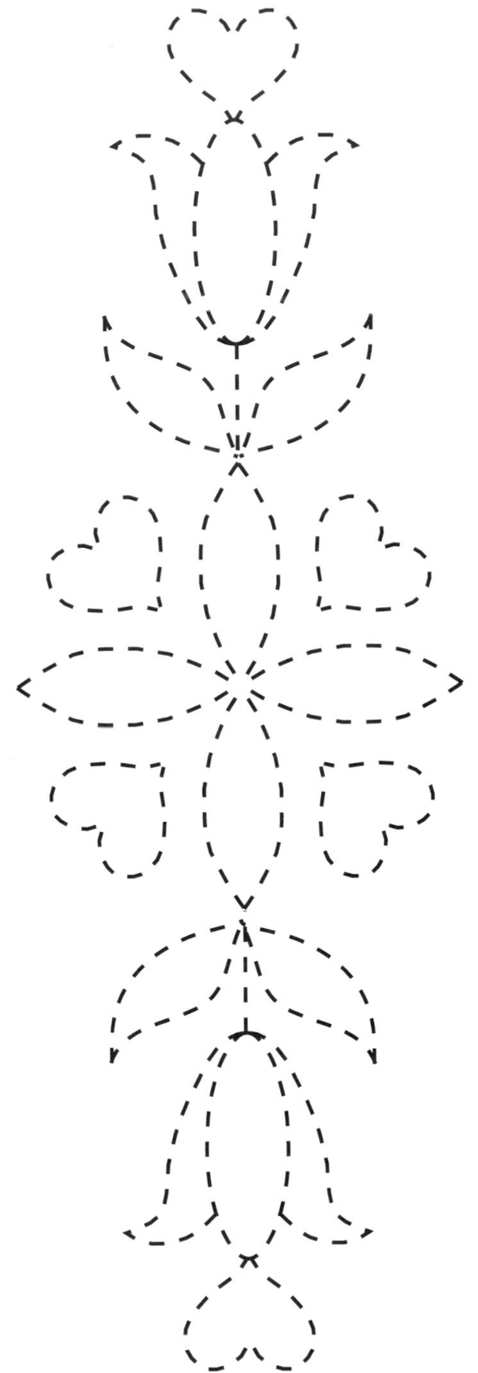

Quilt Assembly Diagram

Quilting Illustration

First Home Tablecloth

First Home Tablecloth

Finished size: 73" x 87"

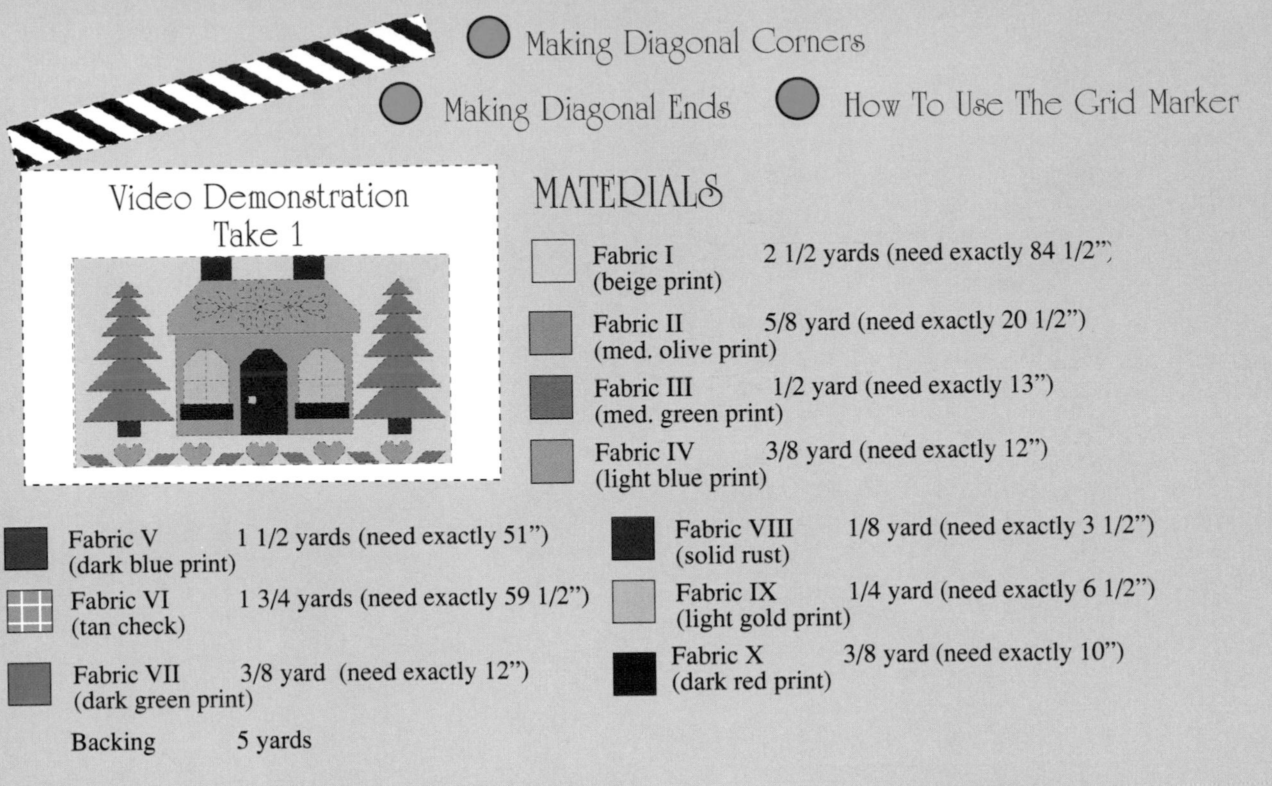

MATERIALS

Fabric I (beige print)	2 1/2 yards (need exactly 84 1/2")
Fabric II (med. olive print)	5/8 yard (need exactly 20 1/2")
Fabric III (med. green print)	1/2 yard (need exactly 13")
Fabric IV (light blue print)	3/8 yard (need exactly 12")
Fabric V (dark blue print)	1 1/2 yards (need exactly 51")
Fabric VI (tan check)	1 3/4 yards (need exactly 59 1/2")
Fabric VII (dark green print)	3/8 yard (need exactly 12")
Fabric VIII (solid rust)	1/8 yard (need exactly 3 1/2")
Fabric IX (light gold print)	1/4 yard (need exactly 6 1/2")
Fabric X (dark red print)	3/8 yard (need exactly 10")
Backing	5 yards

CUTTING

Cutting instructions shown in red indicate that the quantity of units are combined and cut in 2 or more different places to conserve fabric.

From Fabric I, cut: (beige print)

- One 12 1/2" wide strip. From this, cut:
  - One – 6 1/2 x 12 1/2" (T1)
  - Four – 4 1/2" x 12 1/2" (T11)
  - Four – 3 1/2" x 12 1/2" (T8)
  - **Sixteen – 1 1/2" squares (A1a)**
- One 6 1/2" wide strip. From this, cut:
  - Four – 6 1/2" square (T12a)
  - **Two – 5 1/2" x 6 1/2" (T4)**
  - **Six – 2" x 2 1/2" (D2)**
  - **Two – 2 1/2" x 6 1/2" (B5a)**
- Two 6" wide strips. From this, cut:
  - Four – 6" x 16 1/2" (T5)
  - Four – 3" x 6" (B4a)
- One 5 1/2" wide strip. From this and scrap, cut:
  - **Two – 5 1/2" x 6 1/2" (add to T4)**
  - Four – 4 1/2" x 5 1/2" (T3)
  - **Three – 3" x 5 1/2" (B3a)**
  - **Two – 2" x 2 1/2" (add to D2)**
- Three 5" wide strips. From these, cut:
  - Four – 5" x 7 1/2" (T2)
  - Four – 5" squares (C4a)
  - Eight – 3 1/2" x 5" (B2a, C3)
  - Four – 2 1/2" x 5" (B6a)
  - **Twenty-six – 2 1/2" squares (D3, G1a)**
- Three 4 1/2" wide strips. From these, cut:
  - Two – 4 1/2" x 24 1/2" (T9)

* Eight – 4 1/2" squares (B1a)
* Two – 3 1/2" x 10 1/2" (T7)
* One – 3" x 5 1/2" (add to B3a)

• Three 3 1/2" wide strips. From these, cut:

* Two – 3 1/2" x 8 1/2" (C1)
* Twenty-four – 3 1/2" squares (A1b, E1a)
* Two – 2 1/2" x 6 1/2" (add to B5a)

• From scrap, cut:

* Ten – 2 1/2" squares (add to D3, G1a)
* Sixteen – 1 1/2" squares (add to A1a)

• Three 2 1/2" wide strips. Two for Strip Set 1. From remaining strips, cut:

* Four – 2 1/2" x 23 1/2" (T6) piece two together to = two 2 1/2" x 46 1/2"
* Eight – 2" x 2 1/2" (add to D2)

• One 1 1/2" wide strips. From these, cut:

* Four – 1 1/2" x 6 1/2" (C9)

From Fabric II, cut: (medium olive print)

• One 7 1/2" wide strip. From this, cut:

* Four – 7 1/2" squares (T12)
* Six – 3 1/2" squares (G1)

• Two 3 1/2" wide strips. From these, cut:

* Twenty-two – 3 1/2" squares (add to G1)

• Four 1 1/2" wide strips for Strip Sets 1 and 2.

From Fabric III, cut: (medium green print)

• Two 6 1/2" wide strips. From these, cut:

* Twenty – 3 1/2" x 6 1/2" (E1, F1)

From Fabric IV, cut: (light blue print)

• One 3 1/2" wide strip. From this, cut:

* Four – 3 1/2" x 9 " (C11)

• Two 2 1/2" wide strips. From these, cut:

* Two – 2 1/2" x 23 1/2" (C12)
* Twelve – 2 1/2" squares (C5a, C6a)

• One 2" wide strip. From this, cut:

* Four – 2" x 8 1/2" (C7)

• One 1 1/2" wide strip. From this, cut:

* Four – 1 1/2" x 8 1/2" (C8)

From Fabric V, cut: (dark blue print)

• Two 7 1/2" wide strips. From these, cut:

* Two – 7 1/2" x 25 1/2" (C4)
* Twelve – 1 1/2" x 7 1/2" (C10, D1)
* Sixteen – 1 1/2" x 2 1/2" (D4)

• Eight 2 1/2" wide strips for straight grain binding.

• Eight 2" x 42 1/2" wide strips.

* - Four for (Border T20) piece 2 together to = two 84 1/2" borders.
* Four 2" x 37" for (Border T21) piece 2 together to = two 73 1/2" borders.

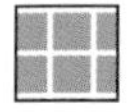

From Fabric VI, cut: (tan check)

• One 6 1/2" wide strip. From this, cut:

* Four – 6 1/2" squares (T12b)
* Twelve – 2 1/2" squares (G1b)

• Eight 3 1/2" wide strips. From these and scrap, cut:

* Two – 3 1/2" x 24 1/2" (T16)
* Four – 3 1/2" x 15 1/2" (T17)
* Four – 3 1/2" x 12 1/2" (T15)
* Two – 3 1/2" x 10 1/2" (T13)
* Four – 3 1/2" x 8 1/2" (T14)
* Twenty-four – 3 1/2" squares (F1a)
* Sixteen – 2 1/2" squares (add to G1b)

• Ten 2 1/2" wide strips. Two strips for Strip Set 2. From remaining strips, cut:

* Four – 2 1/2" x 40 1/2" (T18) piece 2 together to = two 80 1/2" strips.
* Four – 2 1/2" x 35 1/2" (T19) piece 2 together to = two 70 1/2" strips.

From Fabric VII, cut: (dark green print)

• Two 4 1/2" strips. From these, cut:

* Four – 4 1/2" x 12 1/2" (B1)
* Two – 2 1/2" x 4 1/2" (B5)
* Two – 3 1/2" x 9 1/2" (B2)
* One – 3" x 7 1/2" (B3)

• One 3" wide strip. From this, cut:

* One – 3" x 7 1/2" (add to B3)
* Two – 3" x 6 1/2" (B4)

From Fabric VIII, cut: (solid rust)

• One 3 1/2" wide strip. From this, cut:

* Four – 3 1/2" x 4 1/2" (C2)
* Two – 2 1/2" x 3 1/2" (B6)

From Fabric IX, cut: (light gold print)

• One 6 1/2" wide strip. From this, cut:

* Four – 6 1/2" x 8 1/2" (C6)

From Fabric X, cut: (dark red print)

• One 6 1/2" wide strip. From this, cut:

* Two – 6 1/2" x 11 1/2" (C5)
* Five – 3 1/2" x 5 1/2" (A1)

• One 3 1/2" wide strip. From this, cut:

* Three – 3 1/2" x 5 1/2" (add to A1)

ASSEMBLY

STRIP SETS

1. Refer to illustrations below and make Strip Set 1 as shown, using fabrics I and II. Cut segments as directed. Make Strip Set 2 using Fabrics II and VI. Cut segments as directed.

BLOCK A

1. Use diagonal corner technique to make two each of mirror image Unit 1.
2. Join two mirror image units 1 together as shown. Make a total of 4 Block A hearts from fabrics I and X.

Strip Set 1
Make 2

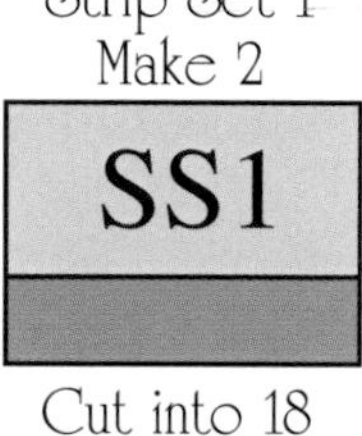

Cut into 18
4 1/2" segments

Strip Set 2
Make 2

Cut into 14
4 1/2" segments

Block A.
Make 4

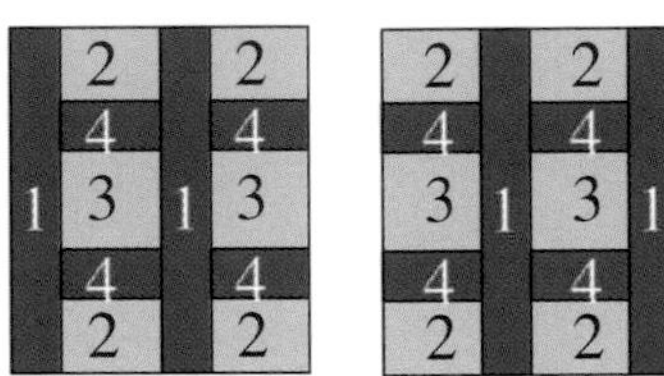

Block D. Make 2 of each

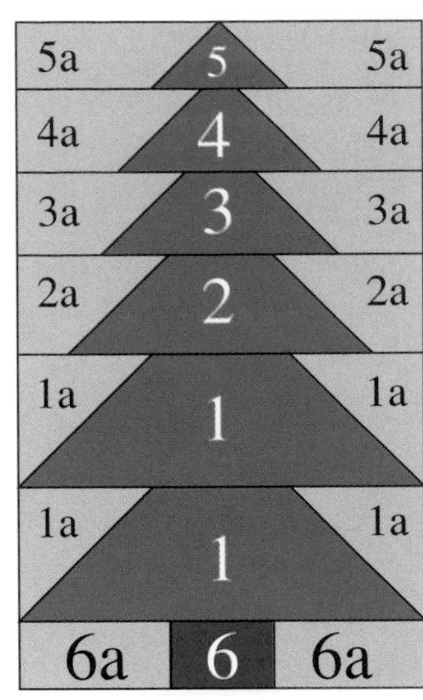

Block B. Make 2

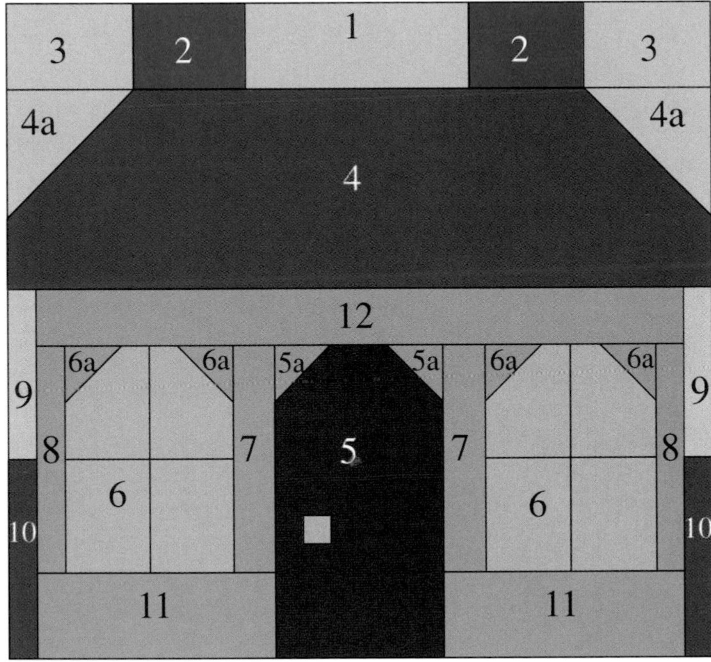

Block C. Make 2

TREE BLOCK B

1. Use diagonal corner technique to make two each of Unit 1. Use diagonal end technique to make one each of units 2, 3, 4, and 5.
2. To assemble, join units 6a-6-and 6a in a horizontal row as shown. Join two of Unit 1 together; then add remainder of units in numerical order working up in a vertical row. Make two trees.

HOUSE BLOCK C

1. Use diagonal corner technique to make one each of units 4 and 5. Use diagonal corner technique to make two of Unit 6.
2. To assemble, begin by joining units 3-2-1-2-and 3 in a horizontal row as shown. Join this row to top of Unit 4.
3. Join units 9 and 10 and set aside. Make two windows by joining units 8-6-7 (left window) and units 7-6-8 (right window; then add Unit 11 to bottom of both windows.
4. Join left and right window section to opposite sides of door; then join Unit 12 to top. Join combined units 9-10 to opposite sides of house as shown; then add roof section to house bottom as shown. Make 2 houses.

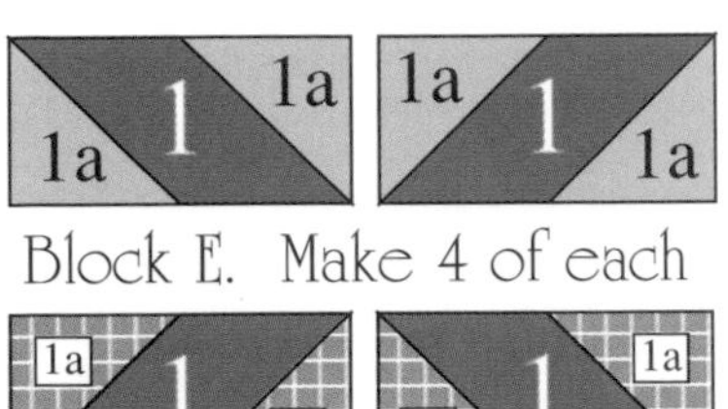

Block E. Make 4 of each

Block F. Make 6 of each

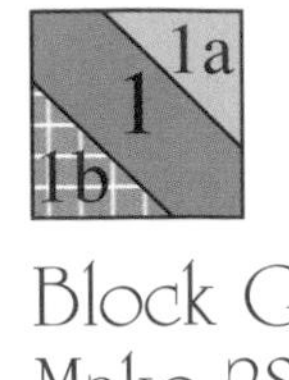

Block G.
Make 28

FENCE BLOCK D

1. Refer to Fence Block D illustration, and begin by making four vertical rows of units 2-4-3-4-2 as shown. For mirror image fences, join Unit 1 to vertical combined unit rows as shown. Make two fence sets.

LEAF BLOCKS E & F

1. Use diagonal corner technique to make Unit 1 for each block as shown. Refer to illustrations for correct placement of mirror image units. For Block E, use Fabrics I and II. For Block F, use fabrics II and VI.

VINE BLOCK G

1. Use diagonal corner technique to make twenty-eight of Block G.

TABLECLOTH ASSEMBLY

TABLECLOTH TOP SECTION

**Please note that all (T) units refer to "Tablecloth Top" units.*

1. To assemble tablecloth, begin by joining Block B trees on opposite side of Unit T1 as shown in Tablecloth Assembly diagram.
2. Join Units 2 to sides of fence, referring to illustration for correct placement of Unit 2. Make four sections. Join units 4-Block A-and 3 in a vertical row, again checking diagram for correct placement of all four sections. Join Unit 5 to side of combined units 4-BlockA-and 3 as shown.
3. Join combined Unit 2-Block D to combined heart section, again checking illustration for correct placement. Join these combined heart-fence sections to opposite sides of House Block C as shown; then add Unit 6 to house bottom.
4. Join the house sections to opposite sides of the tree section.
5. Join units 8-Block E-7-Block E-and 8 in a row. Make 2 and add them to opposite sides of tablecloth top as shown.
6. Referring to illustration, make two horizontal rows by joining Strip Set 1-Block G-Strip Set 2-Block G-Strip Set 1-Block G-Strip Set 2-Block G-Strip Set 1-Block G-Strip Set 2-Block G-and Strip Set 1. Add these rows to opposite ends to tablecloth top.
7. To assemble side section of tablecloth, make two horizontal rows as follows: Unit 15-Block F-Unit 14-Block F-Unit 13-Block F-Unit 14-Block F-and Unit 15. Join to opposite sides of tablecloth.

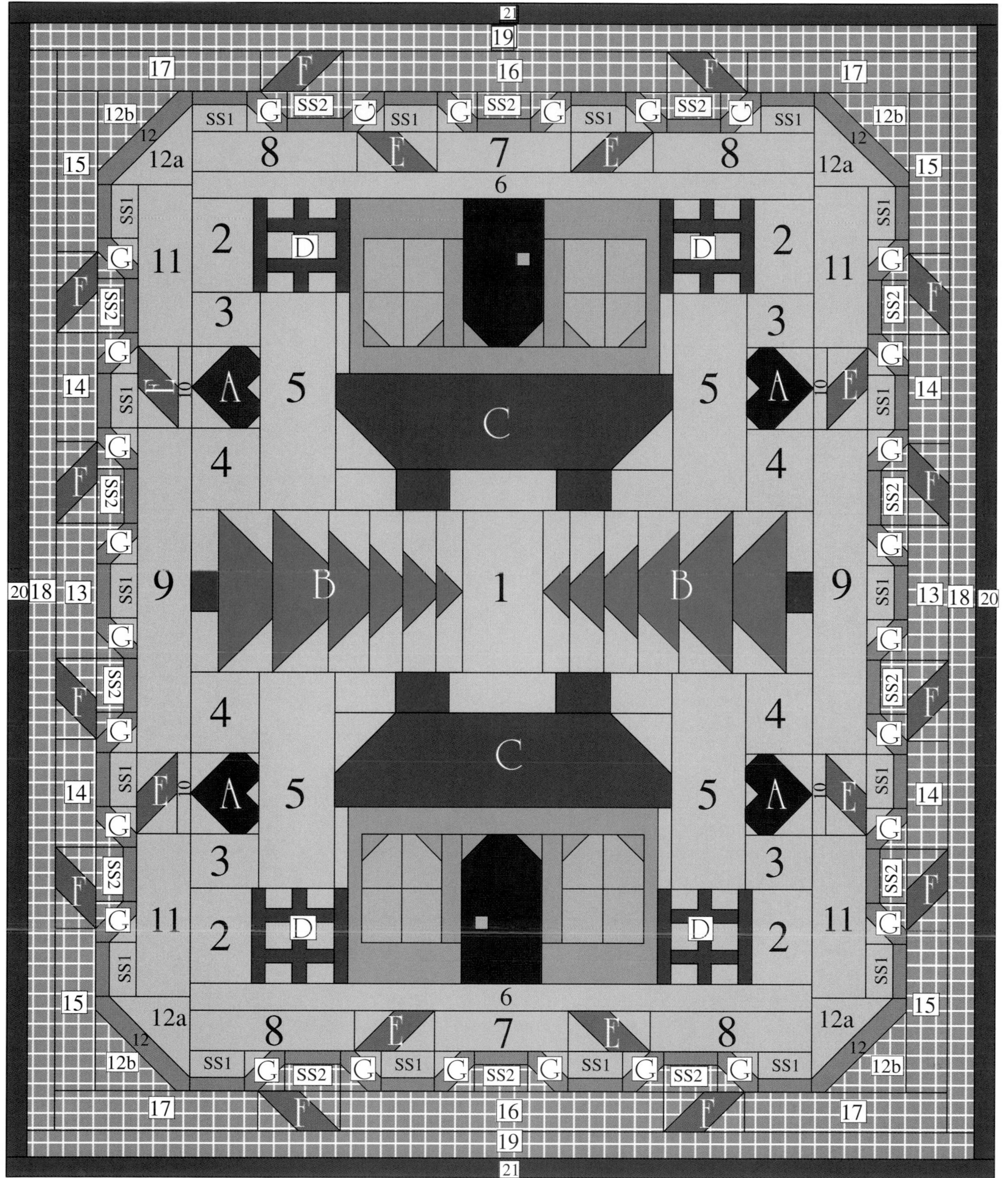

8. Complete top and bottom leaf rows by joining Unit 17-Block F-Unit 16-Block F-and Unit 17 in a horizontal row. Make two, and join to top and bottom of tablecloth.

9. For borders, follow instructions in cutting list to join borders. Begin by joining completed Border 18 to opposite sides of tablecloth as shown; then add Border 19 to top and bottom. Join Border 20 to opposite sides; then add Border 21 to top and bottom to complete tablecloth top.

Quilting Illustration

10. Make 330" of straight-grain, french fold binding, and bind the tablecloth.
11. Refer to illustration above for quilting suggestions. Use June Tailor's Grid Marker for house roofs.
12. Refer to quilt instructions for finishing of flower boxes and yo yo flowers. Use buttons for door knobs if desired.

My first home projects:
My Home

Quilts from my garden
that bloom forever

From My Garden.....

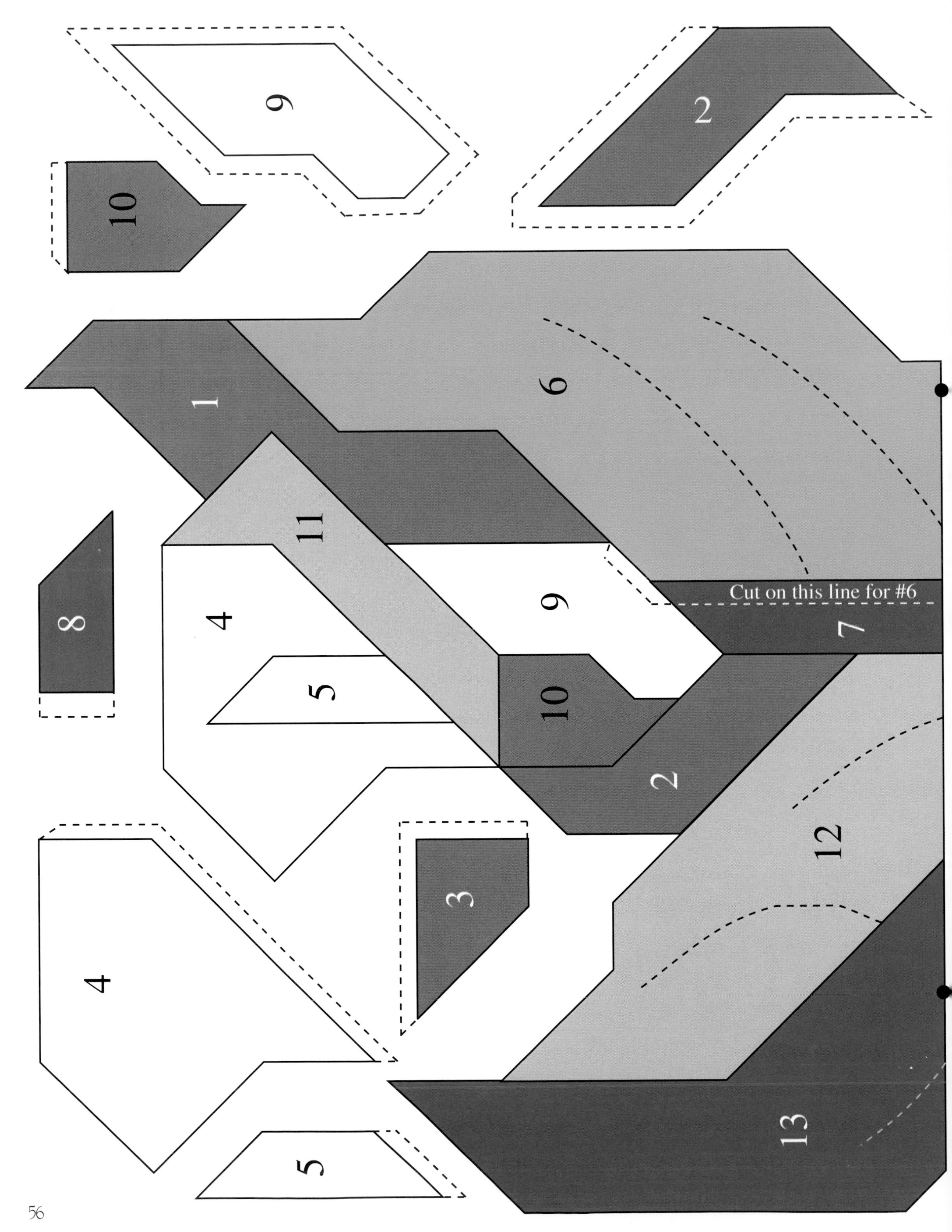
Cut on this line for #6

Four different greens were used for the leaves on the Calla Lily. We suggest a strong dark green, a solid light green chintz, a nice contrasting medium olive print, and a softer green, leaning towards the light side that coordinates with the medium olive.

CUTTING

For #'s 1, 2 and 3: One each medium olive print	3" x 8" scrap
For #'s 4 and 9: One each white chintz	3 1/4" x 5 1/4" scrap
For #11: One med.pink textured print	3 1/4" square scrap
For #12: One solid medium/light olive chintz	2 1/4" x 8" scrap
For #6: One soft medium/light green print	3 3/4" x 9" scrap
For #'s 7, 8, and 13: One each dark forest green print	5 1/4" x 7" scrap
For #5: One soft yellow print	1" x 2 1/2" scrap
For #10: One dark rose print	1 1/2" x 2" scrap

Calla Lily

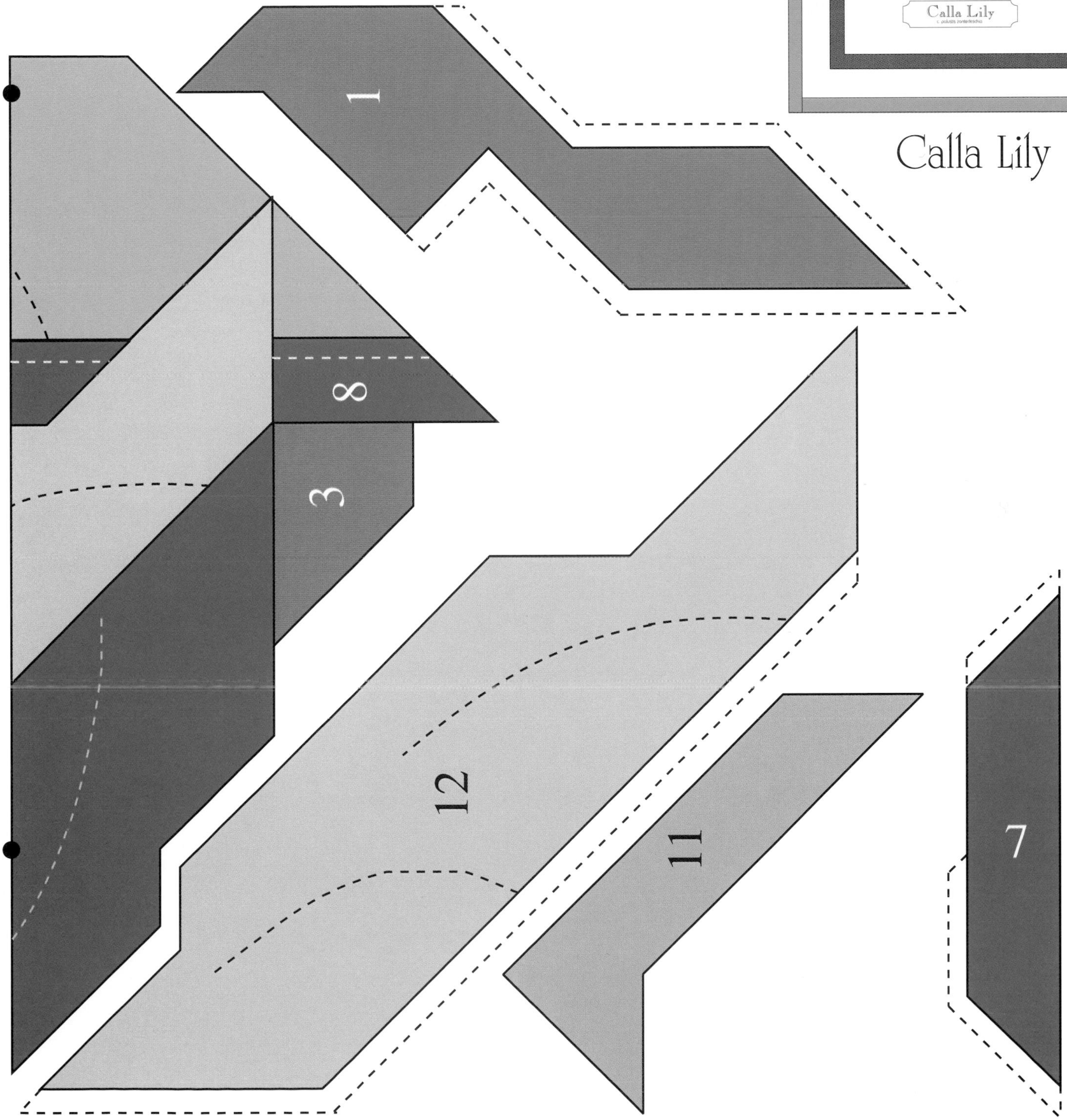

1

8

3

12

11

7

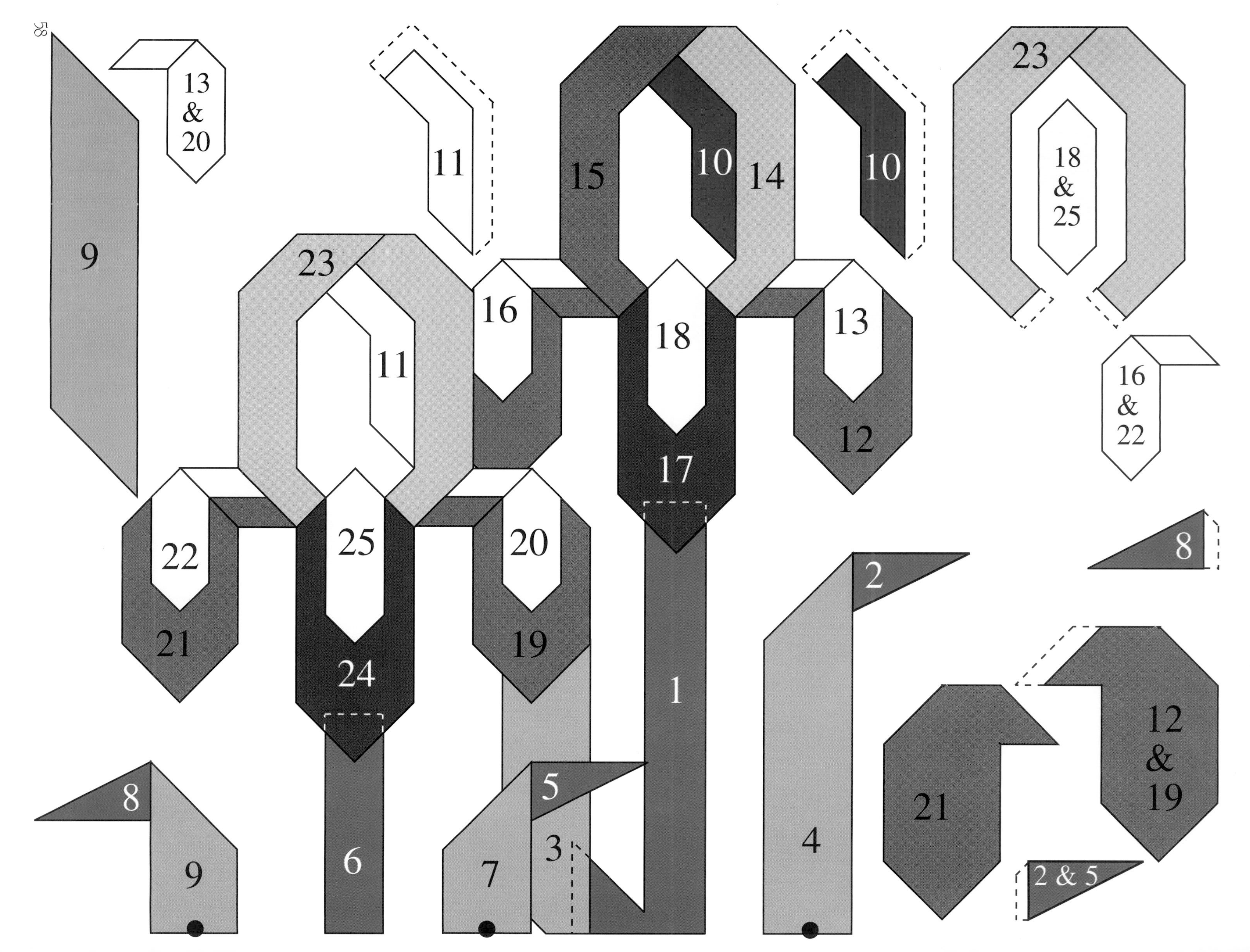

CUTTING

For #'s 1, 2, 5, 6, and 8: One each dark forest green print	4" x 8" scrap
For #'s 3, 4, 7, and 9: One each soft medium/light green print	4 1/2" x 5 1/2" scrap
For #'s 17 and 24: One each dark lavender print	2 3/4" square scrap
For #'s 12, 15, 19, and 21: One each medium lavender print	5" square scrap
For #'s 13, 16, 18, 20, 22, and 25: One each soft yellow print	3 " x 3 1/2" scrap
For #'s 14 and 23: One each solid pale lavender	3" x 4" scrap
For #11: One solid white chintz	1 1/2" x 2 1/2" scrap
For #10: One solid dark purple	1 1/2" x 2 1/2" scrap

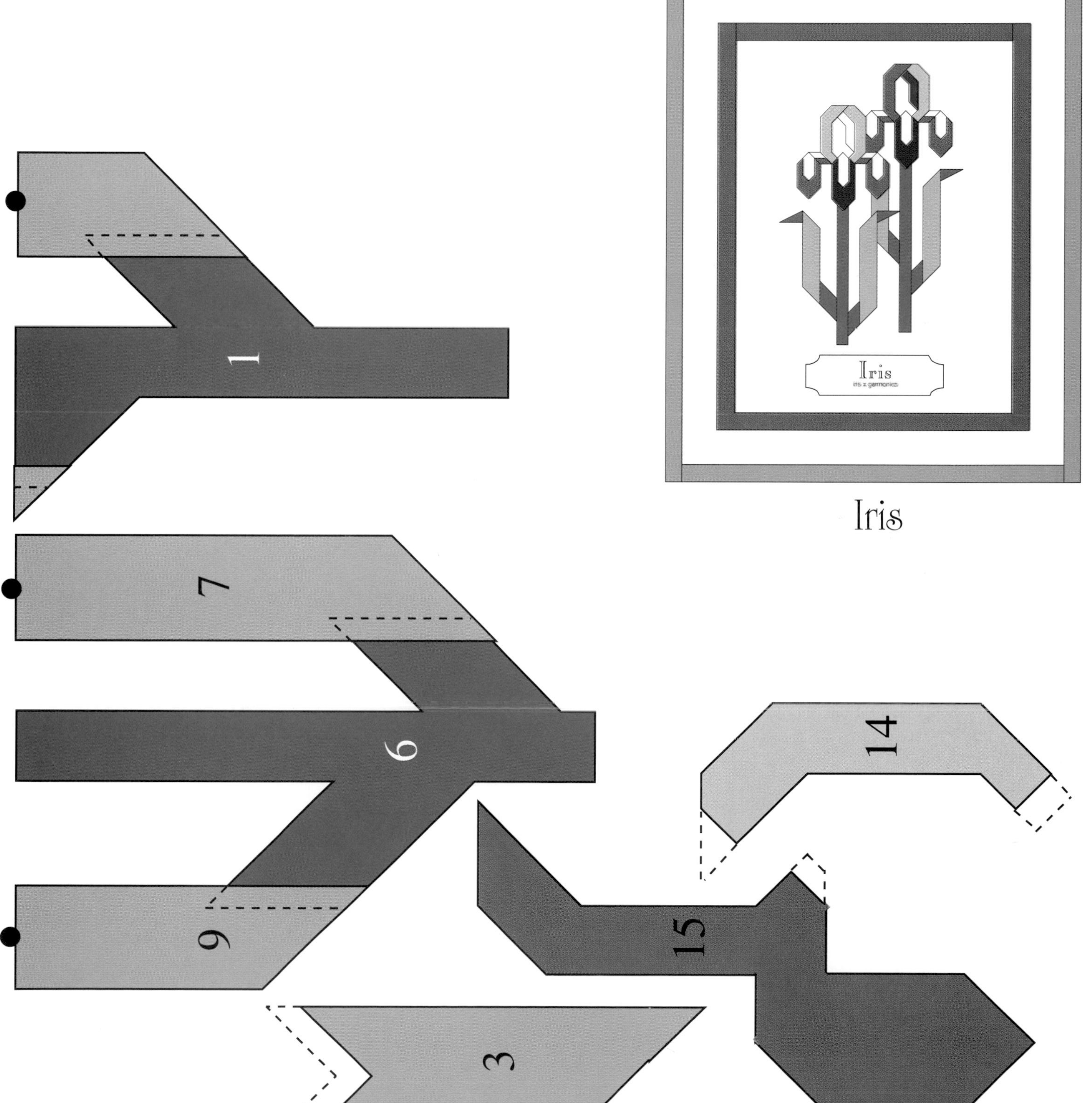

Iris

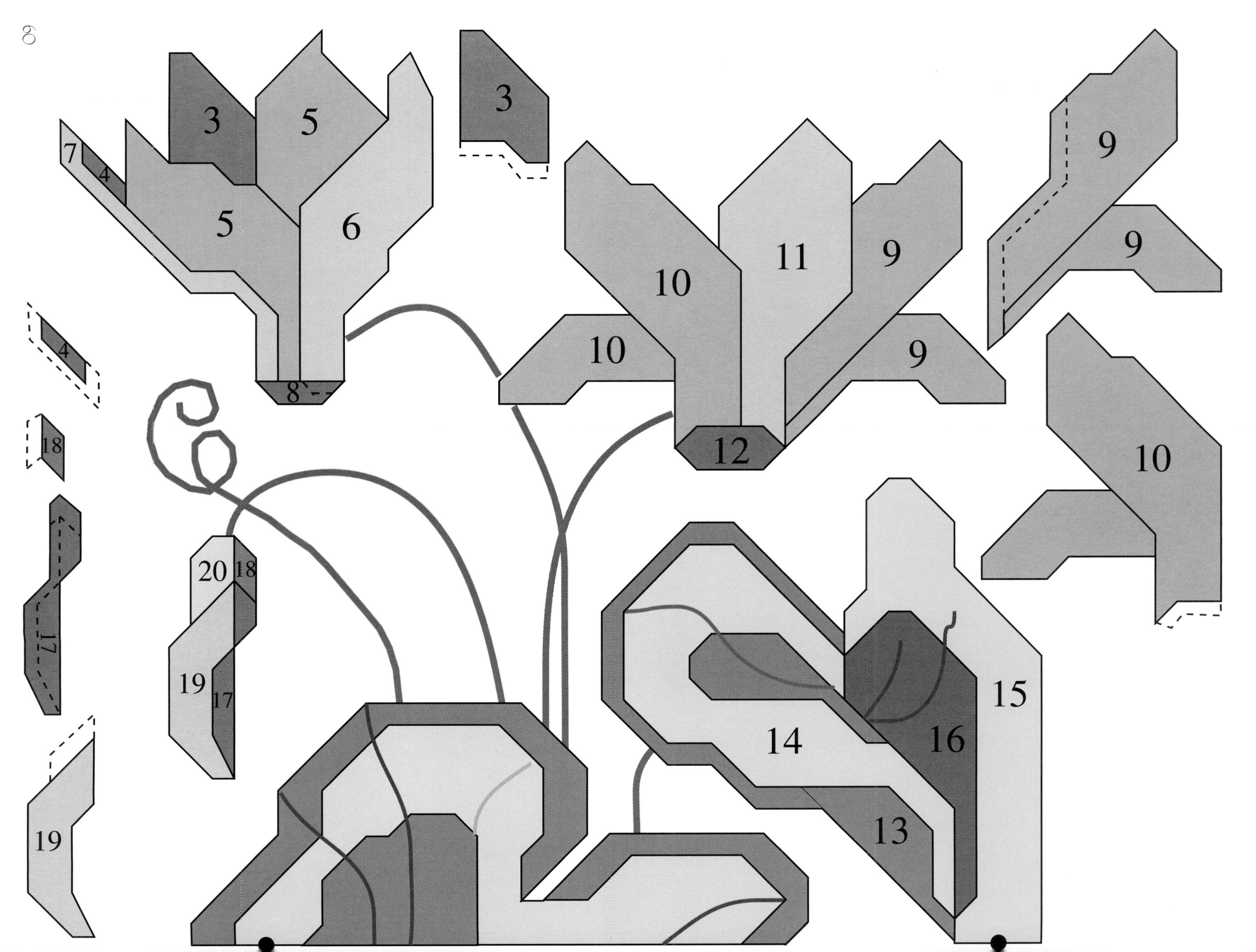
3
5
7
4
5
6
3
10
11
9
9
9
10
9
4
8
12
10
18
20
18
17
19
17
14
16
15
13
19

CUTTING

For #'s 1, 13, and 18: One each medium dusty olive green print	4 1/2" x 10" scrap
For #'s 2, 14, 15, and 20: One each light olive green batik	5 1/2" x 11" scrap
For # 16: One dark olive green print	1 1/2" x 3" scrap
For #'s 5, 9, and 10: One each medium dusty print	3" x 8 1/2" scrap
For #'s 6, 7, 11, and 19: One each light pink print	2" x 8 1/2" scrap
For #'s 3, 4, 8, 12,and 17: One each dark rose chintz	1 " x 5 1/2" scrap

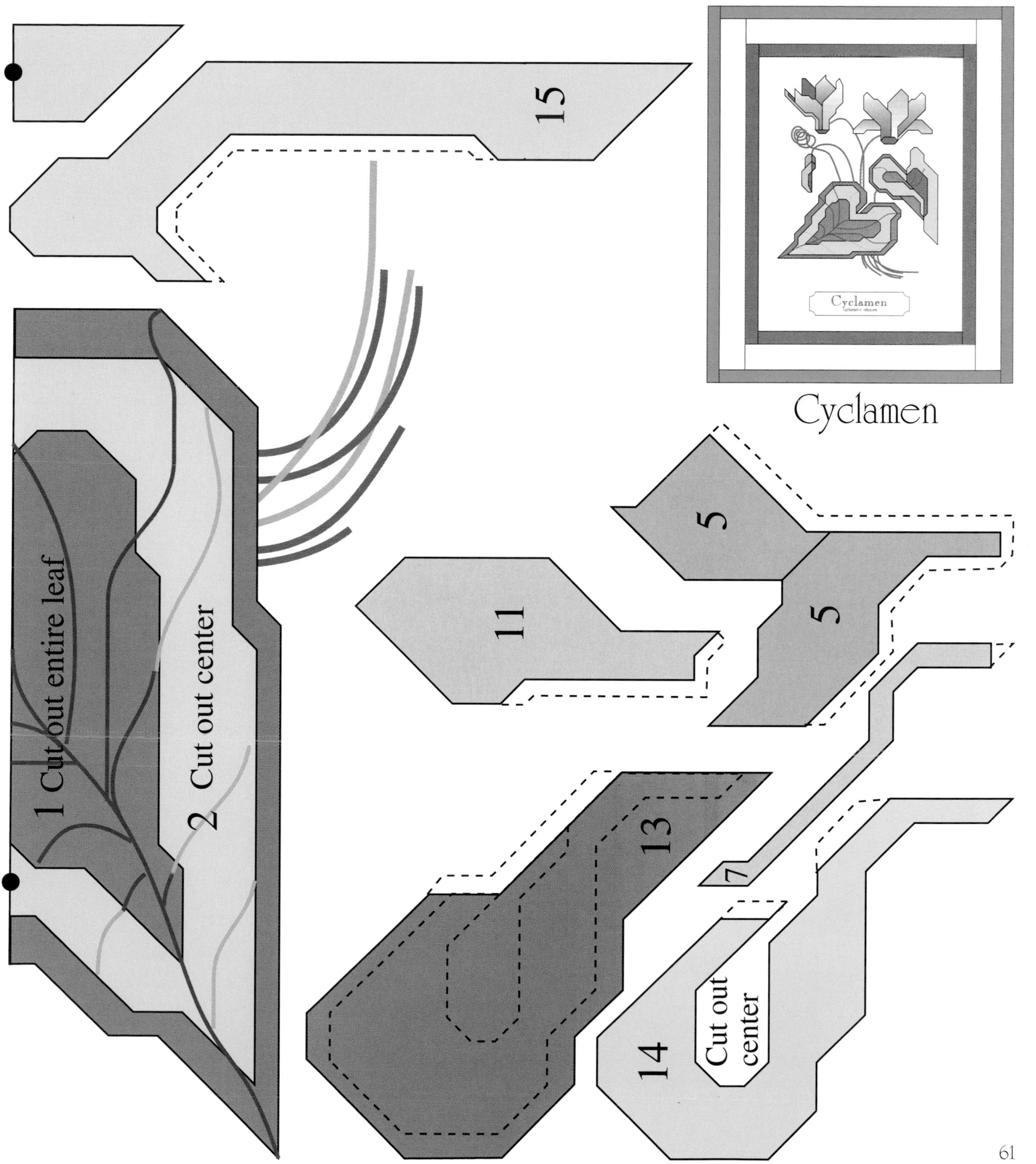

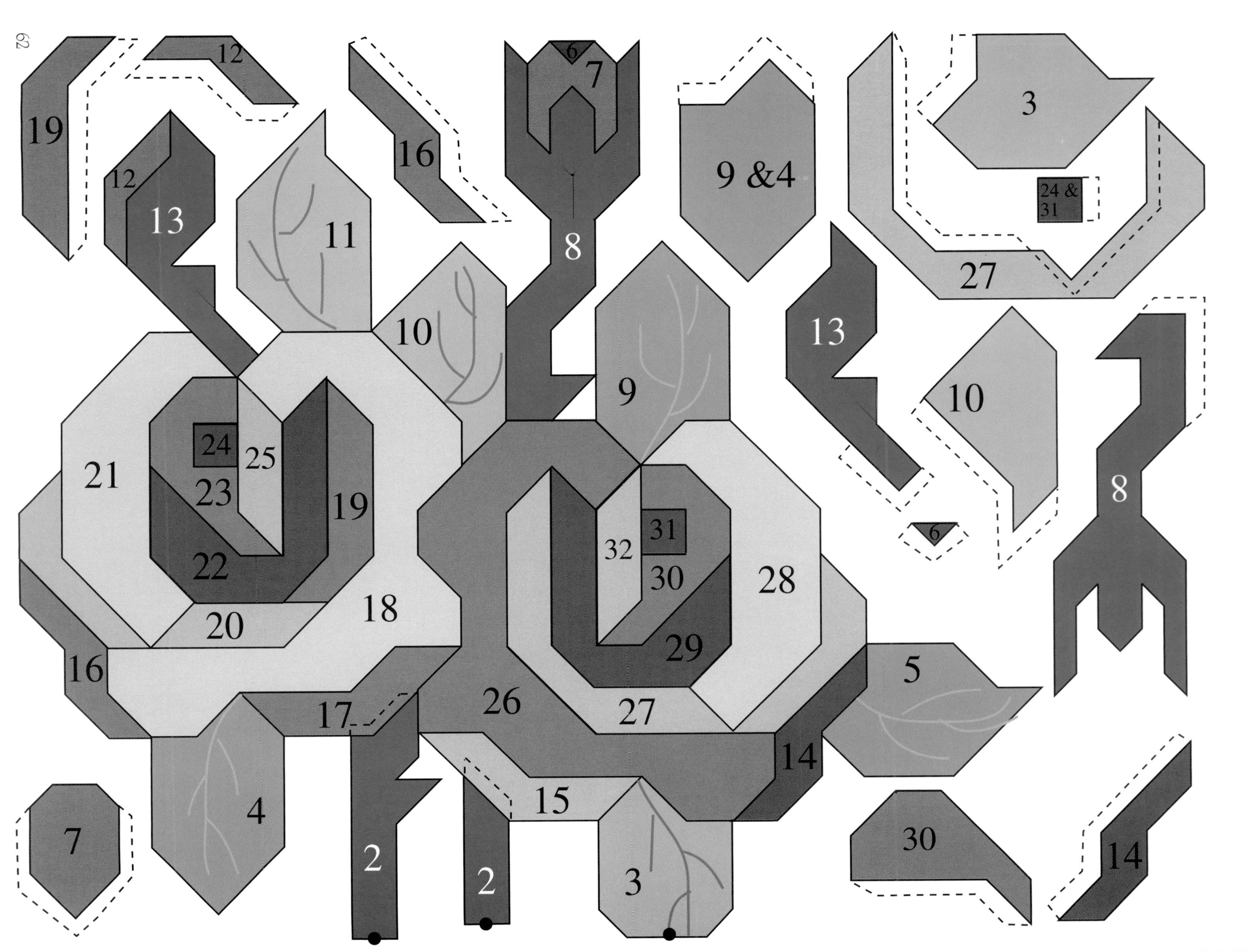
19
12
16
6
7
9 &4
3
24 &
31
12
13
11
8
27
10
13
10
9
8
24
25
21
23
19
31
32
6
22
30
28
18
20
29
16
26
27
17
5
14
15
4
30
7
2
2
3
14

Rose

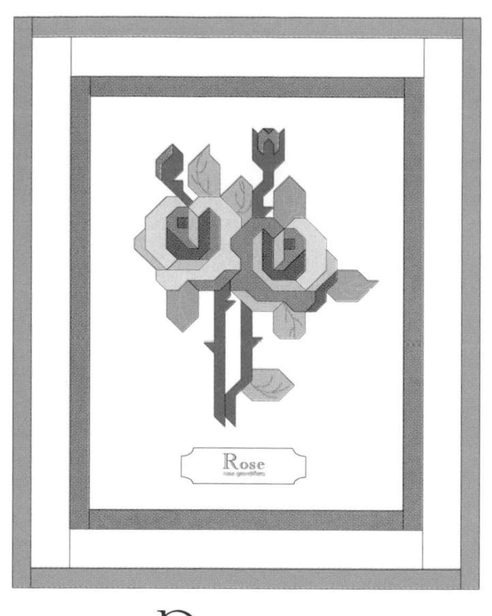

Rose

CUTTING

For #'s 4, 5, and 9: One each medium dusty olive green print	3" x 3 1/2" scrap
For #'s 1, 3, 10, and 11: One each solid medium/light olive chintz	4" x 4 1/2" scrap
For #'s 2, 8, and 13: One each dark olive green print	5" x 5 1/2" scrap
For #'s 15, 20, 25, 27, and 32: One each bright pink print	4" square scrap
For #'s 18, 21, and 28: One each light pink print	4" x 6" scrap
For #'s 14, 22, 24, 29, and 31: One each dark rose print	4" square scrap
For #'s 7, 12, 16, 17, 19, 23, 26, and 30: One each rose chintz	5" square

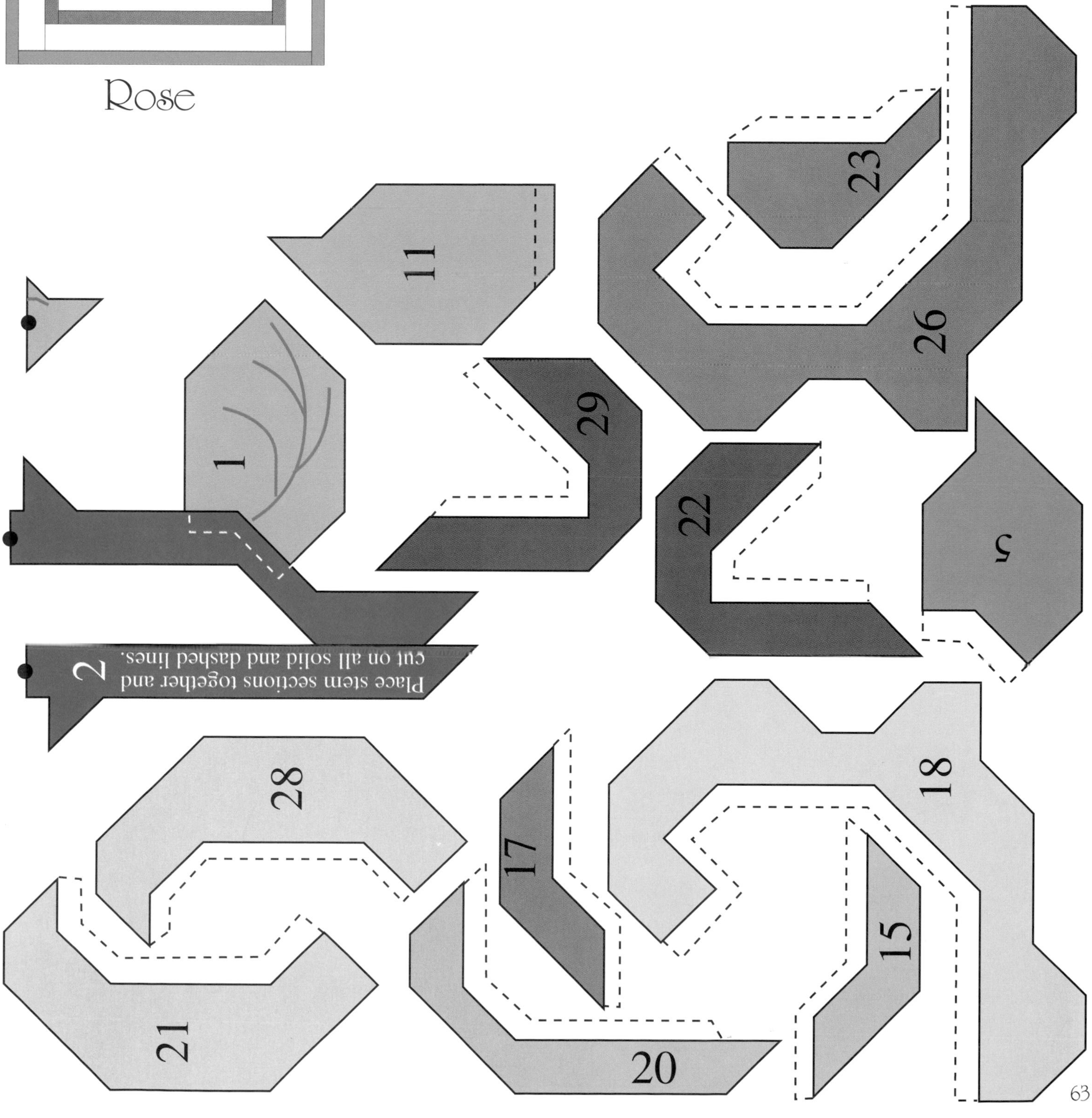

23
11
26
1
29
22
5
2
Place stem sections together and cut on all solid and dashed lines.
28
18
17
15
21
20

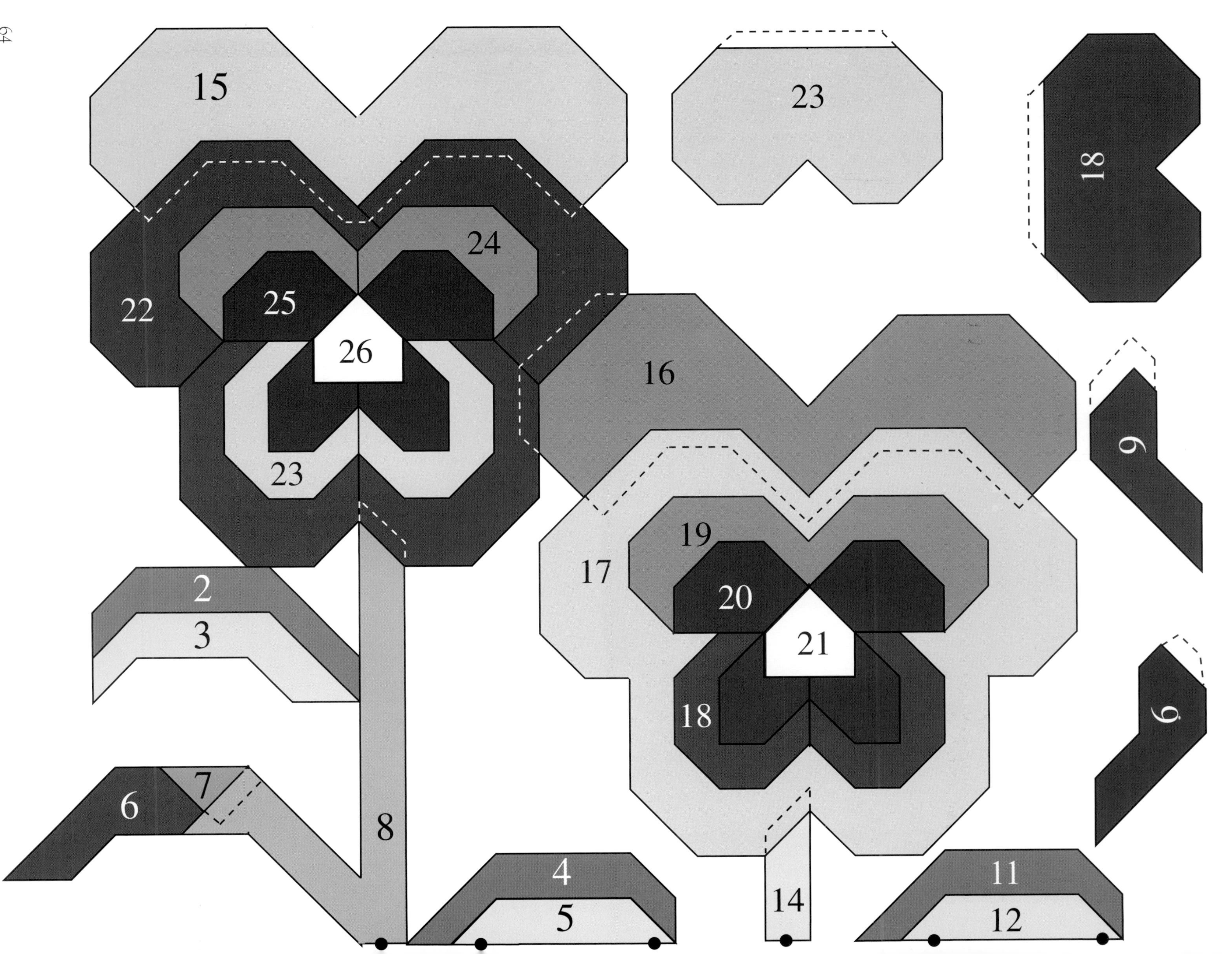

CUTTING

For #'s 3, 5, 12,and 14: One each light olive green batik	5 1/2" square scrap
For # 8: One soft medium/light green print	3" x 6 3/4" scrap
For #'s 1, 2, 4, 11, and 13: One each medium olive print	5" square scrap
For #'s 7, and 10: One each solid medium olive	1 1/2" square scrap
For #'s 9, 20, and 25: One each very dark purple print	4" square scrap
For #'s 6, 18, and 22: One each very dark majenta batik	4" x 6 1/2" scrap
For #'s 16, 19, and 24: One each medium lavender print	5 1/4" square scrap
For #'s 15, 17, and 23: One each light lavender print	7" square scrap
For #'s 21 and 26: One each light yellow print	1" x 2" scrap

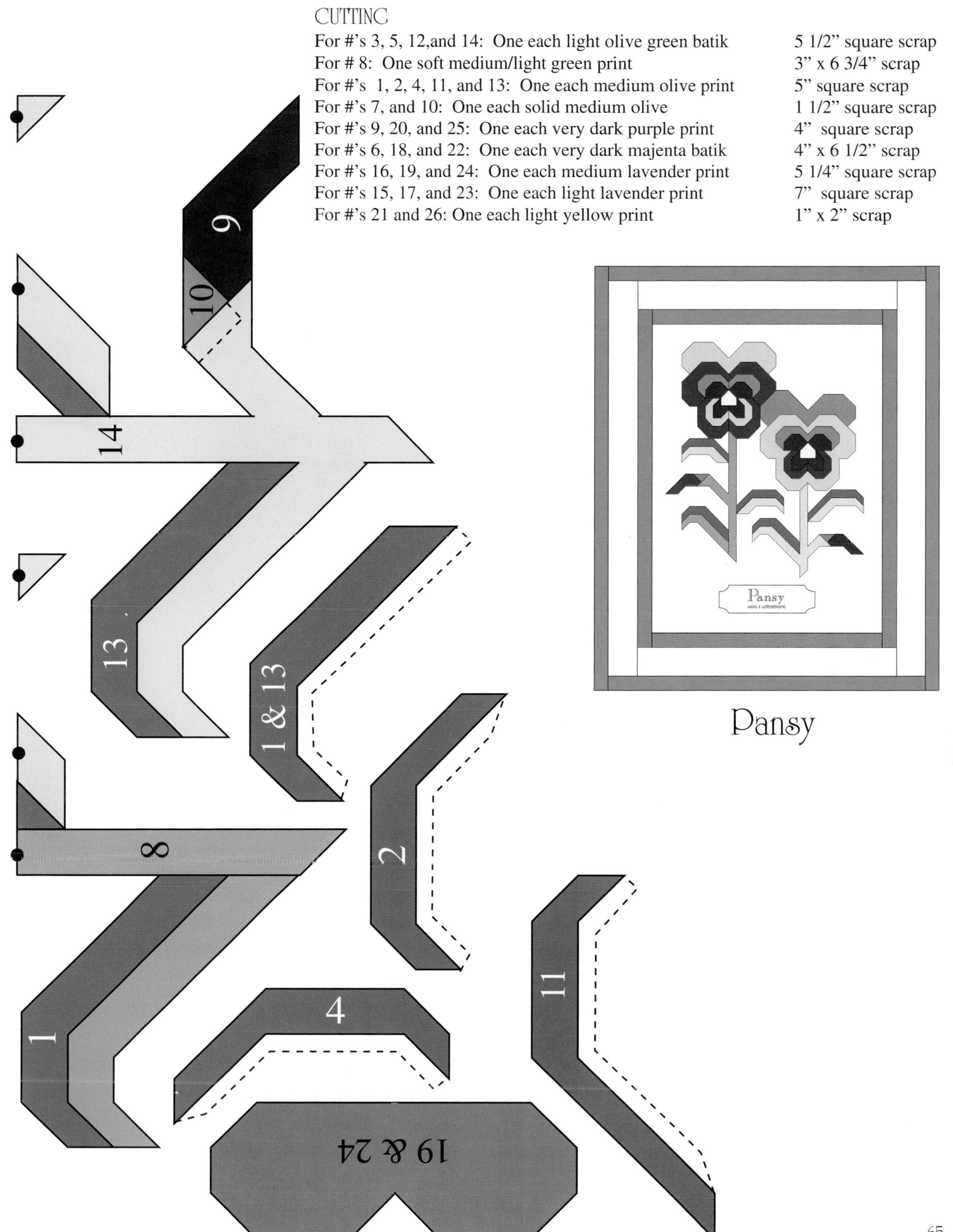

Pansy

Morning Glory

CUTTING

For #'s 2, 6, 12, 16, 20, 21, and 22: One each solid medium olive chintz	3" x 10" scrap
For #'s: 5, 13, 17, and 19 One each medium olive print	3" x 7" scrap
For #'s 1, 3, 4, 11, 14, and 18: One each light olive print	3" x 7" scrap
For #'s 7, 25, 27, 32, and 35: One each dark blue print	3" x 8 1/2"" scrap
For #'s 28, 29, 30, 36, 37, and 38: One each solid navy chintz	2" x 8 1/2" scrap
For #'s 8, 24, 26, 30, and 34: One each medium blue print	2" x 4" scrap
For #'s 9, 10, 15, 23, and 31: One each pale blue print	4" x 6" square scrap
For #'s 39 and 40: One each light yellow print	1" square scrap

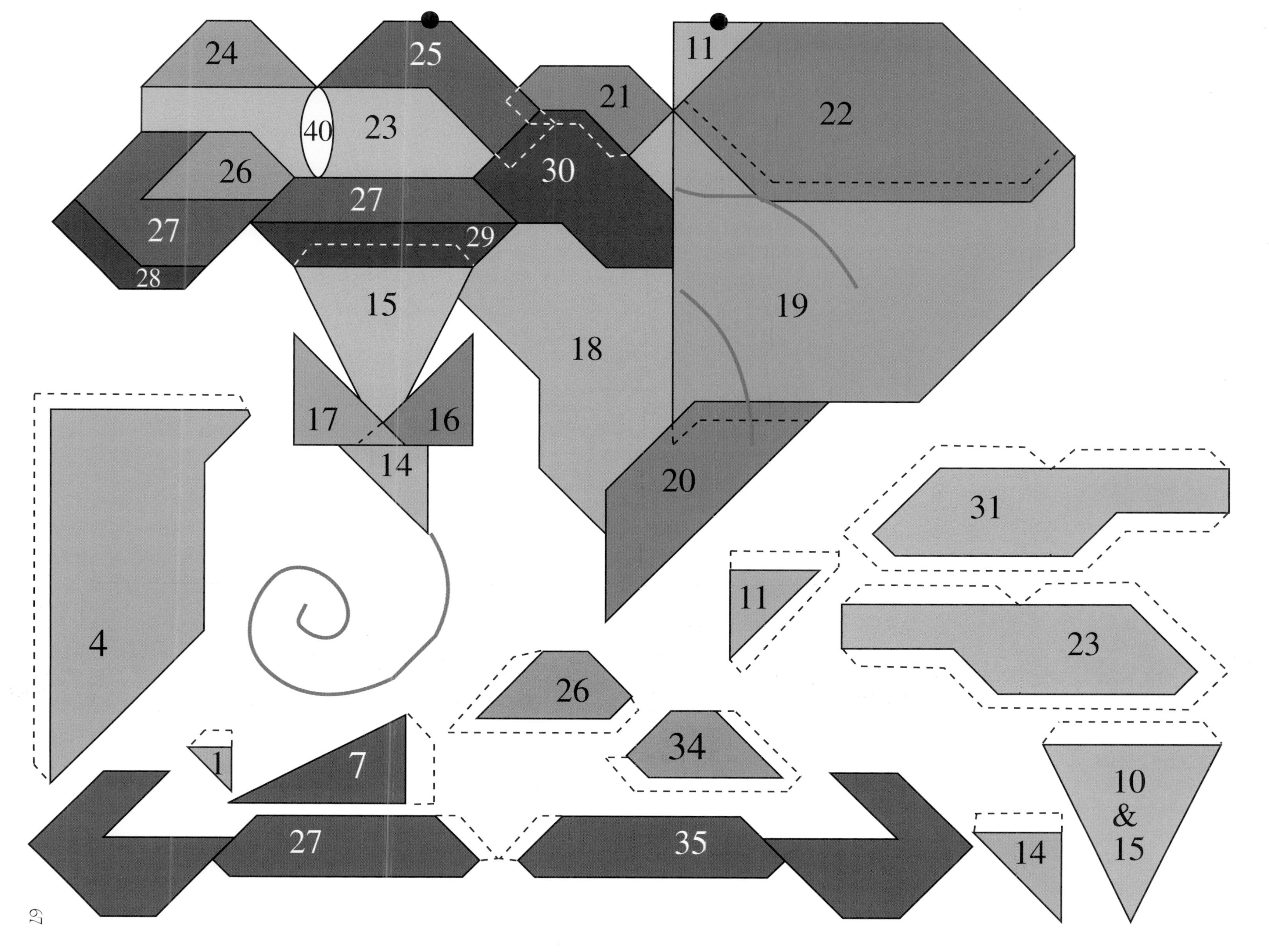
24
25
11
22
21
40
23
30
26
27
27
29
28
15
19
18
17
16
14
20
31
4
11
23
26
34
1
7
10
&
15
27
35
14

Finished size quilt: 70 1/2" x 97"

Finished size framed blocks: 18" x 22"

MATERIALS

Fabric I 1 yard (need exactly 33")
(solid parchment chintz)

Fabric II 2 yards (need exactly 68")
(medium soft olive green print)

Fabric III 1 1/8 yards (need exactly 39 1/4")
(solid rose chintz)

Fabric IV 1/4 yard (need exactly 5")
(solid medium lavender chintz)

Fusible pellon 4 yards
Tear-away pellon 4 yards

Fabric V 3/4 yard (need exactly 24")
(solid light yellow chintz)

Fabric VI 1/8 yard (need exactly 2 1/2")
(solid medium blue chintz)

Fabric VII 1/2 yard (need exactly 15")
(dark olive print)

Fabric VIII 2 1/4 yards (need exactly 78")
(floral print on ivory background)

Backing: 5 3/4 yards

CUTTING

From Fabric I, cut: (solid parchment chintz)

- Two 16 1/2" wide strips. From these, cut:
  - * Six - 12 1/2" x 16 1/2" (flower block background)

From Fabric II, cut: (medium soft olive green print)

- Eight 8 1/2" wide strips. From these, cut:
  - * Two - 8 1/2" x 42" (large side borders)
  - * Four - 8 1/2" x 30" (large side borders)

NOTE; Join 30" strips to opposite short ends of 42" long strip. for quilt side borders. Center and trim off to fit. Make two.

- * Two - 8 1/2" x 28" (quilt bottom border)

NOTE: Join together at short ends. Center seam and trim off to fit.

From Fabric III, cut: (solid rose chintz)

- Nine 3" wide strips for straight-grain binding.
- Six 1 1/2" wide strips. From these, cut:
  - * Two - 1 1/2" x 42" (side border 2)
  - * Two - 1 1/2" x 24" (side border 2)

NOTE: Join 24" strips to opposite short ends of 42" long strip for quilt side border 2.1 Center and trim off to fit. Make two.

* Two - 1 1/2" x 28" (bottom border 1) Piece short ends together to = 55 1/2" long. Center seam and join to quilt bottom.

- From scrap, cut:
  - * Four - 1 1/4" x 18" (rose and cyclamen block inner side borders)
  - * Two - 1 1/4" x 12 1/2" (rose block inner top and bottom borders)
- Three 1 1/4" wide strips. From these, cut:
  - * Two - 1 1/4" x 18" (calla lily block inner side borders)
  - * Four - 1 1/4" x 12 1/2" (cyclamen and calla lily block inner top and bottom borders)

From Fabric IV, cut: (solid medium lavender chintz)

- Four 1 1/4" wide strips. From these, cut:
  - * Four - 1 1/4" x 18" (pansy & iris block inner side bor ders)
  - * Four - 1 1/4" x 12 1/2" (pansy and iris block inner top and bottom borders)

From Fabric V, cut: (solid light yellow chintz)

- Twelve 2" wide strips. From these, cut:
  - * Twelve - 2" x 21" (flower block side frames)
  - * Twelve - 2" x 14" (flower block top & bottom frames)

From Fabric VI, cut: (solid medium blue chintz)

- Two 1 1/4" wide strips. From these, cut:
  - * Two - 1 1/4" x 18" (morning glory block inner side borders)
  - * Two - 1 1/4" x 12 1/2" (morning glory block inner top and bottom borders)

From Fabric VII, cut: (dark olive print)

- Twelve 1 1/4" wide strips. From these, cut:
  - * Twelve - 1 1/4" x 22 1/2" (outer flower block side frame)
  - * Twelve - 1 1/4" x 17" (outer flower block top and bot tom frame)

From Fabric VIII, cut: (floral print on ivory back ground)

- Thirteen 6" wide strips. From these, cut:
  - * Three - 6" x 42" (long sashing strips)
  - * Six - 6" x 24" (long sashing strips)

NOTE: Join 24" strips to opposite short ends of 42" long strip for long quilt sashing strips. Make three.

- * Eight - 6" x 18 1/2" (short sashing strips)

ASSEMBLY

BLOCK PREPARATION

1. Begin your quilt by first assembling the blocks for each flower. Use the 12 1/2" x 16 1/2" parchment chintz for the center of each block. Refer to the cutting instructions for the correct colored inner border for each flower. Each of these borders should be marked according to the flower that it frames.
2. Join the 1 1/4" x 12 1/2" strips of the inner border to the top and bottom of each block. Press out. Join the 1 1/4" x 18" strips of the inner border to opposite sides of each block and press out.
3. Join a 2" x 14" strip of Fabric V to top and bottom of each flower block; then add the 2" x 21" strips of Fabric V to opposite sides of each block.
4. To complete block frames, join the 1 1/4" x 17" strips of Fabric VII to top and bottom of each block; then add the 1 1/4" x 22 1/2" strips to opposite sides to complete block frames.

APPLIQUE PREPARATION

1. Each flower illustration in the following pages is divided in half. Use tracing paper to trace the top half, including the dot placement.

Trace the bottom section by matching the dots up. This is now your placement pattern.
2. Each part of the flower is numbered according to the appliqué placement order. Notice that the individual pattern templates match the numbers on the placement pattern. If there is not a separate template, the pattern piece is to be traced around for a template on the placement pattern itself. This includes solid and dashed lines. When pieces are pressed down for appliqué, most of the pieces overlap each other.
3. There are two ways in which to draw your appliqué pieces. As our pattern is not reversed, so that placement of pieces is easier, you may trace each pattern piece onto a piece of tracing paper. Mark each template number, and turn the paper over; then trace each pattern piece onto the smooth side of fusible pellon. Press the rough side of the fusible pellon onto the *wrong* side of your fabric, and cut out the pieces as drawn.
4. Should you choose the second method, trace all appliqué pieces onto rough side of fusible pellon. We utilized as much of the appliqué film as possible, butting pieces up to each other. Cut out around pieces drawn together. This method is a bit harder to see if you have a dark colored fabric.
5. Place rough side of appliqué film with drawn shapes on *wrong* side of fabric. Press with hot, dry iron for 10 seconds. Move iron from one pressed place to another, until all of the paper has been pressed down.
6. Cutting instructions for scrap fabrics used in the flowers are given for each piece. Cut all pieces out.
7. For plaques, use our CD-ROM, and open the file for Botanical Plaques. Place a piece of June Tailor Colorfast Fabric™ Sheets in your inkjet printer, and print the plaques. Tear away the backing from the fabric, and press a piece of fusible pellon (rough side to back of fabric) behind the plaques. Cut out each plaque.
8. Each plaque should be placed exactly 1 1/4" from bottom inner border of block and centered. Use a press cloth and hot, dry iron and press the plaque in place.
9. Center your placement drawing of the flower over the plaque, leaving plenty of "air" around the flower appliqué. Pin your placement pattern in place. If you choose, you may use dressmakers carbon to trace the placement pattern. Trace any vines, stems or veins in leaves as necessary.
10. Begin with piece #1. Peel paper off of appliqué piece and place the appliqué down in proper position under placement pattern. Lift pattern and lay hot, dry iron on top of appliqué for 10 seconds. Appliqué should now be fused to the background block.
11. Continue adding units in numerical order, and press each one in place as they are added until flower is complete. Remember that pieces overlap each other. Pin tear-away pellon behind each flower before stitching.
12. Use a close, medium wide satin stitch and coordinating thread, and stitch around each appliqué piece. Stitch detail lines for vines, etc. as traced. Stitch around each name plaque with matching yellow thread. When all pieces have been stitched, tear the pellon away on the back side of the block.

QUILT ASSEMBLY

1. To assemble quilt, refer to quilt diagram and join short floral sashing strips with blocks pictured in two vertical rows. Refer to cutting instructions for piecing all sashing strips and borders, and join pieced long sashing strips to opposite sides of rows, joining the quilt top.
2. Join Border 1 to bottom of quilt; then add Border 2 to opposite sides as shown.
3. Join large pieced bottom border; then add large pieced borders from Fabric II to opposite sides.

QUILTING & FINISHING

1. We quilted around each flower in the blocks and the plaques. Block frames were "stitched in the ditch", and the flowers on the large sashing strips were quilted.
2. We made our binding wide. Make 345" of straight-grain, french fold binding and bind your quilt.

CD-ROM EXTRA'S

Your CD-ROM includes the lovely matching "Little Botanical" quilt for framing or quilting. This is an easy project for any beginner. An "extra" flower block is also included.
Matching sachet's, towel borders, coasters, bookmarks, cards, quilt labels and stationery are included as well. All of these "Extra's" can be easily printed on your Colorfast Fabric™ Sheets and used as any fabric. Watch our video demonstration for this special fabric.

Small Sashing
Small Sashing
Morning Glory
Rose
Small Sashing
Small Sashing
Large Sashing
Large Sashing
Large Sashing
Border 2
Border 2
Cyclamen
Pansy
Small Sashing
Small Sashing
Iris
Calla Lily
Small Sashing
Small Sashing
Border 1

Perennial Pleasures

Making Multi Diagonal Corners · Making Diagonal Ends · Making Diagonal Corners · Making Half Square Triangles

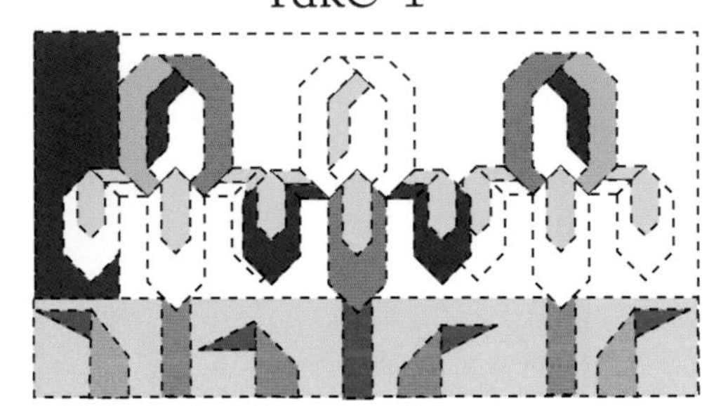

Finished size: 32" x 53"
Blocks A & B: 11 1/2" x 22"

On A Personal Note:

This quilt is considered to be our "challenge" quilt. It has some interesting unit assembly steps in it, however if illustrations are followed in the order shown, and instructions are read carefully it is sure to become one of your all time favorites. This one could take 1st place at your quilt show or the county fair! See the "color picker" on our CD-ROM for alternate color choices - or create your own!

MATERIALS

- Fabric I 1/2 yard (need exactly 15") (dark teal print)
- Fabric II 3/8 yard (need exactly 10 3/8") (light green batik)
- Fabric III 1/8 yard (need exactly 4") (medium green batik)
- Fabric IV 1/8 yard (need exactly 4") (dark green print)
- Fabric V 1/2 yard (need exactly 14") (pale teal print)
- Fabric VI 3/8 yard (need exactly 11 1/2") (pale yellow print)
- Fabric VII 1/4 yard (need exactly 5 1/2") (solid ivory)
- Fabric VIII 1/8 yard (need exactly 3") (light gold print) add 12" for 1" wide bias
- Fabric IX 1/8 yard (need exactly 3") (navy print) add 12" for 1" wide bias
- Fabric X 7/8 yard (need exactly 27") (solid dark navy) add 12" for 1" wide bias
- Fabric XI 1/4 yard (need exactly 7 7/8") (medium teal print) add 12" for 1" wide bias
- Backing 1 5/8 yards

CUTTING

Cutting instructions shown in red indicate that the quantity of units are combined and cut in 2 or more different places to conserve fabric.

NOTE: All "Q" units in cutting instructions stand for "quilt top". These are units that are not incorporated into blocks.

From Fabric I, cut: (dark teal print)

- One 11 1/2" wide strip. From this, cut:
  - Two – 3" x 11 1/2" (A28)
  - Two – 1 1/2" x 11" (A20)
  - Two – 2" x 10 1/2" (A32)
  - Two – 2" x 9 1/2" (A18)
  - Two – 1 1/2" x 9 1/2" (A19)
  - Two – 1 1/2" x 6 3/4" (A25)
  - Two – 2" x 6 1/2" (A30)
  - Two – 3 1/2" x 5" (A31a)
- From scrap, cut:
  - Four – 2 1/2" x 4 1/2" (A7)
  - Four – 1 1/2" x 4 1/2" (A17)
  - Two – 3" x 3 1/4" (A27a)
  - Two – 2" x 3" (A26)
  - Two – 1 1/2" x 3" (A1)
  - Four – 2" squares (A29a, A31b)
  - Two – 1 1/2" x 2" (A35)

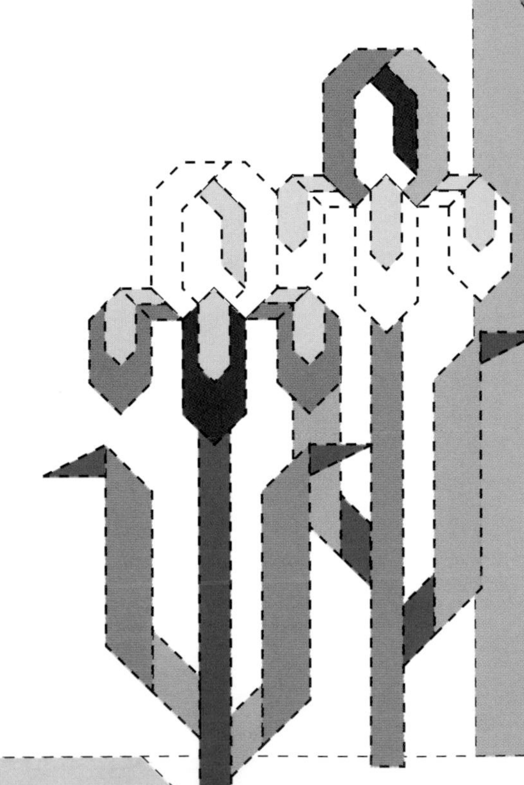

* Twelve– 1 1/2" squares (A2a, A5d, A6a, A8b, A27b)
* Twelve – 1" squares (A5b, A6b, A11b, A12a, A13b)

- One 2 1/2" wide strip. From this, cut:
  * Four – 2 1/2" x 3" (B10)
  * Eight – 2 1/2" squares (A10a, A10b)
  * Eight – 1 1/2" x 2 1/2" (B8)
- One 1" wide strip. From this, cut:
  * Twenty – 1" x 1 1/2" (A16a, B8a, B9, B11a, B13a)

From Fabric II, cut: (light green batik)

- One 2 7/8" strip. From this, cut:
  * Two – 2 7/8" squares (Q3 triangle-squares)
  * Eight – 2 1/2" x 3 " (A28a, A34, B28a, B34 template)
  * One – 1 1/2" x 11 1/2" (A23, B23)
- One 1 1/2" wide strip. From this, cut:
  * Three – 1 1/2" x 11 1/2" (add to A23, B23)
  * Seven – 1" x 1 1/2" (A16a, A37, B16a, B37)
- Six 1" wide strips. From these, cut:
  * Two – 1" x 27 1/2" (Q4)
  * Four – 1" x 25" (Q5) piece 2 together to = 1" x 49 1/2"
  * Five – 1" x 1 1/2" (add to A16a, A37, B16a, B37)

From Fabric III, cut: (medium green batik)

- One 4" wide strip. From this, cut:
  * Four – 2" x 4" (A31, B31)
- Cut remainder into two 2" wide strips. From these, cut:
  * Two – 2" x 6 3/4" (A24)
  * Two – 2" x 6 1/2" (A29)
  * Two – 2" x 3 1/2" (A27)
  * Two – 2" squares (A26a)
  * Two – 1 1/2" x 3 1/2" (B27)

From Fabric IV, cut: (dark green print)

- Two 2" wide strips. From these, cut:
  * Two – 2" x 6 3/4" (B24)
  * Two – 2" x 6 1/2" (B29)
  * Four – 2" x 4" (A31, B31)
  * Two = 2" x 3 1/2" (B27)
  * Two – 2" squares (B26a)
  * Two – 1 1/2" x 3 1/2" (A27)

From Fabric V, cut: (pale teal print)

- One 11 1/2" wide strip. From this, cut:
  * Two – 3" x 11 1/2" (B28)
  * Two – 1 1/2" x 11" (B20)
  * Two – 2" x 10 1/2" (B32)
  * Two – 2" x 9 1/2" (B18)
  * Two – 1 1/2" x 9 1/2" (B19)
  * Two – 1 1/2" x 6 3/4" (B25)
  * Two – 2" x 6 1/2" (B30)
  * Two – 3 1/2" x 5" (B31a)
  * Four – 2 1/2" x 4 1/2" (B7)
  * Four – 1 1/2" x 4 1/2" (B17)
- From scrap, cut:
  * Two – 3" x 3 1/4" (B27a)
  * Two – 1 1/2" x 3" (B1)
  * Four – 2" squares (B29a, B31b)
  * Two – 2" x 3" (B26)
  * Two – 1 1/2" x 2" (B35)

  * Twelve – 1 1/2" squares (B2a, B5d, B6a, B8b, B27b)
  * Twelve – 1" squares (B5b, B6b, B11b, B12a, B13b)
- One 2 1/2" wide strip. From this, cut:
  * Eight – 2 1/2" squares (B10a, B10b)
  * Four – 1" x 1 1/2" (B16a)

From Fabric VI, cut: (pale yellow print)

- Four 2 1/2" wide strips. From these, cut:
  * Four – 2 1/2" x 22 1/2" (Q2)
  * Four – 2 1/2" x 12" (Q1)
  * Four – 2 1/2" x 3" (A10)
  * Two – 2" squares (B6)
  * Two – 1 1/2" x 2" (B13)
- One 1 1/2" wide strip. From this, cut:
  * Two – 1 1/2" x 3" (B4)
  * Two – 1 1/2" squares (B5c)
  * Sixteen – 1" x 1 1/2" (A8a, A9, A11a, A13a)

From Fabric VII, cut: (solid ivory)

- One 2 1/2" wide strip. From this, cut:
  * Two – 2 1/2" squares (A16)
  * Four – 1" x 2 1/2" (A14)
  * Two – 2" x 3" (B5)
  * Two – 1 1/2" x 3" (B3)
  * Two – 1 1/2" x 2" (B11)
  * Two – 1" x 10 1/2" (A33)
  * Eight – 1" squares (A11c, A13c, A15a)
- Three 1" wide strips. From these, cut:
  * Two – 1" x 22 1/2" (A40)
  * Four – 1" x 11" (A21, A22)
  * Four – 1" x 5 1/2" (A38, A39)
  * Two – 1" x 1 1/2" (A36)

From Fabric VIII, cut: (light gold print)

- One 3" wide strip. From this, cut:
  * Two – 1 1/2" x 3" (B2)
  * Two – 2" squares (B5a)
- Cut remainder into two 1 1/2" wide strips. From these, cut:
  * Twelve – 1 1/2" x 2 1/2" (A8, A15, B8, B15)
  * Four – 1 1/2" squares (A12, B12)
  * Sixteen – 1" x 1 1/2" (A8a, A11a, A13a, B8a, B11a, B13a)
  * Sixteen – 1" squares (A9a, B9a)

From Fabric IX, cut: (navy print)

- One 3" wide strip. From this, cut:
  * Two – 2" x 3" (A5)
  * Two – 1 1/2" x 3" (A3)
  * Two – 2 1/2" squares (B16)
  * Four – 1" x 2 1/2" (B14)
  * Two – 1 1/2" x 2" (A11)
  * Eight – 1" squares (B11c, B13c, B15a)

From Fabric X, cut: (solid dark navy)

- Six 2 1/2" wide strips. From these, cut:
  * Two – 2 1/2" x 28 1/2" (Q6 borders)
  * Four – 2 1/2" x 27" (Q7 borders) piece two together to = 2 1/2" x 53 1/2"
  * Two – 2" squares (A5a)
  * Two – 1 1/2" x 3" (A2)

  * Four – 1" x 11" (B21, B22)
  * Two – 1" x 10 1/2" (B33)
  * Four – 1" x 5 1/2" (B38, B39)
  * Two – 1" x 1 1/2" (B36)
- Four 2 1/2" wide strips for straight-grain binding.
- Two 1" wide strips. From these, cut:
  * Two 1" x 22 1/2" (B40)

From Fabric XI, cut: (medium teal print)
- One 2 7/8" wide strip. From this, cut:
  * Two – 2 7/8" squares (Q3 triangle-squares)
  * Fourteen – 2 1/2" squares (Q1a, Q2a, A41, B41)
- Two 2 1/2" wide strips. From these, cut:
  * Eighteen – 2 1/2" squares (add to Q1a, Q2a, A41, B41)
  * Two – 2" squares (A6)
  * Two – 1 1/2" x 2" (A13)
  * Two – 1 1/2" x 3" (A4)
  * Two – 1 1/2" squares (A5c)

ASSEMBLY

GENERAL UNIT CONSTRUCTION

1. There is one basic block in this quilt, although it is a mirror image and has different color combinations. Refer often to the illustrations for correct placement of mirror image units and color changes. General instructions begin below for units that are put together with general diagonal corner or diagonal ends. The units that are more complex are shown graphically and described in detail. Instructions are given for one block only.
2. Use diagonal corner technique to make one each of units 2, 6, 10, 12, 15, 26, and 29. Use diagonal corner technique to make four of mirror image Unit 9.
3. Unit 5 is a good example of the general rule for adding diagonal corners in alphabetical order. Refer to the illustration for

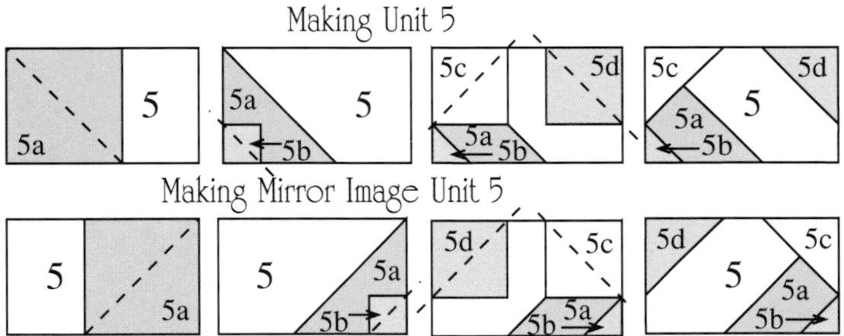

Making Unit 5 that shows how this technique works. Add each diagonal corner in alphabetical order as shown, trimming seams and pressing out as they are added. Refer to block illustrations for Block A color changes.

FLOWER TOP ASSEMBLY

1. For Block A iris top, join units 4-1-2-and 3 in a row. Refer to Block A mirror image illustration and reverse as shown. Assemble Block B in the same manner.
2. Join units 6-5; then add to 4-3 combined flower top units. Join Unit 7 to opposite sides as shown.

FLOWER CENTER UNIT ASSEMBLY

1. For Unit 8, our illustration shows fabrics used in Block B. Two 1" x 1 1/2" strips of Fabric I are joined to opposite sides of a 1 1/2" x 2 1/2" strip of Fabric VIII as shown. For Block A, use two strips of Fabric VI with one of Fabric VIII. For first diagonal corner (B8a), join 1" x 1 1/2" strips of Fabrics I and VIII. This will now become a Multi Diagonal Corner. Place it as shown in illustration and stitch diagonal seam as for any diagonal corner. Trim seam and

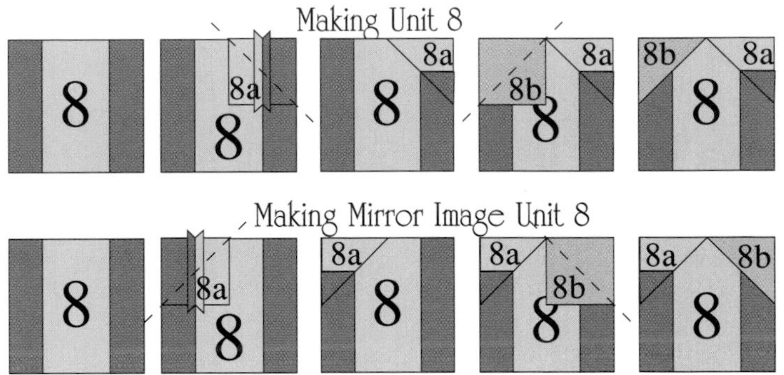

press. Join diagonal corner 8b as shown to complete unit. For Block A Multi Diagonal Corner, use 1" x 1 1/2" strips of fabrics VI and VIII.
2. For Unit 10, diagonal corners overlap each other. Join 10a first, trim seam and press out; then join 10b corner.
3. To make Unit 11, use the same Multi Diagonal Corner technique used in Step 1. For small strip set used in Block B, join 1" x 1 1/2" pieces of Fabric I and VIII. For Block A, use fabrics VI and VIII. Place unit 11a right sides facing on Unit 11 as shown. Stitch diag-

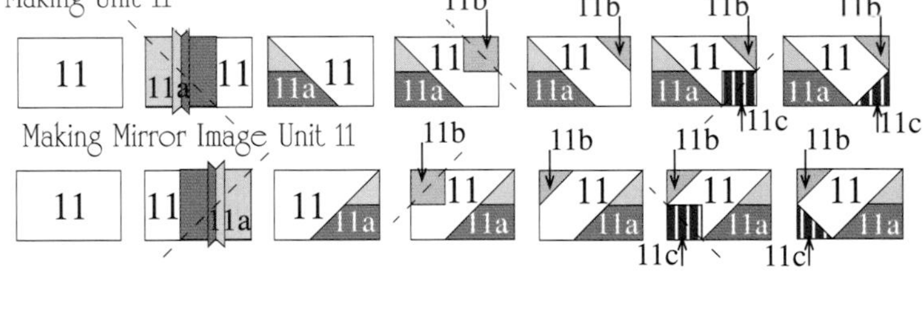

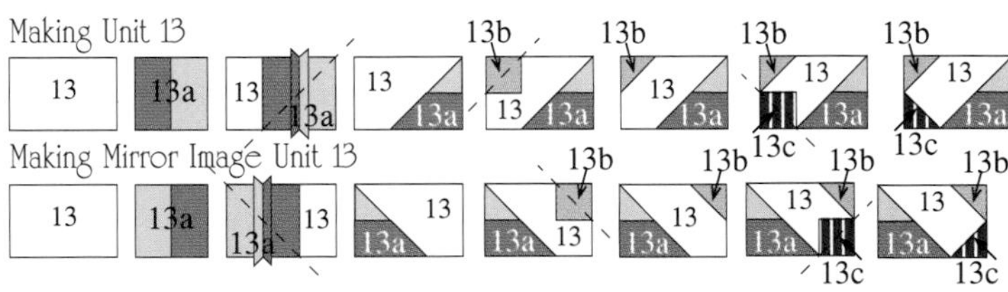

onal, trim seam and press out. Add remaining diagonal corners in alphabetical order.
4. Unit 13 is made the same as Unit 11. Refer to illustration for correct placement of mirror image units and color changes for Block A.
5. To assemble Unit 16, make Multi Diagonal Corner from 1" x 1 1/2" pieces of fabrics II and V for Block B. Make two for each unit and place them as mirror images. For Block A, use fabrics I and II.

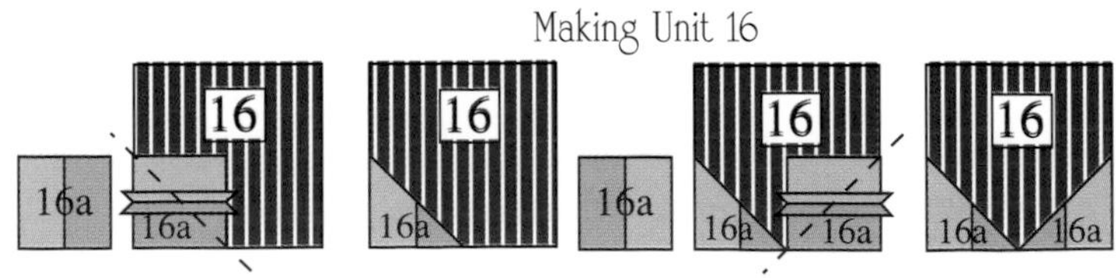

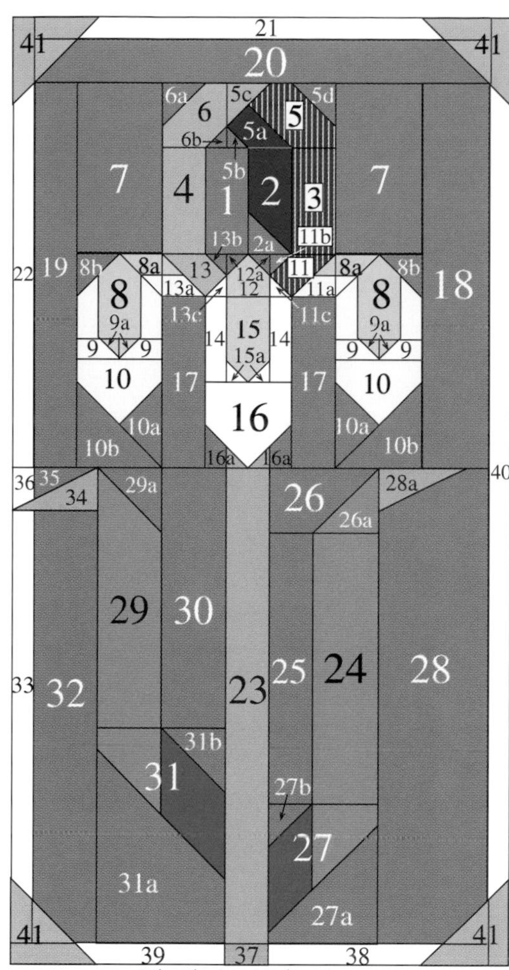

Block A. Make 1

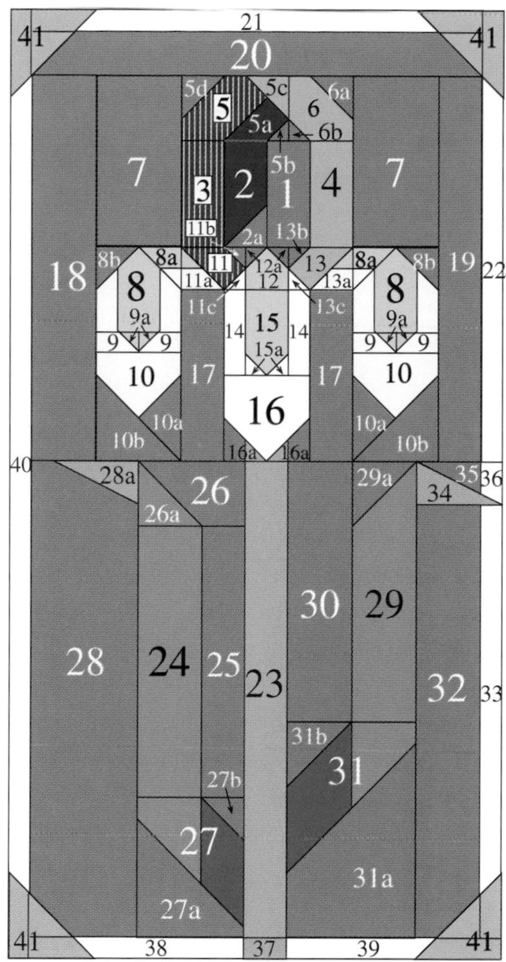

Block A Mirror Image. Make 1

FLOWER CENTER ASSEMBLY

1. To assemble flower center section, begin by joining mirror image units 9 as shown. Join units 8-9-and 10 in a vertical row. Make two for each block, checking illustration for correct placement of mirror image units.
2. Join units 13-12-and 11 in a horizontal row. Reverse for mirror image. Join Unit 14 to opposite sides of Unit 15; then add Unit 16 to bottom. Join Unit 17 to opposite sides of center petal section; then add combined units 13-12-and 11 to top, matching seams.
3. Join combined units 8-10 to opposite sides of center petal. Refer to illustrations for correct placement of mirror image units.
4. Join flower top section to flower center section, matching seams. Join Units 18-19 to opposite sides of flower top as shown; then add Unit 20 to top. Join Unit 21 to Unit 20, to complete flower top. Join Unit 22 to appropriate side as shown.

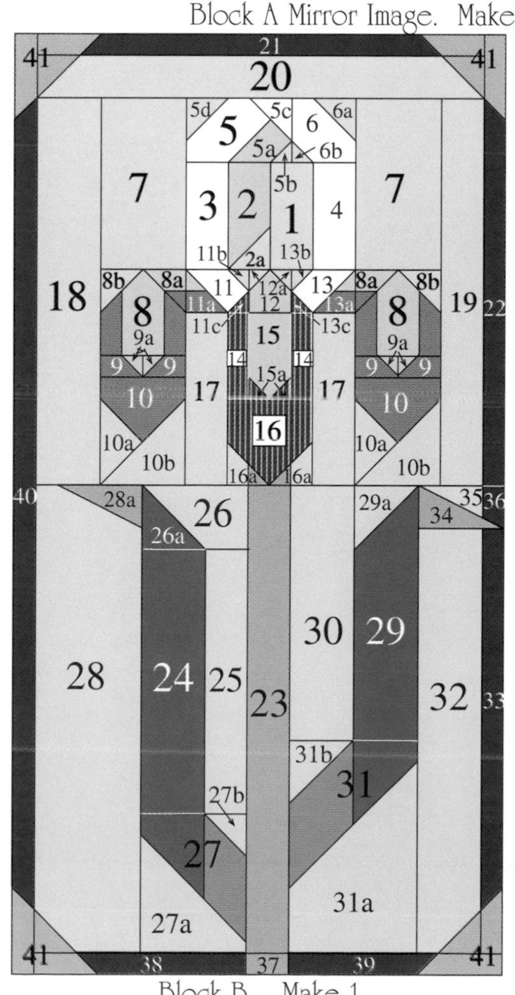

Block B . Make 1

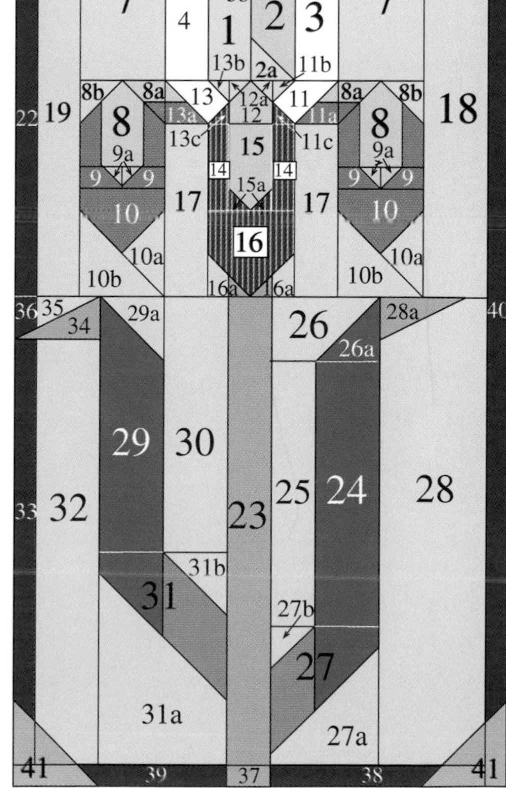

Block B Mirror Image. Make 1

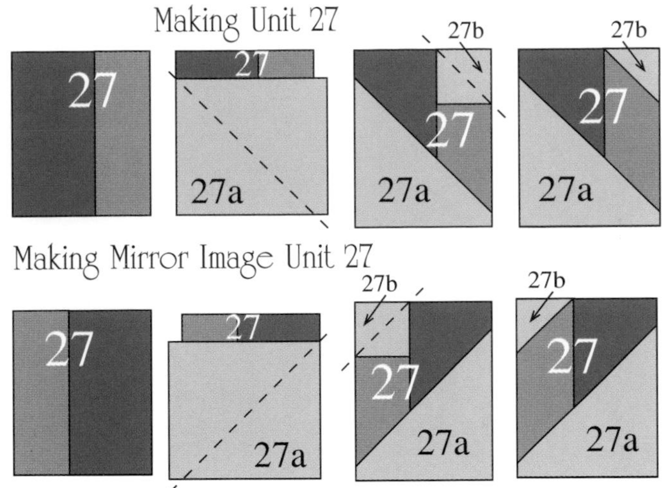

STEM AND LEAF UNIT ASSEMBLY

1. For Block B, Unit 27, join 2" x 3 1/2" strip of Fabric IV and 1 1/2" x 3 1/2" strip of Fabric III to make the small strip set. For Block A use 2" x 3 1/2" strip of Fabric II, and 1 1/2" x 3" strip of Fabric IV.
2. Use diagonal end technique and join Unit 27a to strip set as shown; then add diagonal corner 27b.

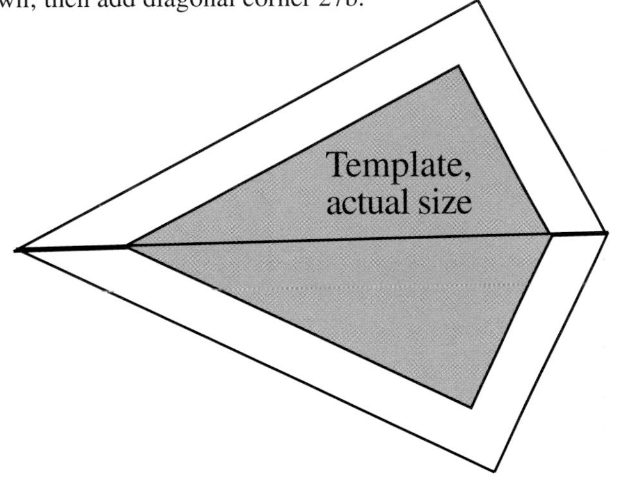

3. Use 2 1/2" x 3" piece of Fabric II and cut out leaf from template. Fold leaf in half wrong sides together. This will now be used at top of Unit 28, and sewn into the seam on two sides as shown with folded edge left loose. You might wish to baste in place.
4. For leaf that extends into border, fold leaf as before. Join units 32 and 33 together as shown.

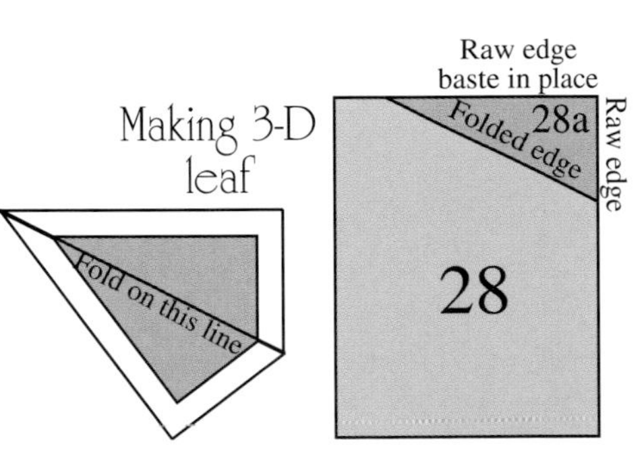

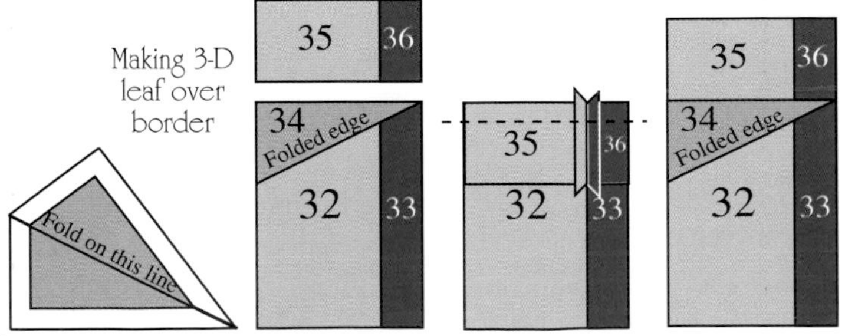

Join units 35 and 36. Baste folded leaf at top of combined 32 and 33 units. Join combined 35-36 units to top of 32-33 units, catching leaf in seam with folded edge loose.
5. Unit 31 is made the same as Unit 27. Join 2" x 4" pieces of fabrics III and IV to make strip set for both A and B blocks. Use diagonal end technique and join Unit 31a to strip set as shown; then add diagonal corner 31b.

Making Unit 31

Making Mirror Image Unit 31

STEM AND LEAF ASSEMBLY

1. To assemble leaf section, begin by joining units 24 and 25; then add Unit 26 to top. Join completed Unit 27 to bottom; then add Unit 23 to one long side and completed leaf Unit 28 to the other.
2. Join units 29 and 30; then add completed Unit 31 to bottom. Join combined leaf units 32-36. Join to center stem Unit 23.
3. Join units 39-37-and 38 in a row as shown. Reverse for mirror image. Join to bottom of leaf section, matching seams.
4. Join stem/leaf section to flower section, matching stem seam carefully. Join Unit 40 to side.
5. Use diagonal corner technique to add Unit 41 to each corner to complete block.

QUILT ASSEMBLY

1. Refer to quilt assembly diagram and join the four blocks together as shown. Match Unit 41 diagonal corner seams.
2. Use diagonal corner technique to make four each of units Q1 and Q2. Join two of Unit Q1 together; then add to top of quilt top as shown. Repeat for quilt bottom.
3. Place 2 7/8" squares of fabrics II and XI right sides together. Make half square triangles following our video instructions using The Angler 2™.
4. Join Units Q2 together in a vertical row; then add half square triangle Unit Q3 to each short end, checking illustration for correct placement. Join these combined units to quilt side.
5. Join border Q4 to top and bottom of quilt; then add Q5 pieced border to opposite sides. Join Q6 border to top and bottom, then add Q7 pieced border to opposite sides to complete quilt top.

QUILTING & FINISHING

1. To make and apply the bias strips around each iris top and outer petals, purchase 1/4" wide bias strips in gold, navy and teal, or make your own.
2. To make your own, add a 12" square to fabrics VIII, IX, X, and XI. Cut 1" wide bias strips from each square and join like colors together. Fold the bias strips wrong side together lengthwise and stitch, using a scant 1/4" seam.
3. Press the bias so that the raw seam is on the back side.
4. Pin the bias strip around your flower, one section at a time. Hand stitch in place, mitering corners and folding under short raw edges.
5. Quilt in the ditch around all patchwork, leaving folded edges of leaves loose.
6. Use the four 2 1/2" wide strips of Fabric X, and make straight-grain, french fold binding. Bind your quilt.

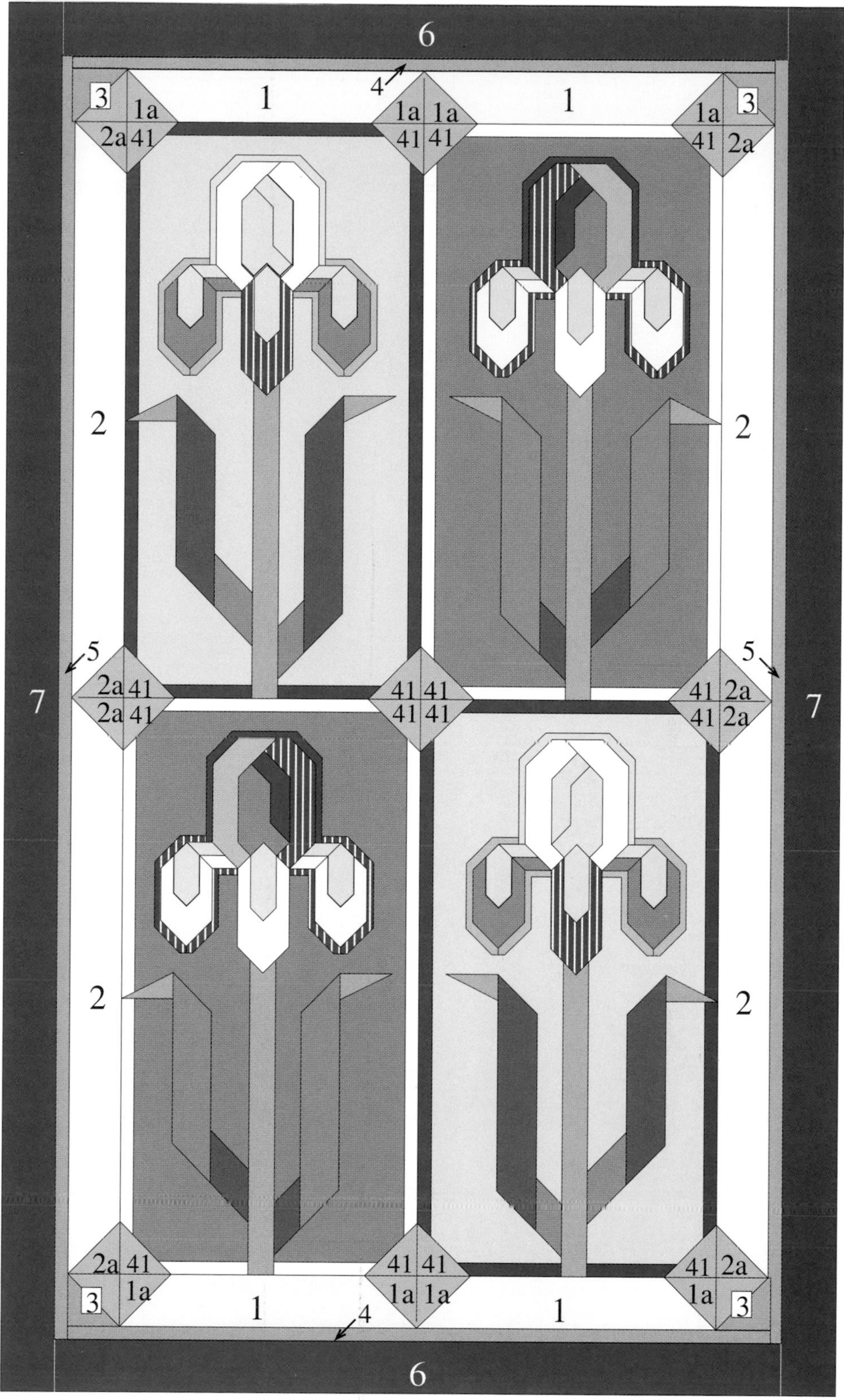

Quilt Assembly Diagram

Glorious Morning

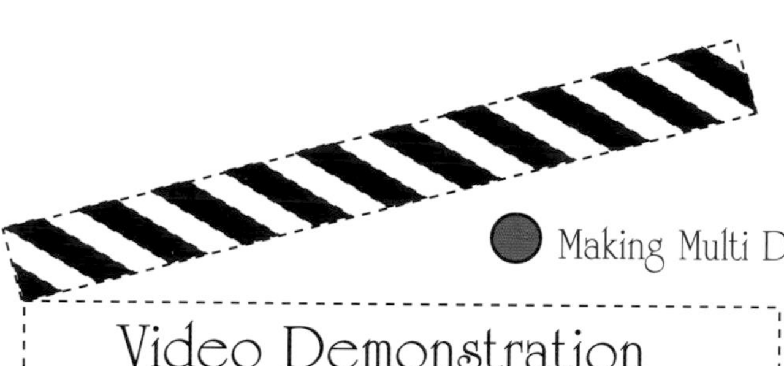

Making Multi Diagonal Corners

Video Demonstration
Take 1

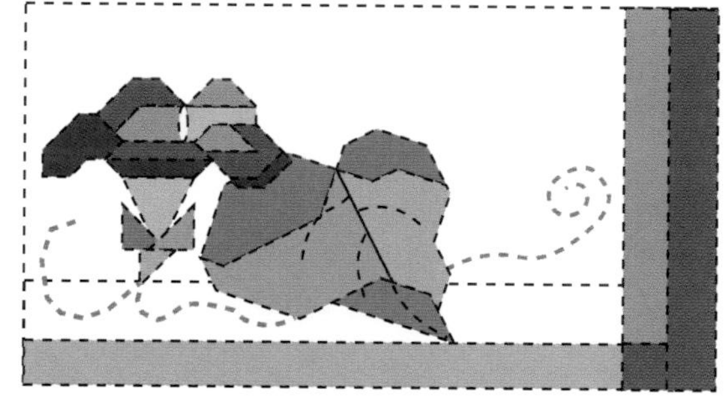

Making Diagonal Ends

Making Diagonal Corners

Finished size: 28 1/8" x 68 5/8"
Morning Glory Blocks A & B:
8 5/8" x 10 1/2"
Bud Blocks C & D: 4 1/8" x 5 5/8"
Leaf Blocks E and F: 10 1/8" x 10 1/2"
Leaf Block G: 7 7/8" square

MATERIALS

Fabric I 7/8 yard (need exactly 28 3/8") (white on white check)
Fabric II 7/8 yard (need exactly 28 3/8") (very dark royal blue print)
Fabric III 1/4 (need exactly 5 3/4") (dark royal blue solid)
Fabric IV 1/8 (need exactly 3 7/8") (medium blue print)
Fabric V 1/4 (need exactly 4 1/2") (light blue print)
Fabric VI 5/8 yard (need exactly 17 7/8") (light green textured print)
Fabric VII 3/8 yard (need exactly 11") (dark green print)
Fabric VIII 1/4 yard (need exactly 8 5/8") (medium green solid)
Fabric IX 1/4 yard (need exactly 5 7/8") (light green print)
Fabric X 3/8 yard (need exactly 9 1/4") (yellow print)
Backing 2 1/8 yards

CUTTING

Cutting instructions shown in red indicate that the quantity of units are combined and cut in 2 or more different places to conserve fabric.*NOTE: All "Q" units in cutting instructions stand for "quilt top". These are units that are not incorporated into blocks.*

From Fabric I, cut: (White on white check)
• One 8 3/4" wide strip. From this, cut:
 * One - 4 1/2" x 8 3/4" (A12, A13, B12, B13 birangles)
• Cut strip lengthwise into one 4 3/8" x 37 1/2" strip, and one 4 1/4" x 37 1/2" strip. From these, cut:
 * One - 4 3/8" x 4 1/2" (C4, D4, birangles)
 * Five - 4 1/4" x 7 1/4" (E3, F3)
 * Five - 1 1/4" x 4 1/4" (E4, F4)
 * Two - 7/8" x 4 1/4" (G1)
 * Four - 3 1/8" x 3 7/8" (A7, B7)
 * Four - 3 1/8" x 3 1/2" (A19, B19)
• Two 3 1/8" wide strips. From these, cut:
 * Twelve - 3 1/8" sq. (E2a, F2a, E10, F10, G6a)
 * Four - 2" x 3 1/8" (A16, B16)
 * Four - 1 5/8" x 3 1/8" (A15, B15)
 * Seven - 2 3/4" sq. (E1a, F1a, G4a)
 * Two - 2" x 5 3/4" (G7)
• Four 2" wide strips. From these, cut:
 * Four - 2" x 6 7/8" (A20, B20)
 * Two - 2" x 5 3/8" (G3)
 * Four - 2" x 4 5/8" (A21, B21)
 * Four - 2" x 3 1/2" (C3, D3)
 * Four - 2" x 2 3/8" (A1, B1)
 * Twenty-four - 2" sq. (A17b, B17b, E1b, E5a, E6b, E8, F1b, F5a, F6b,F8)
 * Four – 1 5/8" x 2 3/4" (A15b, B15b)
 * Four 1 5/8" x 2 3/8" (C2, D2)
 * Four - 1 1/4" x 2" (A18a, B18a)
 * Eight - 1 5/8" sq. (A4b, A6a, A15d, B4b, B6a, B15d, C1a, D1a, D3b, E9a, F9a, G2a, G5a)
• One 1 5/8" wide strip. From this, cut:
 * Twenty-three -1 5/8" sq. (add to A4b, A6a, A15d, B4b, B6a, B15d, C1a, C5d, D1a, D5d, E9a, F9a, G2a, G5a)
• Three 1 1/4" wide strips. From these and scrap, cut:
 * Four - 1 1/4" x 3 7/8" (C6, D6)
 * Eight - 1 1/4" x 3 1/2" (A14, B14)
 * Thirty-nine - 1 1/4" sq. (A11a, A13c, B11a, B13c, C1c, C5b, C7, D1c, D5b, D7, E5b, F5b, G2b)

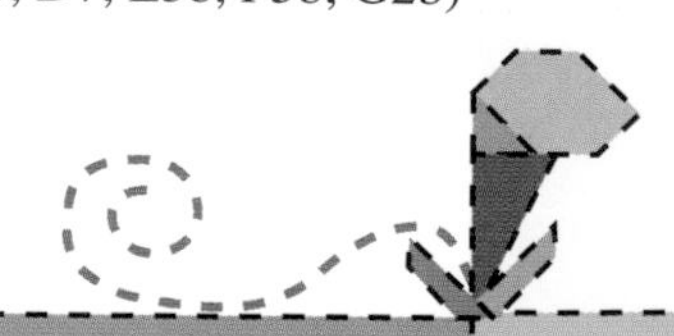

* Four - 7/8" squares (A4c, B4c)

From Fabric II, cut: (Very dark royal blue print)

- Five 3" wide strips from straight-grain binding.
- One 2 3/8" wide strip. From this, cut:
  * Four - 2 3/8" x 3 1/8" (A17, B17)
  * Four - 7/8" x 2 3/8" (A6, B6)
  * Four - 2" squares (A4, B4)
- Six 1 5/8" wide strips. From this, cut:
  * Four - 1 5/8" x 35" (Q29 border) piece two together to = 1 5/8" x 69 1/2"
  * Two - 1 5/8" x 26 3/8" (Q28 border)
- One 1 1/4" wide strip. From this, cut:
  * Four - 1 1/4" x 5" (A11, B11)
  * Four - 1 1/4" x 2 3/8" (A18, B18)
  * Eight - 1 1/4" squares (A9b, A10b, B9b, B10b)

From Fabric III, cut: (Dark royal blue solid)

- One 4 1/2" wide strip. From this, cut:
  * One - 4 1/2" x 8 3/4" (C4, D4 birangles)
- Cut remainder of strip lengthwise, yielding one 2" wide strip, and one 1 5/8" strip. From these strips, cut:
  * Four - 2" sq. (A9a, B9a)
  * Four - 1 5/8" x 3 7/8" (A15c, B15c)
  * Four - 1 5/8" x 2 3/8" (A5, B5)
  * Twelve - 1 5/8" sq. (A1a, A3a, A4a, B1a, B3a, B4a)
- One 1 1/4" wide strip. From this, cut:
  * Four - 1 1/4" x 5" (A10, B10)
  * Four - 7/8" x 1 1/4" (A10a, B10a)
  * Eight - 7/8" squares (A16a, A17a, B16a, B17a)

From Fabric IV, cut: (Medium blue print)

- One 3 7/8" wide strip. From this, cut:
  * Four - 2" x 3 7/8" (A9, B9)
  * Four - 1 5/8" x 3 1/2" (A15a, B15a)
- Cut remaining strip lengthwise into one 1 5/8" x 27 1/2" strip. From this, cut:
  * Four - 1 5/8" x 2 3/8" (A3, B3)
  * Four - 1 5/8" squares (C1b, D1b)
  * Four - 1 1/4" squares (A8a, B8a)
  * Four - 7/8" x 1 1/4" (A10a, B10a)

From Fabric V, cut: (Light blue print)

- One 4 1/2" wide strip. From this, cut:
  * One - 4 1/2" x 8 3/4" (A12, A13, B12, B13 birangles)
  * Four - 2 3/8" x 3 1/2" (C1, D1)
  * Four - 1 5/8" x 2" (A8, B8)
  * Four - 1 1/4" x 2 3/8" (A2, B2)

From Fabric VI, cut: (Light green textured print)

- One 12 1/8" wide strip. From this, cut:
  * One - 6 7/8" x 12 1/8" (Q4)
  * One - 8 3/8" x 11" (Q16)
  * One - 4 1/4" x 10 5/8" (Q24)
  * One - 3 1/8" x 10 5/8" (Q21)
  * One - 4 1/4" x 9 1/8" (Q6)
  * Two - 3 1/8" x 9 1/8" (Q17, Q22)
- From remaining scrap, cut five 1 5/8" x 9" strips. From these, cut:
  * One - 1 5/8" x 7 1/4" (Q19)
  * One - 1 5/8" x 6 7/8" (Q26)
  * One - 1 5/8" x 6 1/8" (Q1)
  * One - 1 5/8" x 5 3/8" (Q11)
  * One - 1 5/8" x 4 5/8" (Q18)
- One 5 3/4" wide strip. From this, cut:
  * One - 4 5/8" x 5 3/4" (Q5)
  * One - 3 7/8" x 6 1/8" (Q14)
  * One - 3 1/8" x 5 3/4" (Q2)
  * One - 2 3/8" x 11" (Q12)
  * One - 2 3/8" x 6 1/8" (Q13)

From Fabric VII, cut: (Dark green print)

- One 3 1/2" wide strip. From this, cut:
  * Five - 3 1/2" x 7 1/4" (E1, F1)
- One 3 1/8" wide strip. From this and scrap, cut:
  * Five - 3 1/8" squares (E3a, F3a)
  * Five - 1 5/8" x 3 1/8" (E9, F9)
  * Four - 2 3/8" squares (A13a, B13a)
  * Four - 2" squares (C5a, D5a)
- One 2 3/8" wide strip. From this, cut:
  * Seven - 2 3/8" x 4 1/4" (E5, F5, G2)
  * Two - 2" x 4 5/8" (G5)
- One 2" wide strip. From this, cut:
  * Seven - 2" squares (E6a, F6a, G4b)
  * Seven - 1 5/8" squares (E7a, F7a, G7b)
  * Two - 1 1/4" squares (G3b)

From Fabric VIII, cut: (Medium green solid)

- One 3 7/8" wide strip. From this, cut:
  * Five - 3 7/8" x 7 1/4" (E2, F2)
  * Five - 1 1/4" squares (E1c, F1c)
- One 2 3/4" wide strip. From this, cut:
  * Two - 2 3/4" x 6 1/8" (G4)
  * Two - 2" x 2 3/4" (G3a)
  * Eight - 2 3/8" squares (A13b, B13b, C5c, D5c)
- One 2" wide strip. From this, cut:
  * Five - 2" squares (E1d, F1d)

From Fabric IX, cut: (Light green print)

- One 3 7/8" wide strip. From this, cut:
  * Five - 3 7/8" x 4 1/4" (E6, F6)
  * Two - 3 1/8" x 6 7/8" (G6)
  * Two - 2" x 3 1/8" (G7a)
- One 2" wide strip. From this, cut:
  * Five - 2" x 2 3/4" (E7, F7)
  * Four - 2" squares (A20a, B20a)
  * Ten - 1 5/8" squares (E5c, E10a, F5c, F10a)
  * Four - 1 1/4" squares (C6a, D6a)

From Fabric X, cut: (Yellow print)

- One 2 3/4" wide strip. From this, cut:
  * One - 2 3/4" x 4 1/4" (Q7)
  * One - 1 5/8" x 35 3/4" (Q23)
- Four 1 5/8" wide strips. From these, cut:
  * Two - 1 5/8" x 24" (Q27) join together to = 1 5/8" x 47"
  * One - 1 5/8" x 20 3/8" (Q9)
  * Two - 1 5/8" x 18 7/8" (Q8, Q25)
  * One - 1 5/8" x 8 3/4" (Q3)
  * Two - 1 5/8" x 6 1/8" (Q10, Q15)
  * One - 1 5/8" x 5 3/4" (Q20)

ASSEMBLY

CUTTING FOR BIRANGLES

1. The illustrations below show how to cut birangles from fabrics I, III, and V. For 4 1/2" x 8 3/4" piece, draw a line down the center, vertically and horizontally. Cut on these lines. Cut rectangular sections from corner to corner as shown. Trim 1/2" off of tip of each triangle.
2. Refer to illustration of 4 1/2" x 4 3/8" piece and trim as shown.

BLOSSOM BLOCKS A AND B

1. A & B blocks are mirror images, refer frequently to illustrations for correct placement of all mirror image units.
2. Use diagonal corner technique to make one each of units 1, 3, 4, 8, 9, 10, 11, 13, 16, 17, and 20.
3. Use diagonal end technique to make one each of units 15 and 18.
4. For Unit 4, join diagonal corners in alphabetical order. Trim seam after joining each one, and press; then join the next.

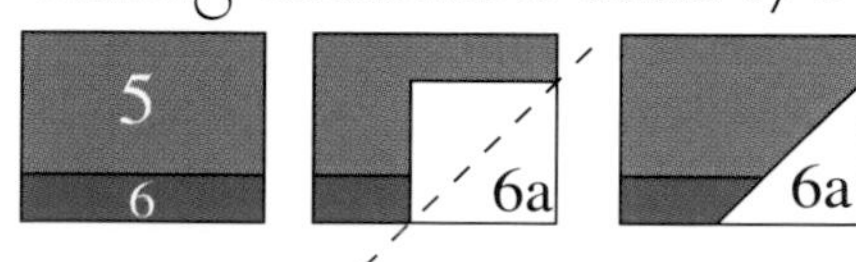

5. To complete combined units 5-6, join 7/8" x 2 3/8" piece of Fabric II with 1 5/8" x 2 3/8" piece of Fabric III as shown. Add diagonal corner 6a to complete combined units.
6. To make Unit 10; join 7/8" x 1 1/4" pieces of fabrics III and IV. Place this small strip set as shown on short end of Unit 10. Stitch diagonally as you would for any diagonal corner. Trim seam and press open. Add diagonal corner 10b to complete the units.

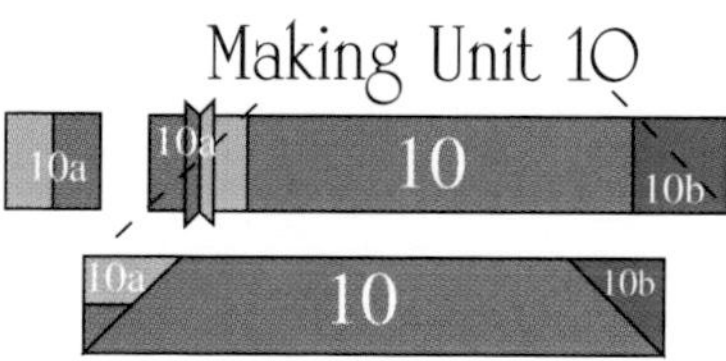

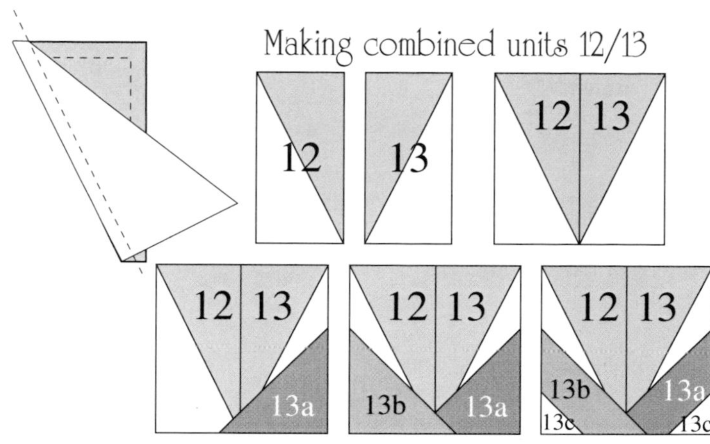

7. To make combined units 12-13, begin by joining birangle pieces as shown above. Make Unit 12 and Unit 13 then join them together. Diagrams show diagonal corners joined in alphabetical order.

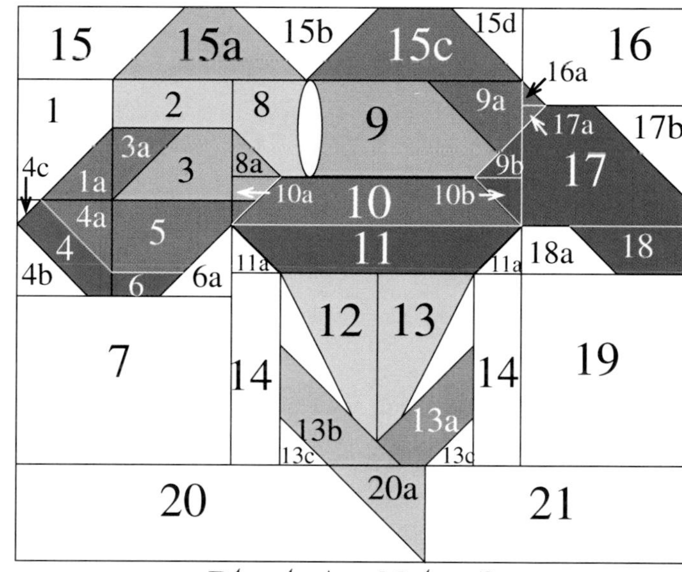

Block A - Make 3.

8. To assemble the Morning Glory blossom, please refer often to mirror image diagrams for correct placement of mirror image units. Begin by joining units 2 and 3; then add Unit 1 to side, matching diagonal seam. Join units 4 and combined units 5-6; then add these combined units to bottom of 1-3 units. Join Unit 7 to bottom.
9. Join units 8 and 9. Join units 10 and 11. Join combined 10-11 units to bottom of 8-9 units. Join Unit 14 to opposite sides of combined 12-13 units as shown; then add to bottom of combined units 8-11. Join this center of the flower to combined units 1-7 as shown.
10. Join units 16-17-18- and 19 in a vertical row as shown; then add to side of flower matching seams.
11. Refer to illustration for making Unit 15. Mirror image illustration for Block B is included. Assemble Unit 15 as shown in diagram, and join to top of flower. Join units 20 and 21 and add to flower bottom to complete blocks A & B.

ASSEMBLING BUD BLOCKS C AND D

1. Use diagonal corner technique to make one each of units 1 and 6.
2. Refer to illustrations frequently as blocks are mirror images. To

assemble combined units 4-5, refer to illustration and begin by joining birangles as shown. Add Unit 5 to side of birangle; then join diagonal corners as shown in alphabetical order.

3. To assemble the bud blocks, begin by joining units 1 and 2. Join units 3 and combined units 4-5 in a row as shown. Join to bottom of combined 1-2 units.

4. Join units 6 and 7; then add to bottom of bud as shown to complete blocks C and D.

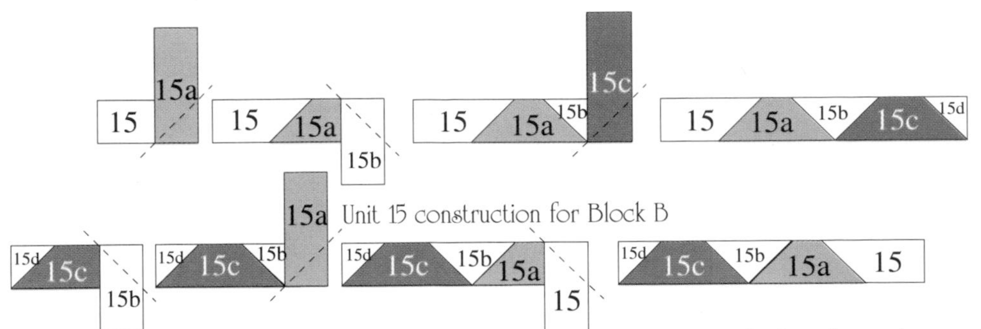

Unit 15 construction for Block B

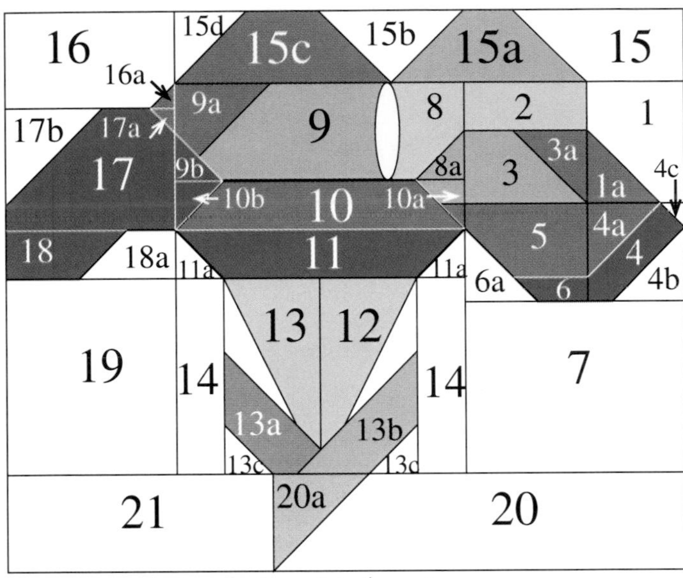

Block B - Make 1.

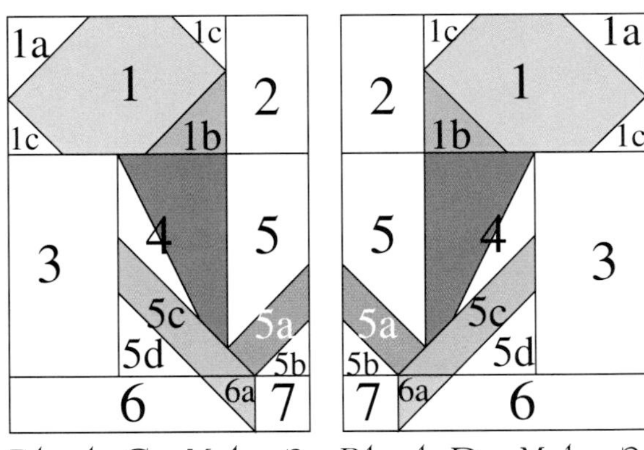

Block C - Make 2. Block D - Make 2.

Making combined units 4/5

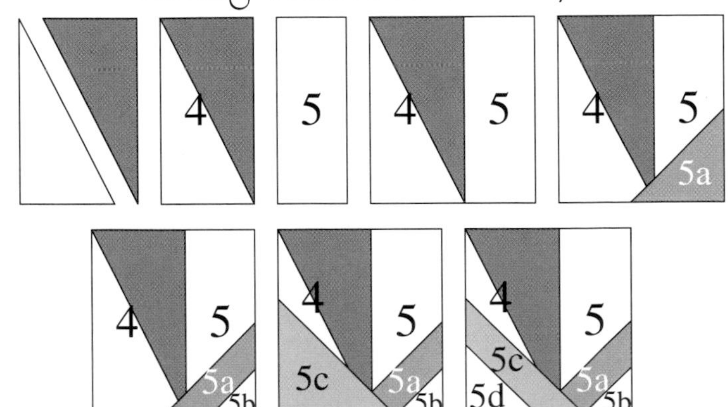

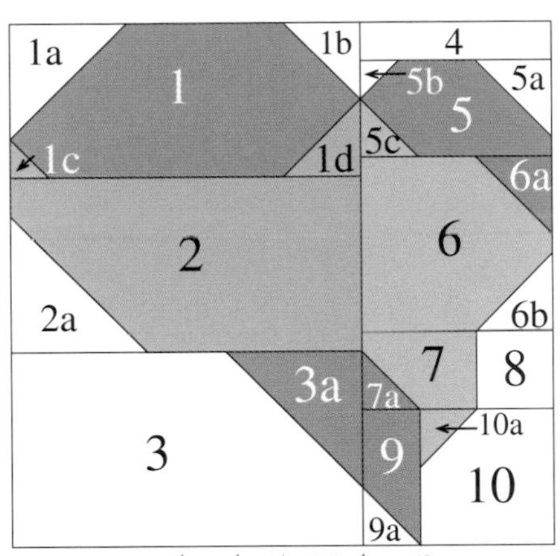

Block E, Make 3.

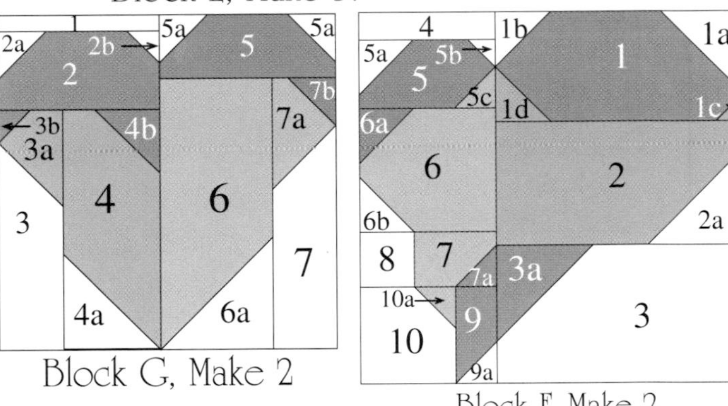

Block G, Make 2

Block F, Make 2.

LEAF BLOCKS E, F, AND G ASSEMBLY

1. For mirror image blocks E and F, use diagonal corner technique to make one each of units 1, 2, 5, 6, 7, 9, and 10.

2. To assemble these blocks, join units 1-2-and 3 in a vertical row. Join units 7 and 8; then join units 9 and 10.

3. Join all remaining units and unit combinations in a vertical row as shown, matching seams.

4. For leaf block G, use diagonal corner technique to make one each of units 2, 4, 5, and 6. Use diagonal end technique to make one each of units 3 and 7.

5. To assemble Leaf Block G, begin by joining units 1 and 2. Join units 3 and 4; then add to bottom of units 1-2. Join units 6 and 7; then add Unit 5 to top of combined units. Join the two leaf sections together to complete Block G.

QUILT ASSEMBLY

1. To assemble quilt top, refer to Quilt Assembly Diagram at right, and begin by joining blocks A and E. Join Unit Q5 with Block D. Join units Q6 and Q7; then add them to left side of combined Unit Q5-Block D. Join Block G to the bottom of this combined section. Join flower and bud sections together; then add Unit Q8 to top, and Unit Q9 to right side..
2. Join Unit Q1 to left side of Block C; then add Unit 2 to top. Join Unit Q3 to left side of Block C combination; then add Unit Q4 to top. Add this section to left side of flower-bud-and leaf sections.
3. For remaining left side of quilt top, begin by joining units Q10 and Q11. Join these to bottom of Block F. Join Block A-Unit Q12-and Block E in a row and add them to bottom of combined Q10-Q11 units.
4. Join Unit Q13-Block C-Q14-and Unit Q15 in a horizontal row; then add Unit Q16 to bottom. Join this bud section to bottom of left row.
5. For right row, begin by joining Block B with Unit Q17. Next join Unit Q18 to bottom of Block D; then add Unit Q19 to right side and Q20 to top. Join this combined section to right side of Block G. Join to bottom of Block B-Unit Q17 combination.
6. Join Block F and Unit Q21 as shown. Join Unit Q22 and Block A as shown. Join these two sections together and add to bottom of Block B-Block G- and Bud combination. Join Unit Q23 to side.
7. Join Block E and Unit Q24; then add to bottom of right row. Join the right and left rows together. Join units Q25 and Q26 and add them to quilt bottom. Join pieced Unit Q27 to left side of quilt as shown. Join the quilt top and bottom together, matching seams.
8. Join Border Q28 to top and bottom of quilt; then add pieced border Q29 to opposite sides of quilt to complete top.
9. Draw vines and veins in leaves with thin felt tipped pen on quilt top as shown. Place tear-away stabilizer behind the vines and using your machine set on a close medium wide satin stitch, satin stitch vines.
10. Before tearing the stabilizer away, we used a wide, yellow satin stitch for flower centers. Tear stabilizer away from quilt back.

QUILTING AND FINISHING

1 This quilt was designed several years ago, and quilted by a friend of ours in Rochester, MN. Her name is Julie Tebay and her business is "Quilting Plus." Julie has several Amish ladies who do lovely hand quilting. This is one of the last quilts that Julie was able to do on her machine before she developed severe wrist problems, and I think it is magnificent. Julie is a talented artist. If you look at the photo closely, you may be able to spot the hummingbird and insects that she quilted among the vines and flowers.
2. Make 200" of straight-grain binding from Fabric II, and bind your quilt.

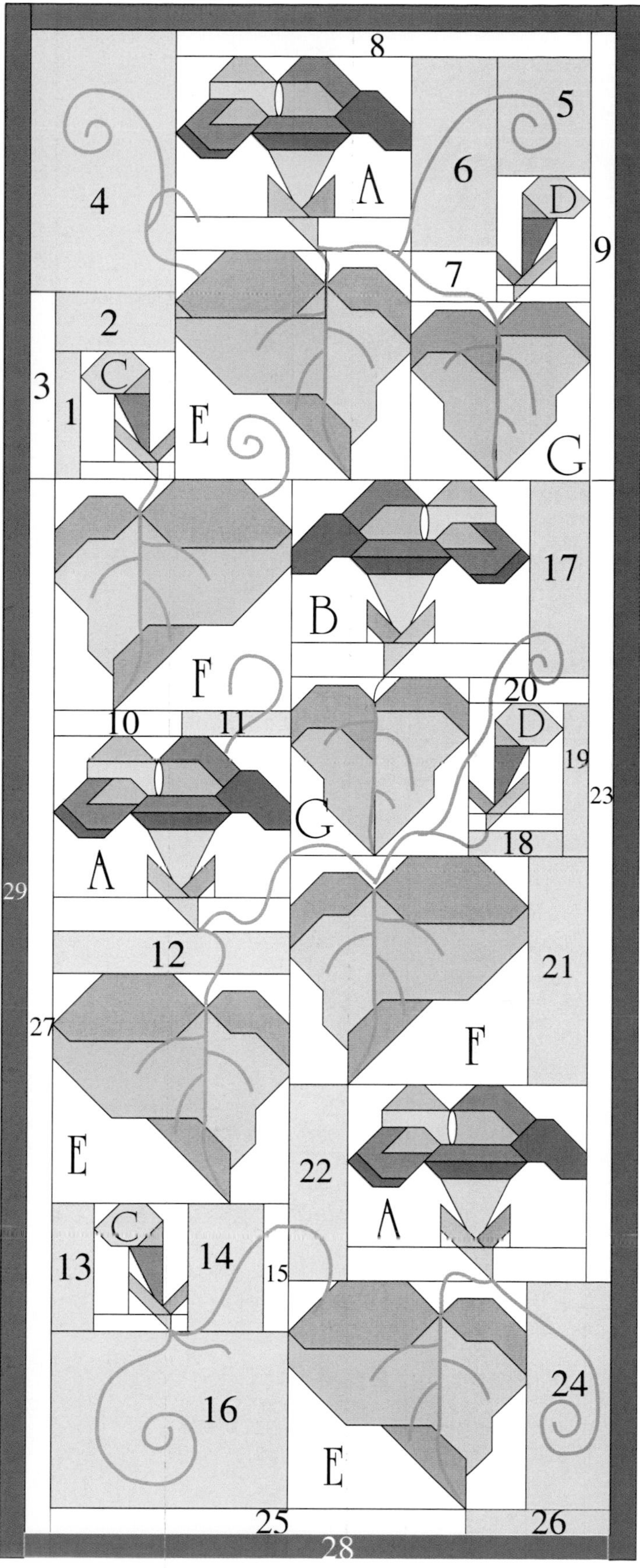

Quilt Assembly Diagram

Floral quilts that bloom in my memory:

Don't Fence Me In Quilt

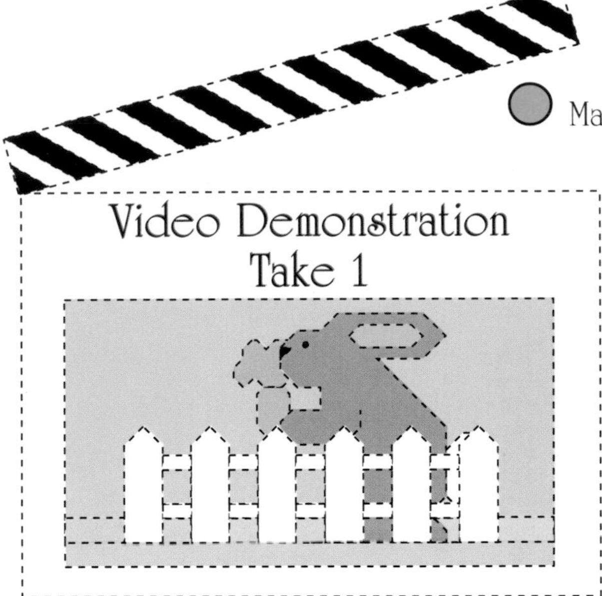

Making Diagonal Corners

Making Diagonal Ends

Finished size: 58" square
Bunny blocks A & B: 12" square
Carrot Block C: 12" square
Heart Block D: 6" square
Fence post Block E: 2" x 6"
Gate Block F: 5" x 6"
Heart Gate Block G: 5" x 6"

MATERIALS FOR QUILT

Fabric I (blue sky print)	**1 3/4 yards (need exactly 59")**
Fabric II (solid white)	**1 1/8 yards (need exactly 38 3/4")**
Fabric III (light orange print)	**1/4 yard (need exactly 5")**
Fabric IV (green daisy print)	**1/2 yard (need exactly 15 3/4")**
Fabric V (brown check)	**3/8 yard (need exactly 9 1/4")**
Fabric VI (dark green print)	**1 yard (need exactly 33 1/4")**
Fabric VII (bright orange print)	**1/4 yard (need exactly 6 1/2")**
Fabric VIII (bright yellow print)	**1/8 yard (need exactly 3 1/2")**
Fabric IX (peach print)	**1/4 yard (need exactly 5 1/4")**
Backing	**3 1/2 yards**

CUTTING

Cutting instructions shown in red indicate that the quantity of units are combined and cut in 2 or more different places to conserve fabric.

NOTE: All "Q" units in cutting instructions stand for "quilt top". These are units that are not incorporated into blocks.

From Fabric I, cut: (blue sky print)

- Two 12 1/2" wide strips. From these, cut:
  - * One – 12 1/2" square (Q1)
  - * Twelve – 2 1/2" x 12 1/2" (Q7)
  - * Four – 1 1/2" x 12 1/2" (A16, B16)
  - * Four – 2" x 10 1/2" (A14, B14)
  - * Four – 1 1/2" x 10 1/2" (A15, B15)
  - * *Do not cut strip down in width unless specified.*
  - * Four – 2 3/4" x 5 3/4" (A9, B9)
- Cut remainder into three 3 1/2" wide strips. From these, cut:
  - * Eight – 3 1/2" x 3 3/4" (C3a)
  - * Four – 1 1/2" x 3 1/2" (C9)
- Two 3 1/2" wide strips. From these, cut:
  - * Eight – 3 1/2" x 4 3/4" (C2)
  - * Six – 3 1/2" squares (A2a, B2a, F1a)
  - * Four – 2 1/4" x 3 1/2" (C5)
  - * Four – 2 1/2" x 3 1/4" (C10)
  - * One – 1 1/2" x 5 1/2" (F4)
- One 2 1/2" wide strip. From this, cut:
  - * Four – 2 1/2" squares (C13)
  - * Four – 2 1/4" x 3 3/4" (A8, B8)
  - * Four – 1 1/2" x 2 1/4" (A6, B6)
  - * Four – 1 1/4" x 2 1/4" (A4, B4)
- Three 2 1/4" wide strips for Strip Set 1.
- Three 2" wide strips for Strip Set 1.
- One 1 3/4" wide strip. From this, cut:
  - * Four – 1 3/4" x 2 3/4" (A13, B13)
  - * Four – 1 3/4" squares (A1a, B1a)
- Five 1 1/2" wide strips, from this and scrap, cut:
  - * 166 – 1 1/2" squares (A1b, B1b, A3a, B3a, A11, B11, C6a, C7a, C8a, C11a, C12a, E1a)
- Two 1 1/4" wide strips. From this, cut:

* Forty – 1 1/4" squares (A1c, B1c, A3b, B3b, A5a, B5a, A10a, B10a, C1b)
* Sixteen – 1" squares (A7a, B7a, A12a, B12a)

From Fabric II, cut: (solid white)

- Four 6 1/2" wide strips. From these, cut:
  * Fifty-one – 2 1/2" x 6 1/2" (E1)
  * One – 4" square (F1)
  * Four – 2 1/2" x 12 1/2" (Q6)
  * Two – 1 1/4" x 5 1/2" (F3)
  * Two – 1 1/4" x 4" (F2)
- One 2 3/4" wide strip. From this, cut:
  * Four – 2 3/4" x 4" (A10, B10)
  * Two – 2 1/2" x 11 1/2" (Q5)
- One 2 1/2" wide strip. From this, cut:
  * Two – 2 1/2" x 11 1/2" (add to Q5)
- Six 1 1/4" wide strips for Strip Set 1

From Fabric III, cut: (light orange print)

- Two 2 1/2" wide strips. From these, cut:
  * Four – 2 1/2" x 12 1/2" (Q2)

From Fabric IV, cut: (green daisy print)

- One 4 1/2" wide strip. From this, cut:
  * Eight – 3 1/2" x 4 1/2" (C3)
  * Eight – 2 1/4" squares (C1a)
- Four 1 1/2 wide strips. From these, cut:
  * Eight – 1 1/2" x 12 1/2" (A17, B17, C4)
  * Four – 1 1/2" x 2 1/2" (Q4)
- Three 1 3/4" wide strips for Strip Set 1.

From Fabric V, cut: (brown check)

- One 6 3/4" wide strip. From this, cut:
  * Four – 1 1/2" x 6 3/4" (A12, B12)
  * Four – 4 1/4" x 6" (A2, B2)
  * Four – 3 3/4" x 6" (A1, B1)
  * Two – 2 1/4" x 3" (A5, B5)
- One 2 1/2" wide strip. From this, cut:
  * Four – 2 1/2" x 6" (A3, B3)
  * Four – 2" x 2 1/2" (A7, B7)
  * Two – 2 1/4" x 3" (add to A5, B5)

From Fabric VI, cut: (dark green print)

- One 3 1/2" wide strip. From this, cut:
  * Four – 3 1/2" x 4 1/2" (C7)
  * Four – 3 1/2" squares (C8)
  * Four – 2 1/2" x 3" (C11)
- One 2 3/4" wide strip. From this, cut:
  * Four – 2 3/4" x 3 1/2" (C6)
  * Four – 2 1/2" x 5 1/4" (C12)
- Six 2 1/2" wide strips for binding.
- Eight 1 1/2" wide strips. From these, cut:
  * Four – 1 1/2" x 29 1/2" (Q10) piece two together to = two 58 1/2" strips.
  * Four – 1 1/2" x 28 1/2" (Q9)

From Fabric VII, cut: (bright orange print)

- One 6 1/2" wide strip. From this, cut:
  * Four – 4" x 6 1/2" (C1)
  * Twelve – 2 1/2" squares (Q8)

From Fabric VIII, cut: (bright yellow print)

- One 3 1/2" wide strip. From this, cut:
  * Four – 3 1/2" x 5 1/2" (D1)
  * Four 2 1/2" x 3 1/2" (D3)
  * Four – 2 1/2" squares (Q3)

From Fabric IX, cut: (peach print)

- One 3 3/4" wide strip. From this, cut:
  * Four – 1 1/2" x 3 3/4" (bunny ear applique)
  * Eight – 1" x 3 1/2" (D2, D4)
  * Four – 3" squares (D5)
  * Four – 1" x 6 1/2" (D7)
  * Two – 1" x 6" (D6)
- One 1 1/2" wide strip. From this, cut:
  * Sixteen – 1 1/2" squares (D1a, D3a)
  * Two – 1" x 6" (add to D6)

ASSEMBLY

Strip Set 1

2"
1 1/4"
2 1/4"
1 1/4"
1 3/4"

STRIP SET 1

1. Refer to illustration of Strip Set 1 and join one 2" wide, and one 2 1/4" wide strip of Fabric I, with two 1 1/4" wide strips of Fabric II, and one 1 3/4" wide strip of Fabric IV as shown. Make three of these strip sets for the quilt. Cut into forty-six 2" wide segments.

MIRROR IMAGE BUNNY BLOCKS A & B

1. It will be essential for you to refer to diagrams of blocks A and B frequently for correct placement of mirror image units.
2. Use diagonal corner technique to make one each of units 1, 2, 3, 5, 7, 10, and 12.
3. Use pattern given for bunny ear appliques and draw the ear on

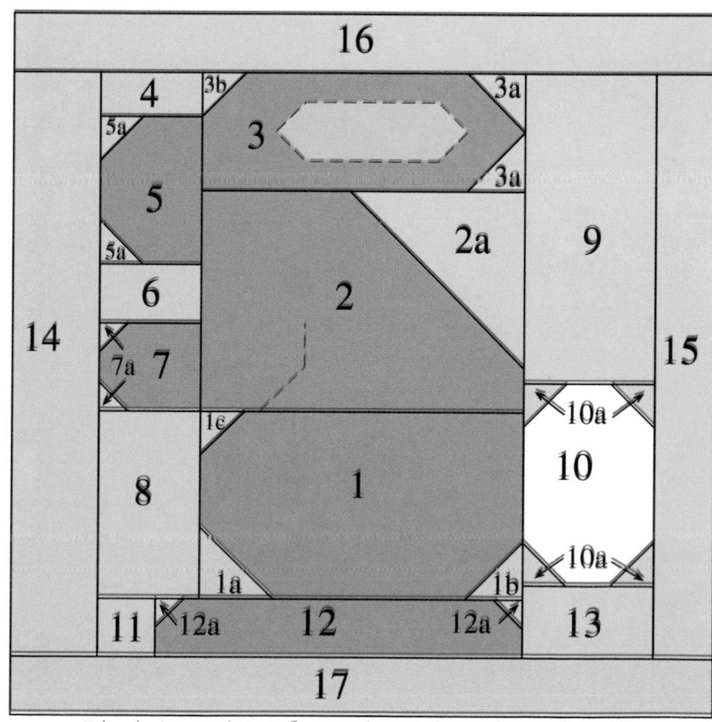

Block A. Make 2 for quilt. Make 1 for wall quilt.

a scrap of fusible pellon. Follow manufacturer's instructions for fusible pellon and press it on four - 1 1/2" x 3 3/4" pieces of Fabric IX. Cut ear out and press in place on Unit 3 as shown. Place tear-away pellon behind ear and sating stitch ear in place with coordinating thread. Tear pellon away.

4. To assemble blocks, begin by joining units 3-2-1 in a vertical row as shown. Join units 4-5-6-7-and 8 in a vertical row and add to combined 1-3 units, matching seams carefully.

5. Join units 11 and 12 in a horizontal row; then add to bottom of combined bunny units.

6. Join units 9-10-13 in a row; then join to back side of bunny as shown. Add Unit 14 to front of bunny; then join Unit 15 to back. Join Unit 16 at top of block, and grass Unit 17 to bottom to complete blocks.

CARROT BLOCK C

1. Use diagonal corner technique to make one each of units 1, 6, 7, 8, 11, and 12.

2. Refer to illustration for making mirror image Unit 3, and use diagonal end technique to make this unit.

3. To assemble carrot, refer to illustration for correct placement, and join units 2 and 3 as shown, making mirror imaged rows for each side of the carrot.

4. Join the 2-3 combined units to opposite sides of Unit 1 carrot; then add Unit 4 to bottom of combined units.

5. Working from left to right, join units 5-6-7-8- and 9 in a vertical row. Join units 10-11-12- and 13 in a vertical row. Join the two rows together and add to carrot top to complete Block C.

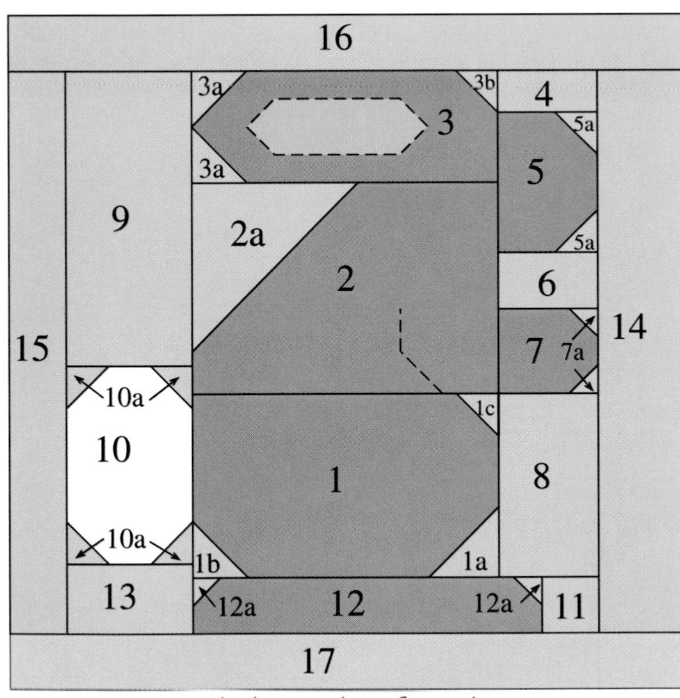

Block B. Make 2 for quilt.

Bunny ear applique, cut 4

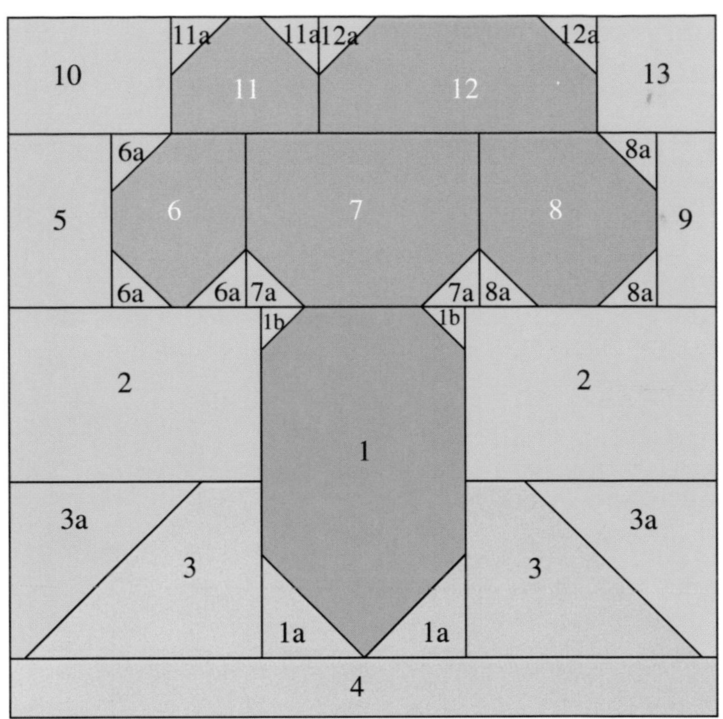

Block C. Make 4 for quilt. Make 2 for wall quilt.

Making mirror image diagonal end, Unit 3

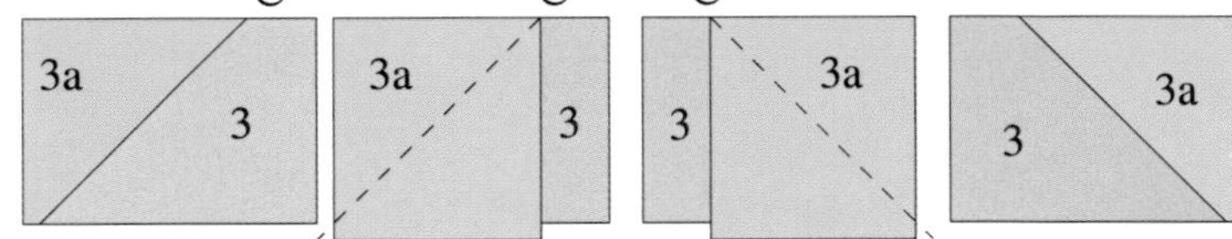

HEART BLOCK D

1. Use diagonal corner technique to make one each of units 1, and 3.

2. To assemble heart, refer to illustration and begin by joining units 1 and 2 as shown. Join units 3 and 4; then add Unit 5 to top of these combined units. Join the 1-2 combined units with the 3-5 units; then add Unit 6 to bottom and Unit 7 to left side as shown.

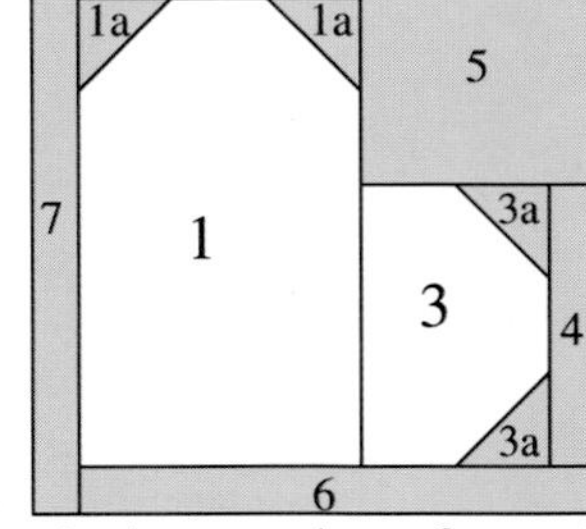

Block D - Make 4 for quilt

Block E

1a 1a

1

FENCE POST BLOCK E

1. This simple unit is made by using diagonal corner technique to make the top of the fence post. Make 51 for the quilt.

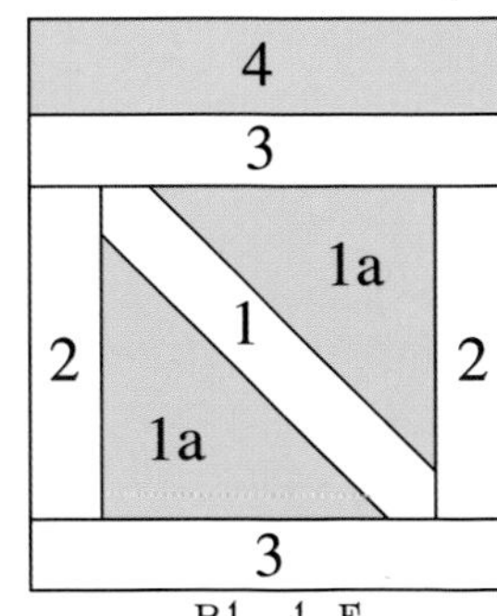

Block F

GATE BLOCK F

1. Use diagonal corner technique to make one of Unit 1.

2. To assemble, join Unit 2 to opposite sides of Unit 1 as shown. Add Unit 3 to top and bottom; then join Unit 4 to top to complete the gate.

QUILT TOP ASSEMBLY

1. Begin assembly with the center portion of the quilt. Refer frequently to the quilt assembly diagram. Start with the top sashing row and join four of Unit Q8 with three of Unit Q7 as shown. Make two of these rows. One for the top of the quilt, and one for the bottom. Set one row aside.
2. Working downward, to assemble second row, join Units Q4 and Q5 as shown in diagram. Make 4. Two are for bottom row. Assemble this row from left to right by joining Unit Q7-Block C-combined Q4-Q5 units-Block A-combined Q4-Q5 units-Block C- and Unit Q7.
3. For second sashing row, join Unit Q8-Q6-Q3-Q2-Q3-Q6-Q8. Make two of these rows and set second aside.
4. Join the first sashing row to carrot-bunny block row top, matching seams. Join the second sashing row to bottom.
5. For center bunny block row, join Unit Q7-Block B-Q2-Q1-Q2-Block A-and Q7. Add second sashing row made in Step 3 to bottom of this bunny row matching seams. Join to top block/sashing section.
6. Make bottom bunny-carrot row by joining Unit Q7-Block C-combined Q4-Q5 units-Block B-combined Q4-Q5 units-Block C-and Unit Q7. Add remaining sashing row made in Step 1 to bottom of this row; then join combined rows to top part of quilt to complete quilt center.
7. For bottom (gate) fence row, refer to quilt diagram and make left fence section first by joining five fence posts with 5 of Strip Set 1 as shown. Repeat for right section, referring to illustration for correct positioning of mirror image Strip Set 1 segments. Join Block F gate between the fence sections and join to quilt bottom.
8. For quilt top, and side fence borders, join thirteen fence posts with twelve of Strip Set 1 segments, beginning and ending with fence posts. Join one of the rows to top of quilt.
9. Join a heart Block D at opposite short ends of side fence borders, checking illustration for correct positioning of hearts. Join to sides of quilt matching seams.
10. Join two 1 1/2" x 28 1/2" strips of Fabric VI together to = 56 1/2" length. Make two and join to top and bottom of quilt for Border 9.
11. Join the 1 1/2" x 58 1/2" strips of Fabric VI to sides of quilt, trimming off at edges for Border 10.

QUILTING & FINISHING

1. Stitch in the ditch around all patchwork. We quilted four hearts in the center block.
2. Make 245" of straight-grain, french fold binding from 2 1/2" wide strips of Fabric VI, and bind your quilt.

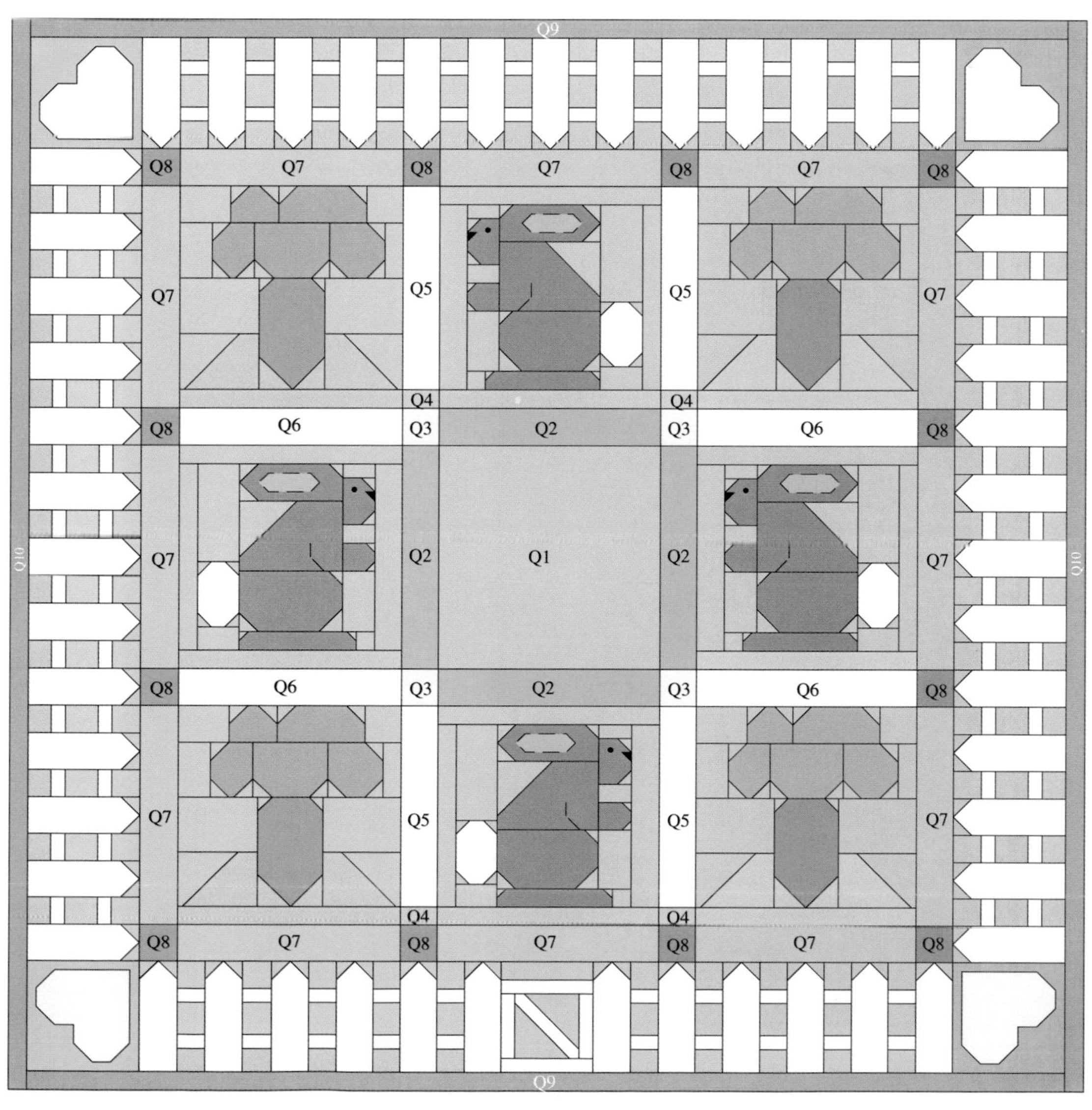

The Special New Child In My Life:

Pick Of The Litter

- Making Diagonal Corners
- Making Diagonal Ends

Finished size: 64" x 99 1/2"
Cat Block A & Blank: 15" x 17 1/2"

Video Demonstration Take 1

On A Personal Note:

This is a beginner quilt utilizing two basic quick piecing techniques. There is one block, and this block gives you a chance to use up those wonderful scraps in your stash! Our yardage requirements give yardage for background and borders. We used our scrappy treasures for the kitties and baskets.

MATERIALS

Background fabric -3 1/8 yards (need exactly 109") We used a grayish blue batik
Shelves and Borders - 1 5/8 yards of woodgrain looking fabric. (need exactly 55")
Backing 5 3/4 yards

CUTTING

Cutting instructions shown in red indicate that the quantity of units are combined and cut in 2 or more different places to conserve fabric.

From background fabric, cut:
- Four 15 1/2" wide strips. From these, cut:
  - * Five - 15 1/2" x 18" (blank block)
  - * Fifteen - 3 1/2" x 15 1/2" (A12)
  - * Fifteen - 2 1/2" squares (A18)
  - * Thirty - 2" x 3" (A6)
  - * Forty-six - 1 1/2" squares (A11b, A14, A17a)
- Three 7 1/2" wide strips. From these, cut:
  - * Thirty - 2" x 7 1/2" (A10)
  - * Thirty - 1 1/2" x 7 1/2" (A9)
  - * Fifteen - 2 1/2" x 4" (A11)
- One 5 1/2" wide strip. From this, cut:
  - * Fourteen - 3" x 5 1/2" (A5)
- Two 4" wide strips. From these, cut:
  - * Fifteen - 4" squares (A20)
  - * Fifteen 2 1/2" x 4" (add to A11)
  - * Twenty-four - 2" squares (A4a)
- One 3" wide strip. From this, cut:
  - * One - 3" x 5 1/2" (add to A5)
  - * Twenty-nine - 1 1/2" squares (add to A11b, A14, A17)
  - * Five - 2" squares (add to A4a)
- Four 2" wide strips. From these, cut:
  - * Fifteen - 2" x 5" (A19)
  - * Thirty - 2" x 3" (A6)

For basket handle, cut: (need equivalent of a 2 1/2" strip).
- One 2 1/2" wide strip. From this, cut:
  - * Two - 2 1/2" squares (A11a)
  - * One - 1 1/2" x 8 1/2" (A7)
  - * Two - 1 1/2" x 7 1/2" (A8)
  - * One - 1 1/2" x 4 1/2" (A13b)
  - * Two - 1 1/2" x 4" (A13, A13d)

For basket, cut: (need equivalent of a 3 1/2" strip)
- One 3 1/2" wide strip. From this, cut:
  - * One - 3 1/2" x 12 1/2" (A15)
  - * One -2" x 8 1/2" (A16b)

For head and tail, cut: (need equivalent of a 3" strip)
- One 3" wide strip. From this, cut:
  - * One - 3" x 8 1/2" (A4)
  - * Two - 2 1/2" squares (A2)
  - * One - 2" x 5" (A17)
  - * One - 2" x 4 1/2" (A16)
  - * Three - 2" squares (A5a ears, A15a)
  - * Four - 1 1/2" squares (A1a, A3a)

For face, cut: (need exactly 3 1/2" x 5")
- Two - 2 1/2" x 3 1/2" (A1)

For tail tip, cut:
- One - 2" x 3 1/2" (A16a)

For nose, cut: (need exactly 1 1/2" x 3")
- Two - 1 1/2" squares (A1c)

For paw tops, cut: (need exactly 3" x 4")
- Two - 1 1/2" x 2 1/2" (A3)
- Two - 1 1/2" squares (A1b)

For paw bottoms, cut: (need exactly 3" x 3 1/2")
- Two - 1 1/2" x 3 1/2" (A13a, A13c)

For shelves and borders, cut:
- Twenty-two - 2 1/2" wide strips. Eight for straight-grain binding. Piece remaining strips together end to end and cut:
  - * Six - 2 1/2" x 60 1/2" (shelves)
  - * Two - 2 1/2" x 100" (side borders)

ASSEMBLY

CAT BLOCK A

1. Use diagonal corner technique to make two each of mirror image units 1, 3, and 11. Use diagonal corner technique to make one each of units 4, 5, 15, and 17.
2. Make one of Unit 13, following graphics for correct placement of continuous diagonal ends as shown below. Use the same technique for Unit 16.

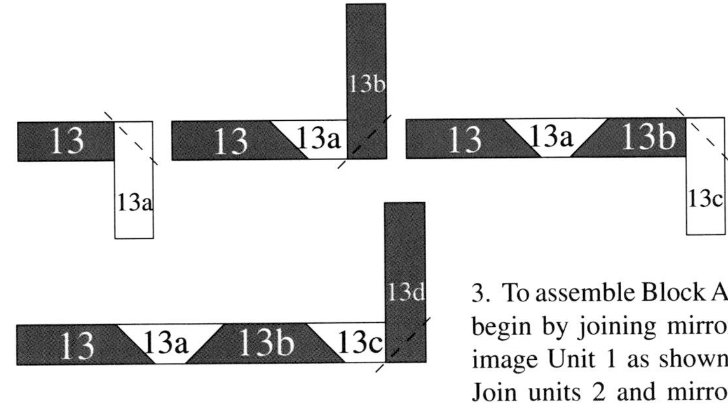

3. To assemble Block A, begin by joining mirror image Unit 1 as shown. Join units 2 and mirror image 3; then add to opposite sides of combined Unit 1.
4. Join units 6-5-6 in a horizontal row; then add Unit 4 to bottom, and Unit 7 to top. Join these combined units to kitty face section.
5. Refer to illustration for mirror image placement, and join units 10-8-and 9 together. Reverse for mirror image. Join mirror image Unit 11 to top of combined 10-8-9 units, matching diagonal seam. Join these combined sections to opposite sides of face section; then add Unit 12 to top.
6. For basket, join Unit 14 to opposite sides of completed Unit 13. Join units 15 and 16; then add Unit 17 to left side of combined units, and Unit 19 to right side.
7. Join diagonal corner 18 to left side of block, and diagonal corner 20 to right side to complete block. Make 15 from scrap fabrics.

QUILT ASSEMBLY & FINISHING

1. Refer to the quilt illustration at right and join the kitty blocks together in rows, with one blank block in each row. We used one completed block to trace the kitty in the basket design onto the blank block for quilting.
2 Cut six 60 1/2" long strips from pieced shelf fabric and stitch under each row of kitties. Join the rows . Add a shelf row to top and bottom of quilt. Join the 100" side border strips to quilt sides.
3. We have included in our book/CD-ROM package, two sheets of June Tailor Colorfast Printer Fabric™ Sheets. You will find graphics for the little printed signs in the card and stationery section of the CD-ROM. Print the signs out on the fabric included, and follow the instructions given in that section for the fabric. After printing and setting the color on the signs, press fusible pellon on the back of each printer fabric sheet. Tear the paper backing away from the fusible pellon and press the signs down as shown on the quilt illustration. Place a piece of tear-away pellon behind each sign, and satin stitch the signs in place. Tear the pellon stabilizer away in back.
4. Quilt in the ditch around all patchwork, and quilt the kitties in their baskets in the blanks.
5. Make 335" of straight-grain french fold binding, and bind your quilt.

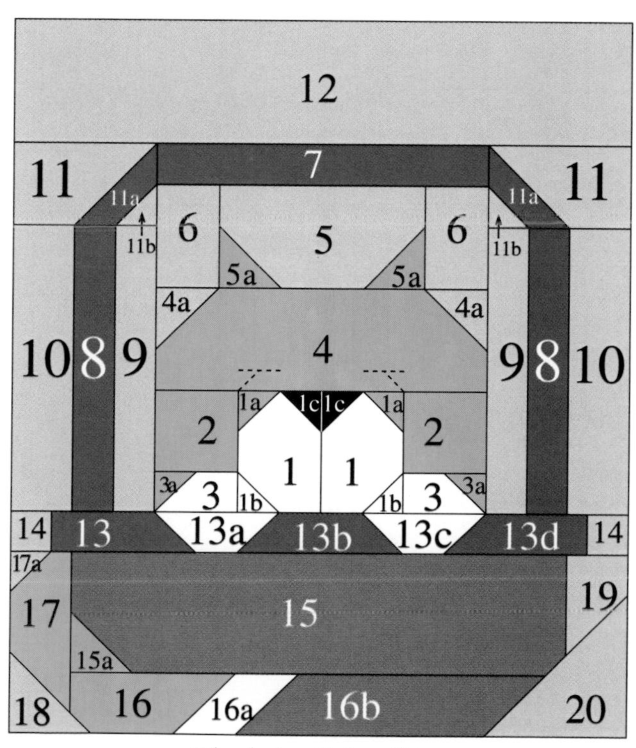

Block A. Make 15

P.S. Luciano, (he sings opera) and Raisin Bono may be seen in the "Blooper"/Credit section of our CD-ROM. Mindy's cat, Charlie talks. He says: "miiiiilk!"

Joyous Projects Inspired By My Pet

Herald Angels Tree Skirt

Finished size: 55 1/2" square
Star center: 27 3/4" square
Star Corner Block A: 9 3/8" sq.
Star Point Block B: 9" x 9 3/8"
Angel Block C: 10 1/2" x 15 3/4"
Corner Block D: 10 1/2" square

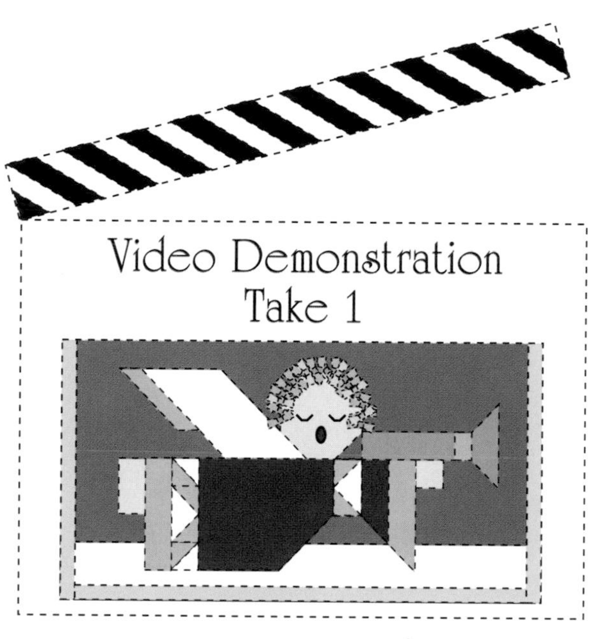

Making Diagonal Corners

Making Diagonal Ends

Making Half Square Triangles

Also On Our CD-ROM:
Herald Angels Wall Quilt
Choose your own colors with our Color Picker
Herald Angels Stockings and Ornaments
Hand towel border
Coordinating cards and stationery
Matching Quilt Label

MATERIALS

Fabric I 1 3/8 yards (need exactly 46 1/4")
(dark burgundy print)
*Add an 18" square if this fabric is used for 2" wide bias binding around center circle.

Fabric II 1 3/4 yards (need exactly 61 3/8")
(metallic gold print)

Fabric III 3/4 yard (need exactly 23 1/4")
(white on white print)

Fabric IV 1/8 yard (need exactly 4")
(majenta print)

Fabric V 1/2 yard (need exactly 15 3/4")
(medium green print)

Fabric VI 1/8 yard (need exactly 3 1/4")
(brassy gold print)

Fabric VII 1/4 yard (need exactly 5 1/2")
(solid flesh)

Backing	2 1/2 yards
4" wide flat lace	1 1/8 yards
1/4" wide rose satin ribbon	10 yards

CUTTING

Cutting instructions shown in red indicate that the quantity of units are combined and cut in 2 or more different places to conserve fabric.

NOTE: All "Q" units in cutting instructions stand for "quilt top". These are units that are not incorporated into blocks.

From Fabric I, cut: (dark burgundy print)

- One 9 1/2" wide strip. From this, cut:
  - * One – 9 1/2" square (Q1)
  - * Two – 8 3/8" squares (D1 triangle-squares)
  - * Four– 4 1/4" x 5 3/4" (C8)
  - * Four – 2" squares (D3)
  - * Six – 1 5/8" squares (A5, C9a)
- One 5 3/4" wide strip. From this, cut:
  - * Four – 4 1/4" x 5 3/4" (add to C8)
  - * Eight – 1 5/8" x 5 3/8" (C12)
  - * Three – 3 1/2" x 5" (C6)
- One 3 1/2" wide strip. From this, cut:
  - * Five – 3 1/2" x 5" (add to C6)
  - * Six – 2 3/4" x 3 1/2" (C11)
- Three 2 3/4" wide strips. From these, cut:
  - * Eight – 2 3/4" x 3 7/8" (C7a)
  - * Two – 2 3/4" x 3 1/2" (add to C11)
  - * Sixteen – 2 3/4" squares (C10a, C16a)
  - * Eight – 2 3/8" x 2 3/4" (C21)
  - * Eight – 1 5/8" x 2 3/4" (C15)
  - * Eight – 1 1/4" x 2 3/4" (C20)
- Two 2 3/8" wide strips. From this, cut:
  - * Twenty – 2 3/8" squares (D2 triangle-squares)
  - * Three – 2" x 11" (C13, D5)
- Four 2" wide strips. From these, cut:
  - * Nine – 2" x 11" (add to C13, D5)
  - * Four – 2" x 9 1/2" (D4)
  - * Seventeen – 1 5/8" squares (add to A5, C9a)
- Four 1 5/8" wide strips. From these, cut:
  - * Eight – 1 5/8" x 11" (C22)
  - * Eight – 1 5/8" x 3 1/8" (A2)
  - * Eight – 1 5/8" x 2 3/8" (C5)
  - * Five – 1 5/8" squares (add to A5, C9a)

From Fabric II, cut: (metallic gold print)

- One 8 3/4" wide strip. From this, cut:
  - * Four – 8 3/4" squares (A1)
  - * Sixteen – 1 5/8" squares (A2a)
- One 8 3/8" wide strip. From this, cut:
  - * Two – 8 3/8" squares (D1 triangle-squares)
- Cut remainder into four 2" wide strips. From these, cut:
  - * Twenty– 2" squares (A3, A4, triangle-squares)
  - * Nineteen– 2" x 3" for paper piecing units (B2, B4, B6, B8, B10, and B12)
- Two 5 1/2" wide strips. From these, cut:
  - * Eight – 5 1/2" x 6 1/2" (paper piecing unit B14)
  - * Sixteen – 1 5/8" x 5" (C7, C18)
  - * Eight – 1 1/4" x 1 5/8" (C2)
- One 2 3/4" wide strip. From this, cut:
  - * Eight – 2 3/4" x 4 5/8" (C11a)
- Six 2 1/2" wide strips for straight-grain binding.
- Eight 2" wide strips. From these, cut:
  - * Four – 2" x 28 1/4" (Q5) piece two together to = 56" border strips.
  - * Four – 2" x 26 3/4" (Q4) piece two together to = 53" border strips
  - * Twenty-nine - 2" x 3" for paper piecing units (B2, B4, B6, B8, B10, and B12)

From Fabric III, cut: (white on white print)

- One 3 7/8" wide strip. From this, cut:
  - * Eight – 3 7/8" squares (C12a)
  - * Four – 2 3/4" x 3 7/8" (C10)
- One 2 3/4" wide strip. From this, cut:
  - * Four – 2 3/4" x 3 7/8" (add to C10)
  - * Eight – 1 5/8" x 2 3/4" (C14)
- Four 2 3/8" x 42 1/8" wide strips. From these, cut:
  - * Four – 2 3/8" x 28 1/4" (Q2)
  - * Twenty – 2 3/8" squares (D2 triangle-squares)
- Four 2" wide strip. From this, cut:
  - * Twenty – 2" squares (A3, A4, triangle-squares)
  - * Forty-eight– 2" x 3" for paper piecing units (B1, B3, B5, B7, B9, and B11)
- Two 1 5/8" wide strips. From these, cut:
  - * Forty – 1 5/8" squares (C9b, C17a)

From Fabric IV, cut: (magenta print)

- One 2 3/8" wide strip. From this, cut:
  - * Four – 2 3/8" squares (Q3)
  - * Sixteen – 1 5/8" squares (C14a)
  - * One – 1 5/8" x 2 3/4" (C17)
- One 1 5/8"wide strip. From this, cut:

* Fifteen – 1 5/8" x 2 3/4" (add to C17)

From Fabric V, cut: (medium green print)

• Three 5 1/2" wide strips. From these, cut:

* Eight – 5 1/2" x 7 1/2" (paper piecing unit B13)
* Eight – 5" x 5 3/4" (C16)
* Eight – 1 5/8" x 5" (C7)

From Fabric VI, cut: (brassy gold print)

• Two 1 5/8" wide strips. From these, cut:

* Eight – 1 5/8" x 3 7/8" (C1)
* Twenty-four – 1 5/8" squares (C3, C5a, C8a)

From Fabric VII, cut: (solid flesh)

• One 3 7/8" wide strip. From this, cut:

* Eight – 3 7/8" squares (C9)
* Six – 1 5/8" x 2 3/4" (C19)

• One 1 5/8" wide strip. From this, cut:

* Two – 1 5/8" x 2 3/4" (add to C19)
* Eight – 1 5/8" squares (C4)

ASSEMBLY

BLOCK A ASSEMBLY

1. Block A is the corner block for the star. Use 2" squares from Fabrics II and III to make a total of 40 half square triangles as shown in our video demonstration.
2. Use diagonal corner technique to make two of Unit 2.
3. To assemble block, working from left to right, join five of half square triangle units 4 and one of Unit 2 as shown. Join to the bottom of Unit 1.
4. Make a vertical unit row, beginning at the top and combining Unit 2, five of half square triangle Unit 3, and one of Unit 5 as shown. Join to left side of square to complete Block A. Make 4.

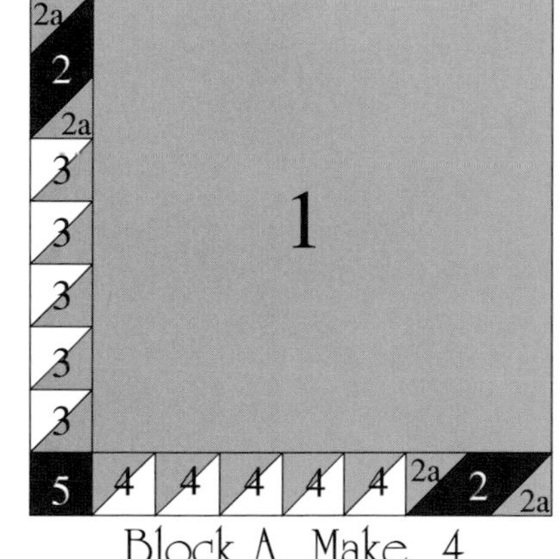

Block A Make 4

BLOCK B ASSEMBLY

1. Block B will look like the diagram below when complete. We have given you a foundation to make Block B on the following page. It can be accomplished easily by using the foundation paper piecing technique.
2. Prepare the block foundations as described on the block foundation illustration. You may also choose to use a tear-away stabilizer as your foundation.
3. The basic rules for paper piecing this block are to sew on all marked lines in numerical order.

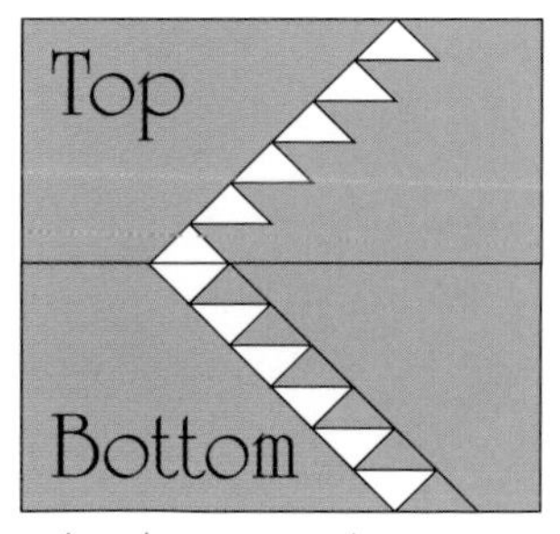

Block B. Make 4

4. All unit pieces are positioned for stitching on the unmarked side of the foundation. Each piece of fabric will overlap the drawn area for the unit. Sizes for each unit are given in cutting instructions and should be cut as directed.
5. When sewing by machine on the marked lines, begin a stitch or two before the line and continue a stitch or two beyond the end of the line. Backstitching is not necessary. Set your stitch length for 15-20 stitches per inch. The smaller stitches make it easier to remove the paper.
6. Begin with units 1 and 2. Place them right sides together; then position them so that they cover the Unit 1 area and extend beyond 1/4". Sew on the line between Unit 1 and Unit 2. Open the two units up and finger press them open so that they cover the Unit 1 and Unit 2 areas. Trim seam to 1/4".
7. Position Unit 3 right sides facing on Unit 2 and stitch on line between Unit 2 and Unit 3. Finger press Unit 3 out. Continue with this method until all units have been sewn in numerical order.
8. For large units 13 and 14, we have given you a rectangle. If you wish to trim the diagonal before stitching you may do so, being careful to trim at the correct angle. Make 4 top sections for Block B, and 4 bottom sections.
9. Tear the paper away from the back side and press gently. Join the top and bottom sections together as shown in Block B illustration and join together.

ANGEL BLOCK C ASSEMBLY

1. Begin by using diagonal corner technique to make one each of units 5, 8, 9, 10, 12a, 14, 16, and 17.

Block C Make 8

3. Use diagonal end technique to make one each of units 7 and 11.
4. To assemble block, begin by joining units 1, 2, and 3 in a horizontal row. Add Unit 8 to top of these combined units. Join units 4 and 5; then add Unit 6 to bottom of 4-5 joined units.
5. To make Unit 7, join 1 5/8" x 5" pieces of Fabrics II and V. This is now to be treated as one unit. Join diagonal end (Unit 7a) as shown to complete Unit 7. Add Unit 7 to side of combined units 4-6 as shown; then join to combined units 1-2-3-8 to complete trumpet section of angel.
6. Join units 9 and 10, taking care to match diagonal seams. Refer to illustration for making com-

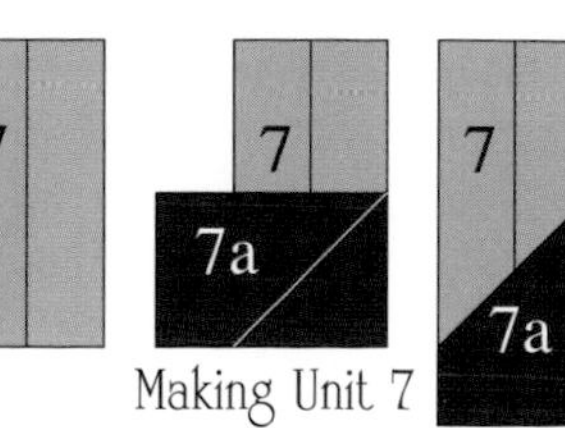

Making Unit 7

bined units 11-12. Begin by using diagonal end technique to complete Unit 11; then add Unit 12 to bottom as shown. Use diagonal corner technique to add Unit 12a, completing wing. Join these combined units to units 9-10; then add Unit 13 to top as shown.

7. Join units 14 and 15. For Unit 16, cut

11a
11a
11
12
12a
11
12
12a
11a
11
12

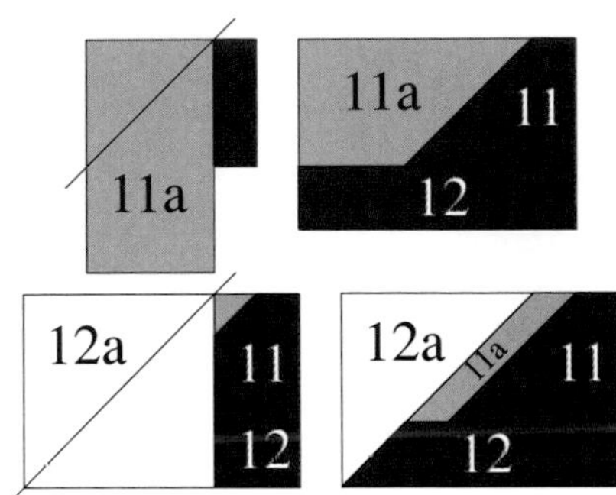

Making combined units 11-12 for Block C.

a piece of 4" wide flat lace 5" long. Pin the lace as shown for Unit 16. Add diagonal corner 16a; then join combined units 14-15 as illustrated, sewing lace into seam. Lace is to be treated as part of Unit 16 and will be sewn into all seams. End result is an angel with a little choir robe on.

sew lace into seams
4" wide flat lace.
add diagonal corner
16
16a

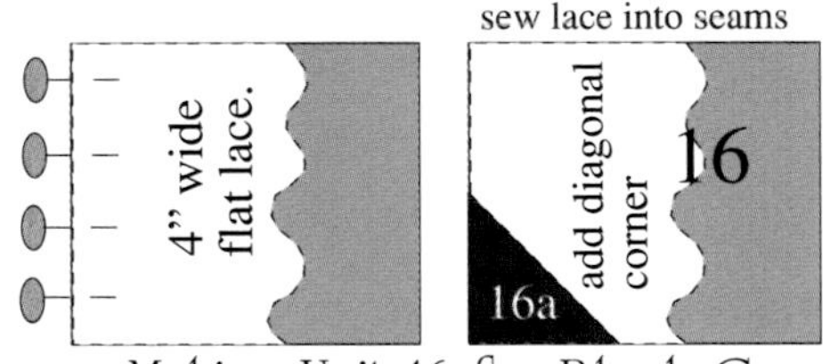

Making Unit 16 for Block C

8. Join mirror image units 17 together as shown; then add Unit 18 to these combined units. Join to combined units 14-16.

9. Join units 19 and 20; then add Unit 21 to bottom. Join to combined angel body units; then join Unit 22 to bottom.

10. To complete angel, join wing section to body section; then add trumpet section as illustrated. Take care to match all seams. Make 8 angels.

11. Use pattern given to trace face onto angels. We used a red fabric pen for mouth, outlined with black, and a black fabric pen to draw eyes.

MAKING BLOCK D

1. Block D is for the tree skirt corners. Refer to illustration for Block D, and use 2 3/8" squares of fabrics I and III to make half square triangle squares. Make a total of 40.

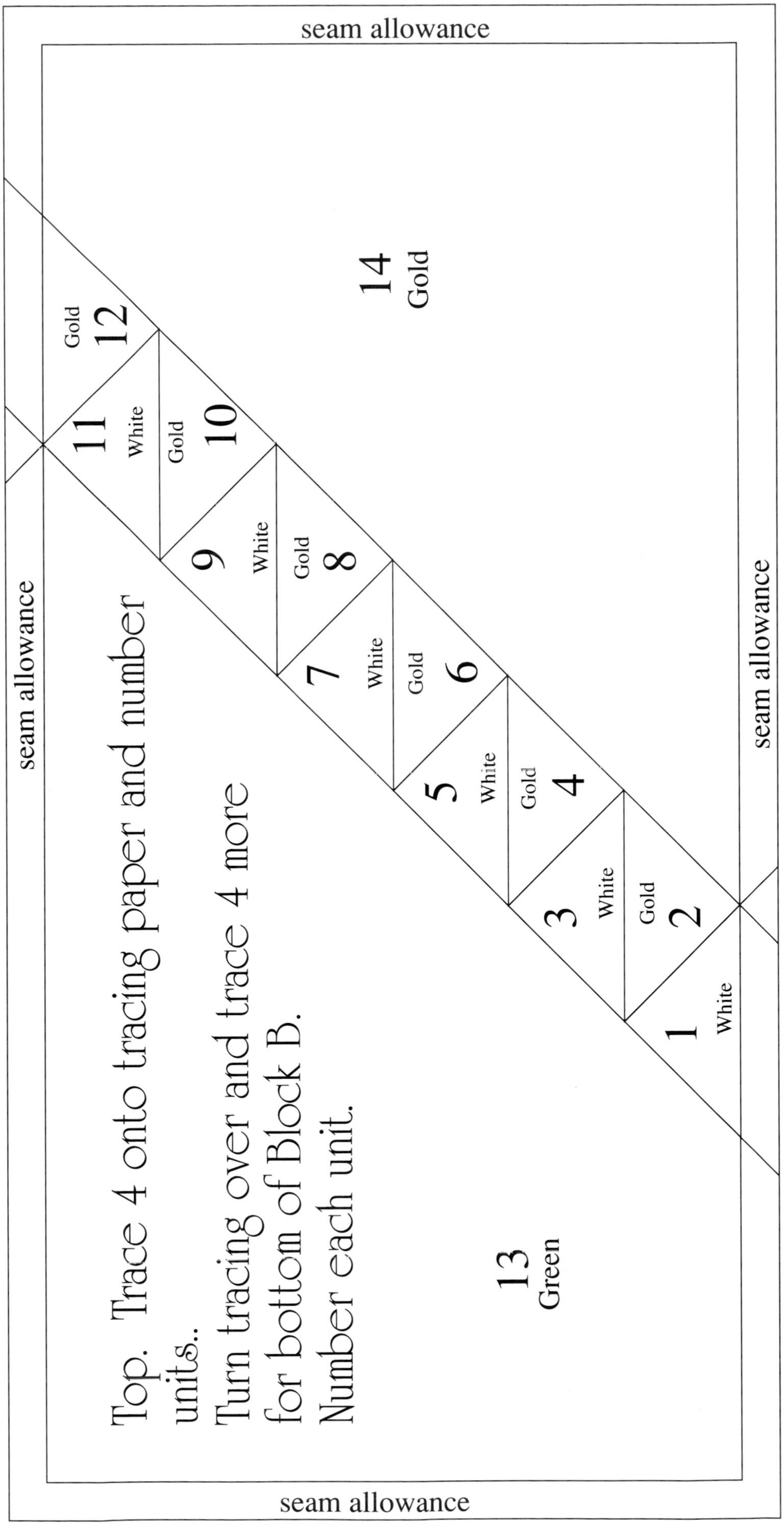

seam allowance
seam allowance
seam allowance
seam allowance
Top. Trace 4 onto tracing paper and number units..
Turn tracing over and trace 4 more for bottom of Block B.
Number each unit.
14
Gold
13
Green
1 White
2 Gold
3 White
4 Gold
5 White
6 Gold
7 White
8 Gold
9 White
10 Gold
11 White
12 Gold

2. Use 8 3/8" squares of fabrics I and II and make a total of four half square triangles for Unit 1.
3. Join five Unit 2 half square triangles in a horizontal row as shown; then join to bottom of Unit 1.
4. Join another row of five Unit 2 half square triangles in a vertical row as shown. Add Unit 3 to bottom of row; then add to right side of Unit 1.
5. Join Unit 4 to left side of Block D; then add Unit 5 to top to complete block.

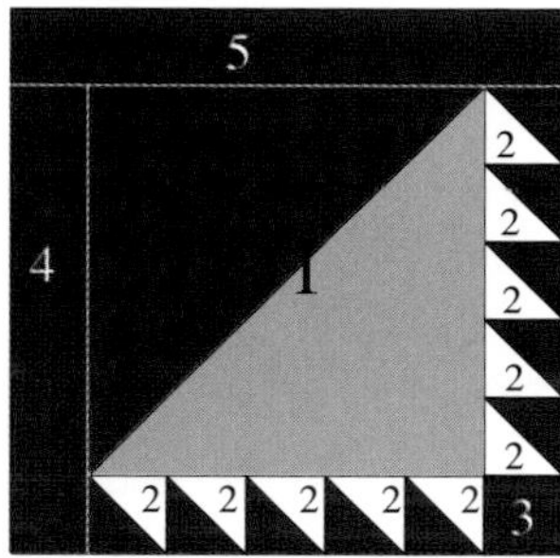

Block D. Make 4.

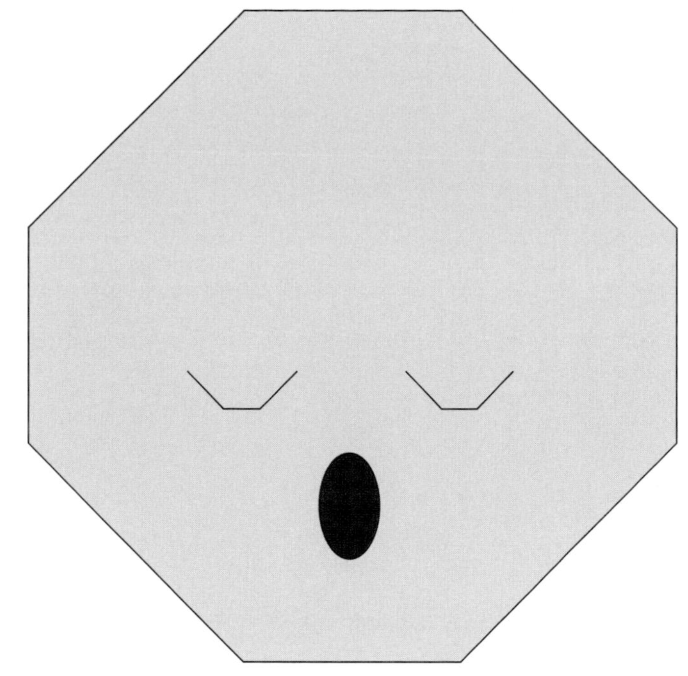

STAR ASSEMBLY
1. To assemble star top, refer to illustration of tree skirt and join Block A-Block B-and Block A in a row as shown. Make two rows, one for star top and one for star bottom.
2. For center row, join Block B-Unit Q1-and Block B in a row. Join rows together to complete star.
3. Join units Q2 to opposite sides of center star. Join Q3 corners to remaining Q2 strips and add to top and bottom of center star, matching seams.

TREE SKIRT ASSEMBLY
1. Begin by joining two Angel C blocks. Make four sets. Join one set to top of tree skirt and another set to bottom as shown.
2. Refer to illustration and join Block D to opposite ends of combined C blocks. Join to sides of tree skirt.
3. Join pieced borders Q4 to top and bottom of tree skirt; then add pieced borders Q5 to opposite sides to complete tree skirt.

QUILTING & FINISHING

1. Stipple star background and stitch in the ditch around all patchwork. We did echo quilting on tree skirt corners.
2. Join the six 2 1/2" wide strips of Fabric II, and make 230" of straight-grain french fold binding for outer edge of tree skirt.
3. Cut an 8" in diameter circle in center of Unit 1 through all thicknesses. Cut from circle straight down one side between angel blocks. Cut 2" wide bias binding from Fabric I and bind around circle to outer edges. Bind outer edges with Fabric II strips.
4. Hair was made by winding doll hair yarn around two fingers so that yarn is in a long row. Stitch down the center of the row to hold it together; then arrange around angel's heads and top stitch down center.
5. Make small bows from satin ribbon (5 for each head), and hot glue in place.

Most Memorable Holiday Projects:

1st Day Of School Quilt

Using Quilt Top Express™

Making Diagonal Corners

Making One Half Square Triangle

Video Demonstration
Take 1

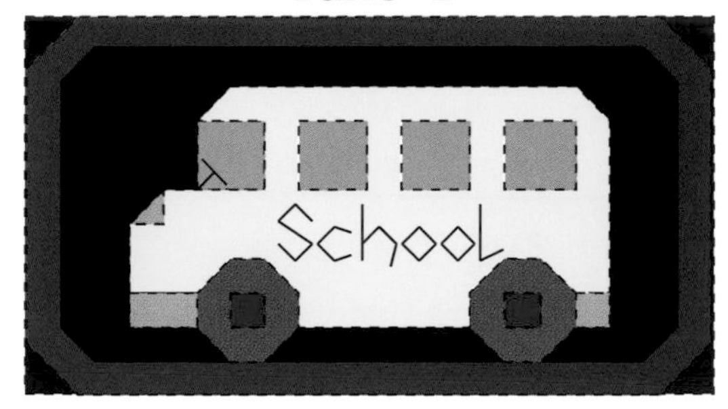

MATERIALS

Fabric I (solid black)	1 1/8 yards (need exactly 38 1/2") 1 yard (need exactly 32 1/2")
Fabric II (bright red print)	1/4 yard (need exactly 8") 1/4 yard (need exactly 6 1/2")
Fabric III (light red print)	Scrap (need exactly 2 1/2" x 11")
Fabric IV (dark green print)	1/4 yard (need exactly 5 1/2") 1/8 yard (need exactly 4")
Fabric V (light green print)	Scrap (need exactly 2 1/2" x 11")
Fabric VI (dark blue print)	1/4 yard (need exactly 5 1/2") 1/8 yard (need exactly 4")
Fabric VII (solid light blue)	Scrap (need exactly 2 1/2" x 21")
Fabric VIII (bright yellow print)	1/4 yard (need exactly 7") 1/8 yard (need exactly 4")
Fabric IX (solid light yellow)	Scrap (need exactly 2 1/2" x 11")
Fabric X (dark gray print)	Scrap (need exactly 1 1/2" x 20")
Fabric XI (metallic silver print)	Scrap (need exactly 1 1/2" x 5 1/2")
Fabric XII (solid light gray)	3/8 yard (need exactly 13")
Fabric XII (dark brown check)	1/4 yard (need exactly 4 1/2")
Backing	1 1/8 yards
QUILT TOP EXPRESS™	1 package

NOTE: Please refer to QUILT TOP EXPRESS™ instructions which are given with "My First Quilt" project.

ON A PERSONAL NOTE: This is a great beginner project, and affords Mom or the leader of a scout troop or 4-H the opportunity to teach a young person to sew. Taking that special child to the fabric store to help pick out brightly colored fabric for the project can be fun as well. You may follow the instructions in BLACK using Strip Sets, or the instructions in RED for using QUILT TOP EXPRESS™. We suggest the latter method. It is quick and teaches accuracy. Please watch the video demonstration and read the instructions thoroughly.

Finished size: Quilt: 34" x 38"
School bus Block A: 8" x 14"
CRAYOLA Block: 2" x 4 1/2"
Apple Block C: 5" x 6"

CUTTING

NOTE: All "Q" units in cutting instructions stand for "quilt top". These are units that are not incorporated into blocks. Cutting instructions shown in blue indicate that the quantity of units are combined and cut in 2 or more different places to conserve fabric.

From Fabric I, cut: (solid black)

- One 6 1/2" wide strip. From this, cut:
  - * One - 6 1/2" x 14 1/2" (Q1)
  - * One - 2 1/2" x 5 1/2" (Q2)
  - * One - 1 1/2" x 5 1/2" (A15)
  - * Two - 2 1/2" x 22 1/2" (Q5)
  - * Fifteen - 1 1/2" squares (A3a, A5, A13b, A18, C1b,C2a)
- Five 2 1/2" wide strips. Four for straight-grain binding. From remaining strip, cut:
  - * One - 2 1/2" x 14 1/2" (Q3)
  - * One - 2 1/2" x 3 1/2" (A4)
  - * Four - 2 1/2" squares (C1a, C3a)
  - * Nine - 1 1/2" x 2 1/2" (A10, CRAYOLA 3)
- Thirteen 1 1/2" wide strips. Eight for Strip Sets 1, 2, 3, and 4. From remaining five strips, cut:
  - * Two - 1 1/2" x 38 1/2" (Q16)
  - * Two - 1 1/2" x 32 1/2" (Q15)
  - * One - 1 1/2" x 14 1/2" (Q4)
  - * Eight - 1 1/2" x 2 1/2" (add to A10, CRAYOLA 3)
  - * One - 1 1/2" square (add to A3a, A5, A13b, A18, C1b, C2a)
- For QUILT TOP EXPRESS™ method, cut nine 1 1/2" wide strips. From these, cut:
  - * 121 - 1 1/2" squares (borders and Unit C2a)
  - * Two - 1 1/2" x 38 1/2" (Q16)
  - * Two - 1 1/2" x 32 1/2" (Q15)
  - * One - 1 1/2" x 14 1/2" (Q4)
  - * Eight - 1 1/2" x 2 1/2" (A10, CRAYOLA 3)

From Fabric II, cut: (bright red print)

- One 3 1/2" wide strip. From this, cut:
  - * Two - 3 1/2" x 5 1/2" (C1)
  - * Two - 3 1/2" squares (C3)
  - * Two - 2 1/2" x 4 1/2" (Q11)
  - * Six - 2 1/2" squares (CRAYOLA 1, Q14)
- Three 1 1/2" wide strips. Two for Strip Set 4. From remaining strip, cut:
  - * Two - 1 1/2" x 2 1/2" (CRAYOLA 5)
  - * Six - 1 1/2" squares (A11, C2b)
- For QUILT TOP EXPRESS™ method, cut two 1 1/2" wide strips. From these, cut:
  - * Thirty- 1 1/2" squares (for checkerboard borders)
  - * Two - 1 1/2" x 2 1/2" (add to CRAYOLA 5)

From Fabric III, cut: (light red print)

- One 2 1/2" wide strip. From this, cut:
  - * Two - 2 1/2" squares (CRAYOLA 4)
  - * Four - 1 1/2" x 2 1/2" (CRAYOLA 2)

From Fabric IV, cut: (dark green print)

- One 2 1/2" wide strip. From this, cut:
  - * Two - 2 1/2" x 3 1/2" (C2)
  - * Two - 2 1/2" squares (CRAYOLA 1)
  - * Two - 1 1/2" x 2 1/2" (CRAYOLA 5)
- Two 1 1/2" wide strips for Strip Set 3.
- For QUILT TOP EXPRESS™ method, cut one 1 1/2" wide strip. From this and scrap, cut:
  - * Thirty - 1 1/2" squares for borders.

From Fabric V, cut: (light green print)

- One 2 1/2" wide strip. From this, cut:
  - * Two - 2 1/2" squares (CRAYOLA 4)
  - * Four - 1 1/2" x 2 1/2" (CRAYOLA 2)

From Fabric VI, cut: (dark blue print)

- One 2 1/2" wide strip. From this, cut:
  - * Two - 2 1/2" squares (CRAYOLA 1)
  - * Two - 1 1/2" x 2 1/2" (CRAYOLA 5)
- Two 1 1/2" wide strips for Strip Set 2.
- For QUILT TOP EXPRESS™ method, cut one 1 1/2" wide strip. From this, cut:
  - * Twenty-four - 1 1/2" squares for borders

From Fabric VII, cut: (solid light blue)

- One 2 1/2" wide strip. From this, cut:
  - * Six - 2 1/2" squares (A1, CRAYOLA 4)
  - * Four - 1 1/2" x 2 1/2" (CRAYOLA 2)

From Fabric VIII, cut: (bright yellow print)

- One 2 1/2" wide strip. From this, cut:
  - * One - 2 1/2" x 13 1/2" (A7)
  - * One - 2 1/2" x 5 1/2" (A14)
  - * Two - 2 1/2" squares (CRAYOLA 1)
  - * Seven - 1 1/2" x 2 1/2" (A2, A8, CRAYOLA 5)
- Three 1 1/2" wide strips. Two for Strip Set 1. From remaining strip, cut:
  - * One - 1 1/2" x 12 1/2" (A3)
  - * Six - 1 1/2" squares (A6, A13a, A16)
- For QUILT TOP EXPRESS™ method, cut two 1 1/2" wide strips. From these, cut:
  - * Forty-two - 1 1/2" squares (36 for borders, and six for units A6, A13a, A16)
  - * One - 1 1/2" x 12 1/2" (A3)

From Fabric IX, cut: (solid light yellow)

- One 2 1/2" wide strip. From this, cut:
  - * Two - 2 1/2" squares (CRAYOLA 4)
  - * Four - 1 1/2" x 2 1/2" (CRAYOLA 2)

From Fabric X, cut: (dark gray print)

- One - 1 1/2" wide strip. From this, cut:
  - * Four - 1 1/2" x 3 1/2" (A13)
  - * Four - 1 1/2" squares (A12)

From Fabric XI, cut: (metallic silver)

- One - 1 1/2" x 2 1/2" (A9)
- Two - 1 1/2" squares (A5a, A17)

From Fabric XII, cut: (solid light gray)

- One 4 1/2" wide strip. From this, cut:

* Four - 4 1/2" squares (Q13)
* Three - 1 1/2" x 20 1/2" (Q9)
* Three - 1 1/2" x 2 1/2" (Q10)

• One 2 1/2" wide strip. From this, cut:

* Two - 2 1/2" squares (Q8)
* One - 1 1/2" x 2 1/2" (add to Q10)
* One - 1 1/2" x 24 1/2" (Q12)

• Four 1 1/2" wide strips. From these, cut:

* Three - 1 1/2" x 24 1/2" (add to Q12)
* One - 1 1/2" x 20 1/2" (add to Q9)
* Twenty-eight - 1 1/2" squares (Q7a, Q11a, CRAYOLA 1a)

From Fabric XIII, cut: (dark brown check)

• Three 1 1/2" wide strips. From these, cut:

* Two - 1 1/2" x 24 1/2" (Q7)
* Two - 1 1/2" x 18 1/2" (Q6)
* Four - 1 1/2" squares (Q5a)

4. Join units 8, 9, and 10 in a vertical row as shown. To make wheels, join units 12-11-12 in a vertical row. Make two. Join mirror image Unit 13 to opposite sides of vertical row to complete wheels.

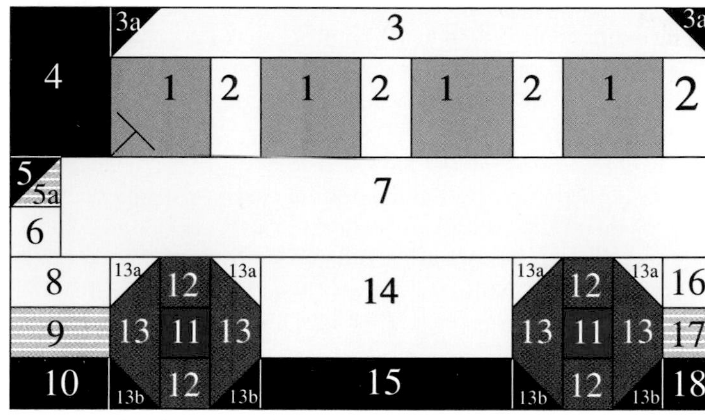

Block A. Make 1. Finishes to: 8" x 14"

5. Join units 14 and 15 as shown. Join units 16, 17, and 18 in a vertical row. To assemble bus bottom, join combined units 8-9-10 to left side of one wheel; then add combined units 14-15 to right side. Add another wheel as shown, and complete bus bottom by joining combined units 16-17-18 to right side of back wheel.

6. Join combined units 5-6-7 to top of wheel section; then add bus top.

7. Using a large, black felt tip fabric pen, and write the word "School" on bus side. You may also satin stitch the word in black thread if desired. Draw a "wheel" in front window of bus, or satin stitch.

CRAYOLA BLOCK

1. This is a simple block for a beginner to make. Use diagonal corner technique to make one of Unit 1. Join units 1-2-3-4-3-2-and 5 in a horizontal row.

2. Follow cutting instructions carefully and make the required number of Crayola's in 4 different colors.

Block CRAYOLA. Make 8.
Make 2 yellow, 2 blue, 2 green, and 2 red.

ASSEMBLY

STRIP SETS

1. If you are using the strip set method for your quilt top, refer to the illustrations, and make each strip set as directed. Cut into the required number of segments. Set aside for later use.

SCHOOL BUS, BLOCK A

1. Use diagonal corner technique to make one of Unit 3. Use diagonal corner technique to make four each of Unit 13, referring often to illustration for correct position of mirror image units.

Strip Set 1

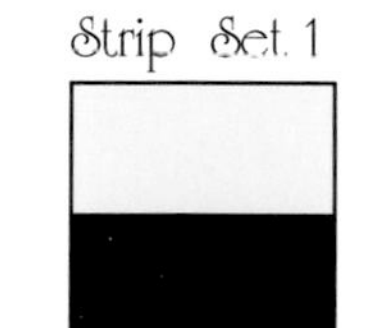

Make 2. Cut into 36 - 1 1/2" segments.

Strip Set 2

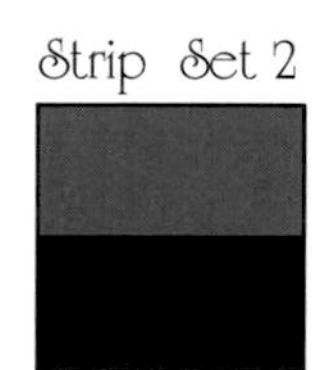

Make 2. Cut into 24 - 1 1/2" segments.

Strip Set 3

Make 2. Cut into 30 - 1 1/2" segments.

Strip Set 4

Make 2. Cut into 30 - 1 1/2" segments.

2. To assemble the bus, working from left to right, join units 1-2-1-2-1-2-1-2 in a horizontal row; then add Unit 3 across the top. Join Unit 4 to left side to complete the top of the bus.

3. Use 1 1/2" squares of Fabric I and XI to make Unit 5. Place the squares right sides together and stitch a diagonal through the center, Trim seam and press out. Join this unit with Unit 6; then add Unit 7 to the two combined units as shown.

APPLE BLOCK C

1. Use diagonal corner technique to make one each of units 1, 2, and 3.

2. To assemble, join units 2 and 3 as shown; then add Unit 1 to right side.

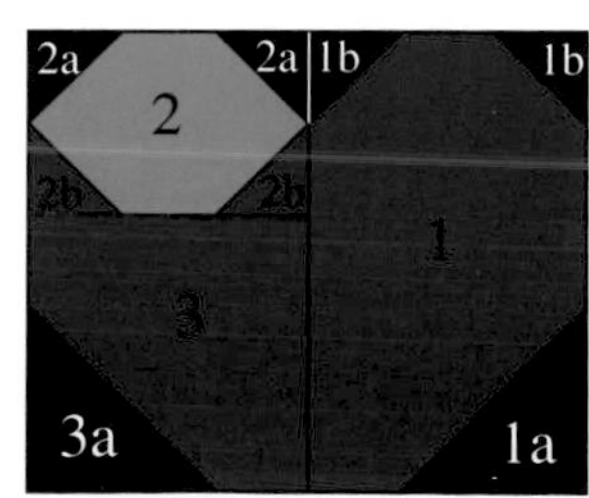

Block C. Make 2.

CHECKERBOARD BORDERS

1. At this time, refer to the quilt illustration, and using the strip set segments previously made, join the checkerboard strip set segments together in the color scheme shown on the quilt top borders. Begin with top and bottom borders; then work on side borders. Accuracy with seams is important on the borders and we suggest taking a full 1/4" seam, rather than a scant 1/4". Take care to match your seams when joining rows, and press segments in opposite directions. Set borders aside.
2. If you are using QUILT TOP EXPRESS™ to make the checkerboard borders, refer to the illustration, and instructions given for this method. Lay each square on grid lines for each border. Squares should be directly next to each other. Stitch as shown in QUILT TOP EXPRESS™ illustrations on CD-ROM and at the beginning of "My First Quilt" project. Clip seams and trim QUILT TOP EXPRESS™ away from border edges after border is pieced, and press on *fabric* side. Set borders aside.

QUILT ASSEMBLY

1. To assemble the quilt top, begin by joining Apple Block C-Unit Q2-and remaining Apple Block C in a horizontal row; then add Unit Q1 to top of row, and Unit Q4 to bottom. Join Unit Q3 to top of School Bus Block A; then join the bus section to Unit Q1 as shown.
2. Before the quilt becomes larger and is more difficult to handle, use a chalk marker if you are going to satin stitch the childs name and date of "1st Day In School", or use white fabric paint. Plan this printed part of the wall quilt carefully as this is the focal point of the quilt, and something to be treasured. We printed ours out on paper and used a light table so that we could see through the black fabric.
3. If you are satin stitching, use white thread, and be sure to put tear-away stabilizer behind your lettering. At this time, use brown thread to satin stitch stems on apples.
4. To complete center section of quilt, use diagonal corner technique to make two of Unit Q5. Join these units to sides of quilt center section, referring to illustration for correct placement.
5. Join Unit Q6 to top and bottom of center section. Use diagonal corner technique to make Unit Q7; then add to quilt top sides, taking care to place this blackboard frame correctly with diagonal corners to the outside.
6. For top crayola border, refer to illustration, and join a red crayola-Unit Q8-and green crayola. Join Unit Q9 to top and bottom of joined crayola row. Join to top of quilt.
7. For bottom crayola border, refer to illustration and repeat procedure for top row using a red and yellow crayola block. Join to bottom of quilt and press out.
8. Use diagonal corner technique to make two of Unit Q11. For left side crayola border, join a blue crayola-Unit Q11- and a green crayola in a vertical row as shown; then add Unit Q12 to opposite sides of crayola row. Repeat this procedure for right side, using a yellow and blue crayola.
9. Join square Unit Q13 to top and bottom of side crayola rows; then join the rows to quilt top sides, matching seams.
10. Join top and bottom checkerboard borders previously made to top and bottom of quilt top. Join square Unit Q14 to opposite short ends of side checkerboard borders; then add to quilt sides.
11. Join Q15 border to top and bottom of quilt; then add Q16 borders to sides to complete quilt top.

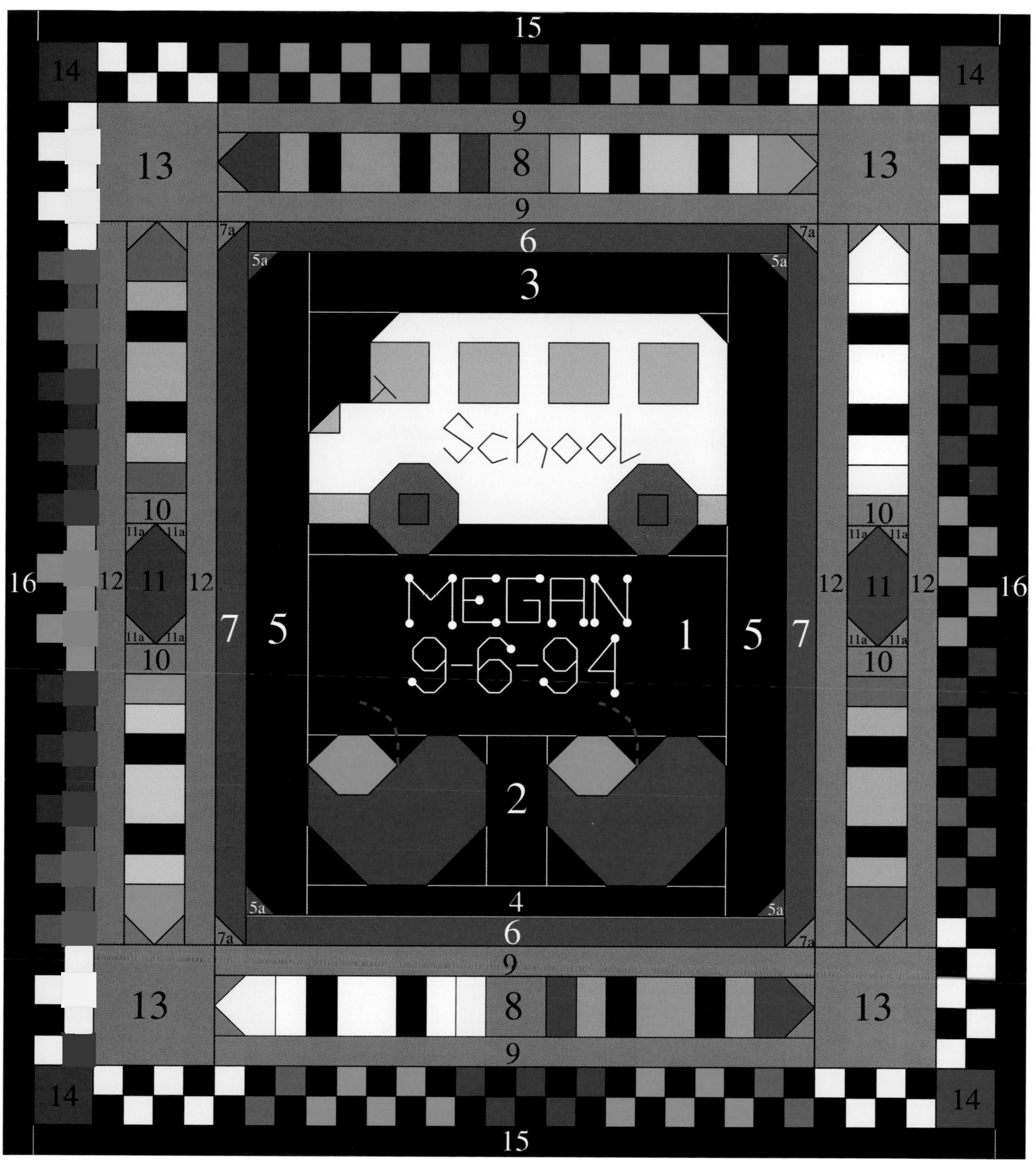

Quilt Assembly Diagram

QUILTING AND FINISHING

1. Quilt all patchwork in the ditch.
2. Use 2 1/2" wide strips of Fabric I and make 155" of straight-grain, french fold binding, and bind your quilt.

Learning projects with the kids:
School

Snug As A Bug

- Making Diagonal Ends
- Making Diagonal Corners

Video Demonstration Take 1

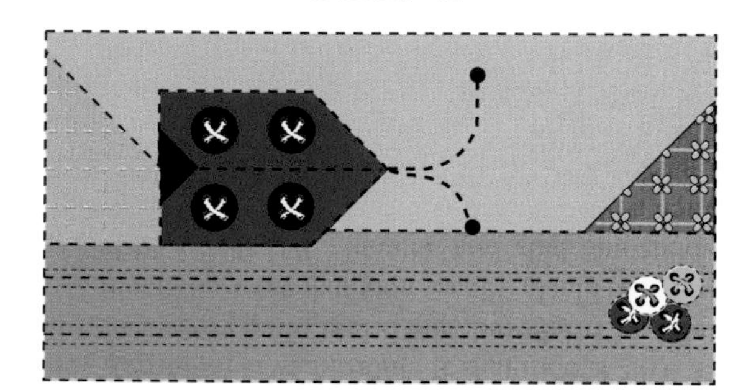

Finished size sign and placemats: 16" x 18 1/2"

MATERIALS

Fabric I (blue sky background print)	3/8 yard (need exactly 11")
Fabric II (olive stripe print)	1/8 yard (need exactly 3 1/2")
Fabric III (green prints)	Scraps of eight different
Fabric IV, (red prints).	Scraps of two different
Fabric V (bright yellow check)	3/8 yard (need exactly 11 1/2")
Fabric VI (orange check)	Scrap
Fabric VII (solid black)	Scrap

Backing and batting for "in" and "out" signs 3/4 yard

Large scrap or skein of black embroidery floss, eight 5/8" black buttons, four 1/2" bright yellow buttons, four 1/2" bright red buttons, four 1/2" olive green buttons, four 3/8" black buttons, eight 5/8" black buttons, a variety of 16 different decorative buttons, (we found some cute lady bug and tulip buttons), one 1/8" wide dowel rod cut 21" long, 1/2 yard 1/4" wide red double-faced satin ribbon, two large black beads for dowel rod ends or decorations of your choice, and a red and black fabric pen for lettering.

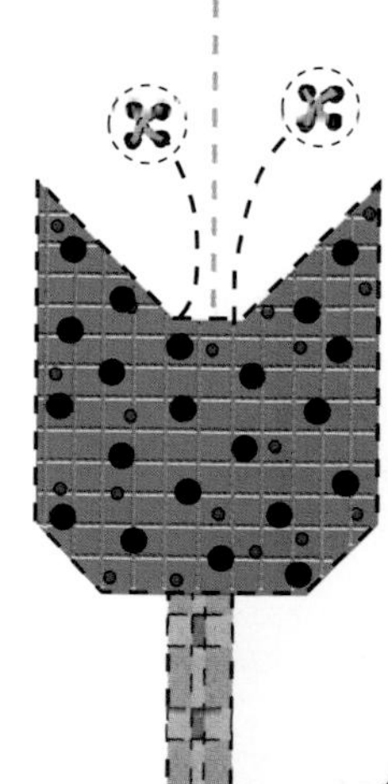

On A Personal Note:

This is a great beginner project. Two basic techniques are used to produce cute results. Use up bright scrap fabrics and buttons to add a whimsical look.

CUTTING FOR SIGN (front and back)

From Fabric I, cut: (Blue sky background print)

- One 3 1/2" wide strip. From this, cut:
  - * Two - 2 1/2" x 3 1/2" (9 "out" sign only)
  - * Four - 2" x 3 1/2" (8, 22)
  - * Two - 1 1/2" x 3 1/2" (6)
  - * Two - 3" x 5 1/2" (5)
  - * Two - 3" x 5" (18)
  - * Two - 2" x 3" (24)
- One 3" wide strip. From this, cut:
  - * Two - 3" squares (16)
  - * Four - 2 1/2" x 3" (1, 25)
  - * Two - 1 1/2" x 3" (11)
  - * Two - 1 1/2" x 2 1/2" (19)
  - * Two - 1" x 2 1/2" (21)
  - * Two - 2" x 7 1/2" (10)
- One 2 1/2" wide strip. From this, cut:
  - * Two - 2 1/2" x 16" (27)
- One 2" wide strip. From this, cut:
  - * Two - 2" x 5" (15)
  - * Four - 1 1/2" x 2" (13)
  - * Twelve - 1 1/2" squares (3, 9a)
  - * Twelve - 1" squares (2a, 12a, 17a)

From Fabric II, cut: (Olive stripe print for grass)

- Two - 3 1/2" x 16" (26)

From Fabric III, cut: (Eight different green print scraps for leaves and stems)

* *The following are to be cut from eight different scraps. Refer to color photo for placement of dark and light prints. Using one stripe scrap adds some interest.*
  - * Two - 2" x 3" (10a)
  - * Two - 3 1/2" squares (8a)
  - * Two - 2 1/2" squares (8b)
  - * Two - 1" x 1 1/2" (4 stem for red tulip)
  - * Two - 1" x 3 1/2" (7 stem for red tulip)
  - * Two - 1" x 2" (14 stem for yellow tulip)
  - * Two - 1" x 2 1/2" (20 stem for yellow tulip)
  - * Two - 2 1/2" x 4" (21a)
  - * Two - 1" x 4" (23 stem for orange tulip)
  - * Two - 2" x 3" (24a)
  - * Two - 2 1/2" x 3 1/2" (25a)

From Fabric IV, cut: (Two different red prints)

* *The following are to be cut from two different red scraps. Refer to color photo for placement of different reds.*
  - * Four - 1 1/2" squares (1a red tulip)
  - * Two - 2 1/2" x 3" (2 red tulip)
  - * Four - 1 1/2" x 3 1/2" (9 lady bugs)

From Fabric V, cut: (Bright yellow check)

- Two 3 1/2" wide strips. From these, cut:
  - * Two - 3 1/2" x 21" (french fold binding for sign top and bottom)
  - * Two - 3 1/2" x 16 1/2" (french fold binding for sign sides)
- Four 2" wide strips. From these, cut:
  - * Four - 2" x 19" (29 sign top and bottom borders)
  - * Four - 2" x 13 1/2" (28 sign side borders)
  - * Four - 1 1/2" squares (11a tulip)
- From scrap, cut:
  - * Two - 2 1/2" x 3" (12 tulip)

From Fabric VI, cut: (Orange check)

- Two - 2 1/2" x 3" (17)
- Four - 1 1/2" squares (16a)

From Fabric VII, cut: (Black solid)

- Four - 1" squares (9b)

SIGN UNIT ASSEMBLY (front and back)

NOTE: Front and back of sign are exactly alike except for the Lady Bug (Unit 9). For back of sign, substitute red Lady Bug (Unit 9) for Fabric I, Unit 9. Making the two at the same time is helpful.

1. Use diagonal corner technique to make one each of units 1, 2, 9, 11, 12, 16, and 17.

Making combined units 6-8

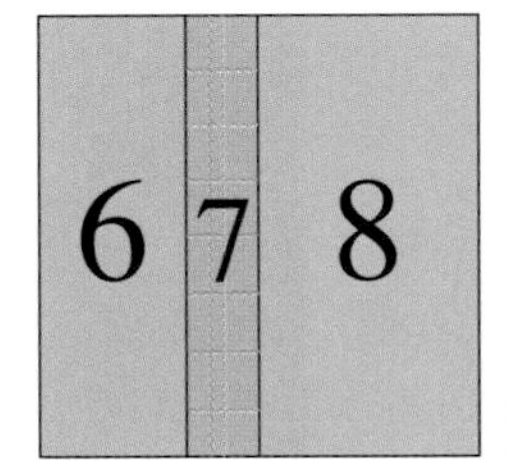

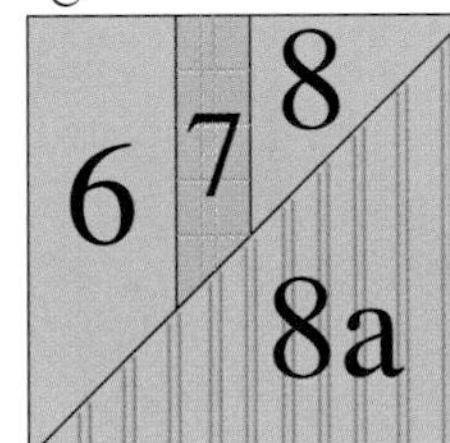

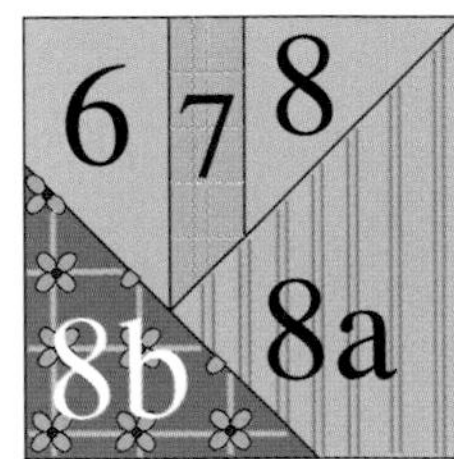

2. Use diagonal end technique to make one each of units 10, and 25.
3. To assemble combined units 6-8, join 1 1/2" x 3 1/2" piece of Fabric I, 1" x 3 1/2" piece of Fabric III scrap, and 2" x 3 1/2" piece of Fabric I as shown. Use diagonal corner technique and add corner 8a. Trim seam and press out; then add diagonal corner 8b.

Making combined units 19-21

Right Side. Join units 19, 20 and 21 as shown.

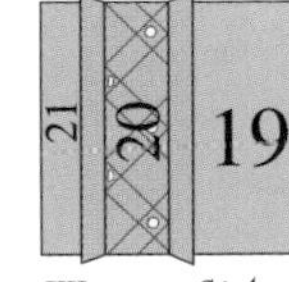

Wrong Side

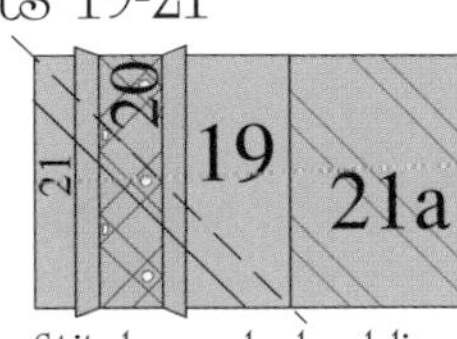

Stitch on dashed line. Trim on solid line

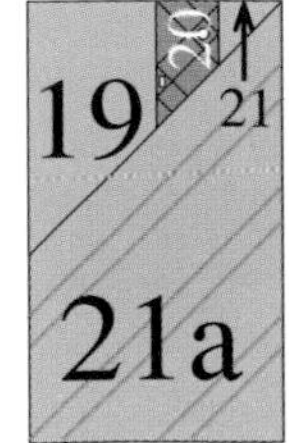

4. To make combined units 19-21a, join 1 1/2" x 2 1/2" piece of Fabric I, 1" x 2 1/2" piece of Fabric III, and 1" x 2 1/2" piece of Fabric I together as shown. This pieced square is now to be used as a diagonal corner. Place the diagonal corner square right sides together on Unit 21a as shown and stitch diagonal seam. Trim seam and press.

SIGN ASSEMBLY (front and back)

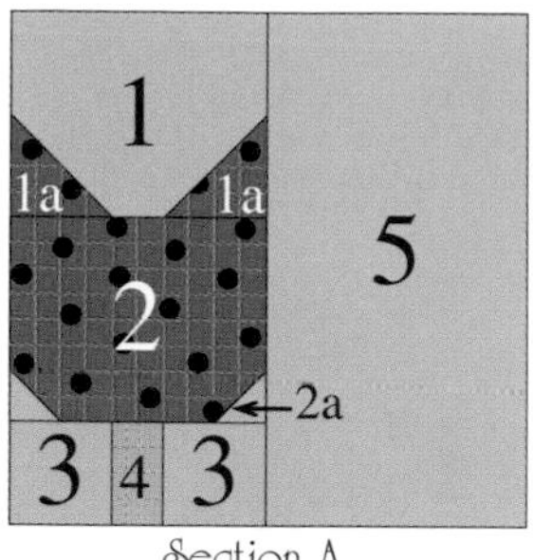

Section A

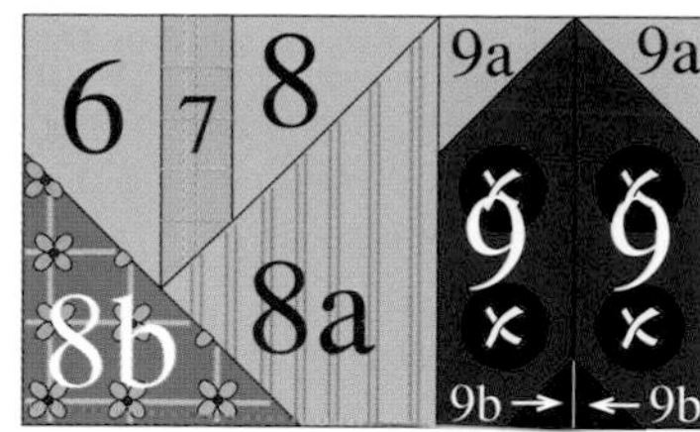

Section B

1. To assemble sign, begin by joining units 3-4-3 in a row as shown. Join Unit 1 to top of Unit 2; then add combined 3-4-3 units to bottom. Join Unit 5 to right side to complete Section A.

2. For Lady Bug, join mirror image units 9 together as shown and join the Lady Bug to right side of combined 6-8b units; then add to combined units 1-5. Add Unit 10 to left side as shown to complete combined sections A and B.

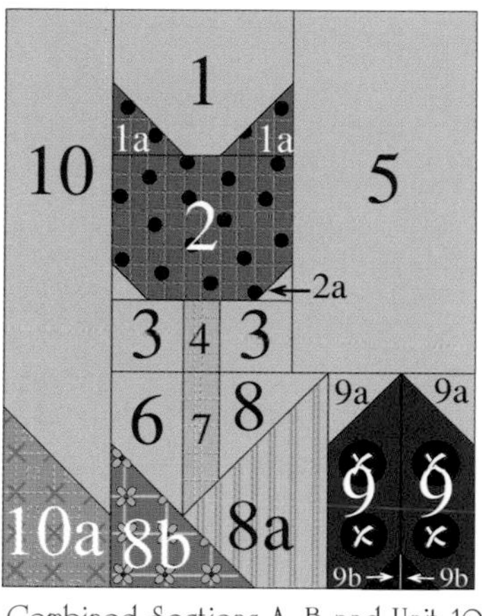

Combined Sections A, B and Unit 10

3. To make Section C, begin by joining units 13-14-13 in a horizontal row. Join Unit 11-Unit 12-and combined 13-14-13 units; then add Unit 15 to right side. Join units 16 and 17; then add Unit 18 to right side. Combine the two tulips to complete Section C.

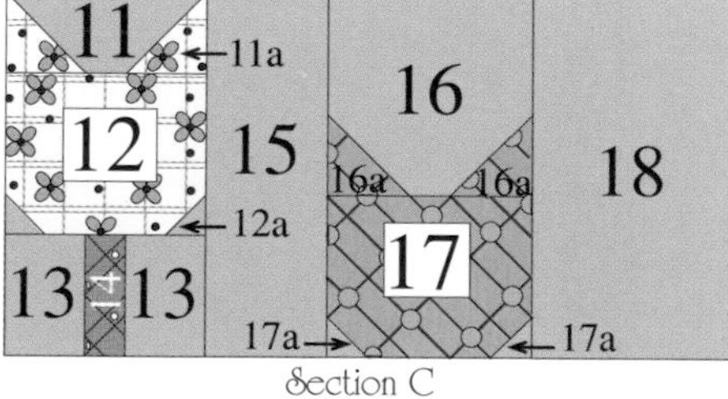

Section C

4. To make Section D, join Units 22 and completed Lady Bug Unit 9. Add these combined units to combined units 19-21a. Join units 23-24-and 25 together as shown; then add them to other combined units to complete Section D.

Section D

5. Combine Sections C and D as shown.

6. Join A-B section to C-D section; then join grass Unit 26 to bottom of combined sections. Join border Unit 28 to opposite sides of sign; then join Unit 29 to top and bottom.

7. Refer to illustrations of "in" and "out" signs. Draw lettering on paper with black marking pen. Center and trace lettering onto grass portion of each sign. Use red fabric pen for lettering. We used a fine tipped black fabric pen to outline the thick red lettering. This helps to make the lettering stand out.

8. For both sides of the sign, cut two 22" x 20" each (batting and backing). We used a muslin backing. Sandwich the three together for each sign, centering sign with batting in the center, and pieced sign top facing right side up. Quilt "in the ditch" around all leaves, stems, and tulips. Quilt grass and sky as desired. We did not quilt in the lettering.

9. Use water erasable pen to mark the stamens of each tulip, and the antenna of each lady bug. Use two strands of black embroidery floss to hand quilt the stamens and antenni.

10. Refer to color photograph, and sew yellow buttons at tips of each stamen on the red tulip, red buttons for the yellow tulip, and olive buttons for the orange tulip. Sew 5/8" black buttons on the backs of each lady bug as shown, and the 3/8" black buttons at each tip of lady bug antenni.

11. Use decorative buttons placed as desired on both sides of the sign. Please note that if Lady Bug buttons are used, we placed one crawling up the stem of the yellow tulip.

12. Using ruler and rotary cutter, trim off batting and backing from both signs. Pin or baste signs together (wrong sides facing).

13. Press side binding pieces in half lengthwise (wrong sides together). Apply this french fold binding to sides of sign, stitching to outside of sign by machine, and hand whipping binding to inside of sign.

14. Measure sign top and bottom and press under 3/4" - 1" on short sides of top and bottom binding so that length matches the sign. Press top and bottom binding pieces in half lengthwise as for Step 13. Apply this french fold binding to top and bottom of sign. There will be open short ends. For sign bottom, whip stitch short ends closed. For sign top, leave them open.

15. Cut 1/8" dowel rod 1" longer on both ends than completed sign top measurement. Using a black marker, paint ends of dowel rod. Insert dowel rod through top binding and glue black beads to each end. Tie red ribbon on each side of dowel rod next to beads for hanging.

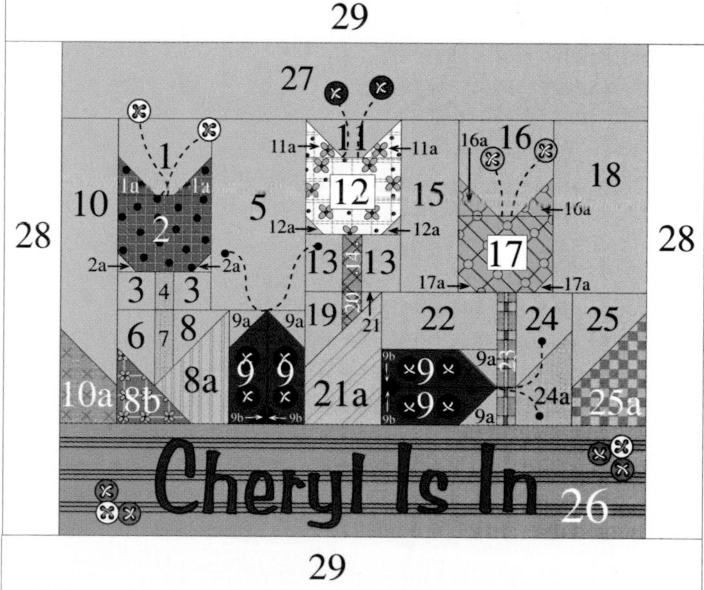

TWO PLACEMATS & NAPKINS

Materials for placemat will be the same as for the sign, with the exception of Fabrics II and V. You will need to purchase 1 yard of Fabric II for the napkins, and 3/4 yard of Fabric V to cover additional

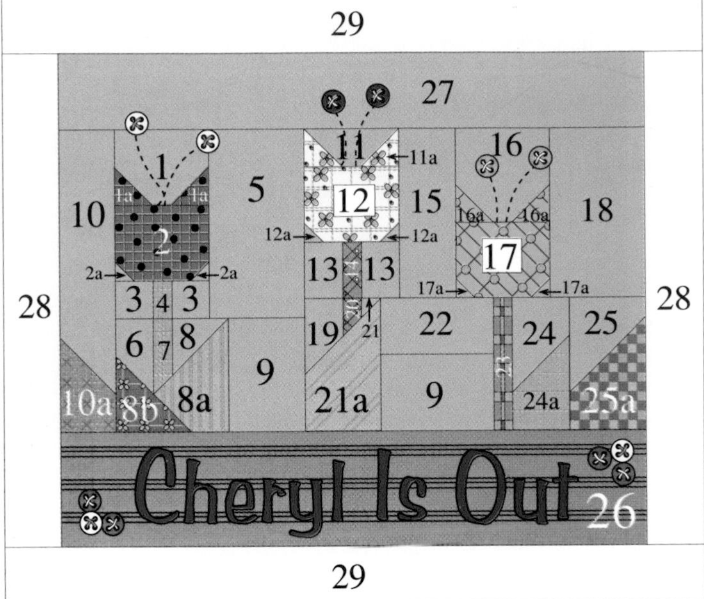

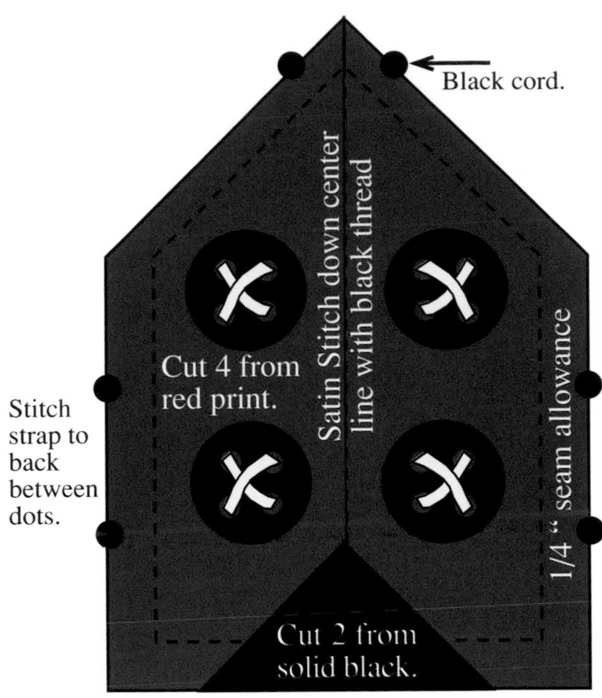

Lady Bug Napkin Ring Pattern

binding. Placemat backing requires one 20" x 22" piece of backing for each placemat. We used the bright yellow check. This is optional. If bright yellow check is used, the purchase of an additional 1 1/3 yards of Fabric V will be necessary.

We used two black buttons on each lady bug and embroidered circle tips of each tulip and lady bug antenni instead of using buttons. Therefore, plates placed on the placemats do not get caught on the buttons. This is optional. If embroidery is preferred, you will need bright yellow, bright red, and bright olive green embroidery floss, along with the black. Please note that we used machine satin stitch for stamens and lady bug antenni. We also used black thread to satin stitch a black line down the center of each lady bug. This too is optional.

You will need to purchase eight 5/8" black buttons for napkin ring lady bugs, and 1/2 yard of 1/8" wide black cording. A scrap of appliqué film will also be necessary.

Placemats are assembled exactly as for "in" side of sign. You will need to cut four lady bugs, rather than for two. See Fabric V cutting instructions for lady bugs and double the cutting of the red fabric.

For Napkins:
Cut four 12" squares of Fabric II. Place two squares each, wrong sides facing. Piece 54" of 2" wide straight-grain Fabric V binding. Use french fold binding and bind edges of each napkin.

For Napkin Rings:

1. Cut four lady bugs around outside line of pattern given for napkin ring. From Fabric VII, cut two solid black triangles. Use appliqué film as directed by manufacturer, and fuse the triangles to bottom of two of the lady bug pieces. Satin stitch around two sides of the black triangles if desired.
2. Using the lady bug as a pattern, cut two thin pieces of batting. Place two lady bugs pieces right sides together. Make certain that you have one piece lady bug with black triangle at bottom and one without. Place cut batting on underside of lady bugs. Cut two 9" lengths of black cording and place one length on top of top lady bug with ends of cording facing in towards lady bug center. Ends should be where black dots are shown on lady bug tip. Baste cording ends in place securely.
3. Stitch on seam line (dashed line on pattern), leaving bottom open to turn. Trim at points for easier turning. Turn right side out, making certain that points are sharp, and that cording is facing outwards. Tie a knot at the end of each end of the cording. Slip stitch the bottom closed.
4. With right side of lady bug up (side with black triangle bottom), satin stitch with black thread on center line of bug through all thicknesses. Make two lady bugs. Sew four black buttons on each lady bug right side.
5. Cut two 2" x 6 1/2" lengths of the same red fabric used for bugs. Press under 1/4" on short ends. Press under 1/4" on each long end. Press strip in half, wrong sides facing, and edge stitch around the three open sides. Place this strip between side dots shown on napkin ring pattern and top stitch in place, forming a ring.
6. Fold napkin as desired and slip rings around napkins.

Sherbert

On A Personal Note:

This is a beginner quilt utilizing the most important basic technique: Diagonal Corners. Watch the video on our CD-ROM for a demonstration of how to use this technique with The Angler 2™.
The size of this quilt is quick and easy to increase by simply adding rows. We used soft pastels for a light, summery look.

Finished size: 58" x 82"
Blocks A, B, C, D, and E: 12" square

Making Diagonal Corners

Video Demonstration
Take 1

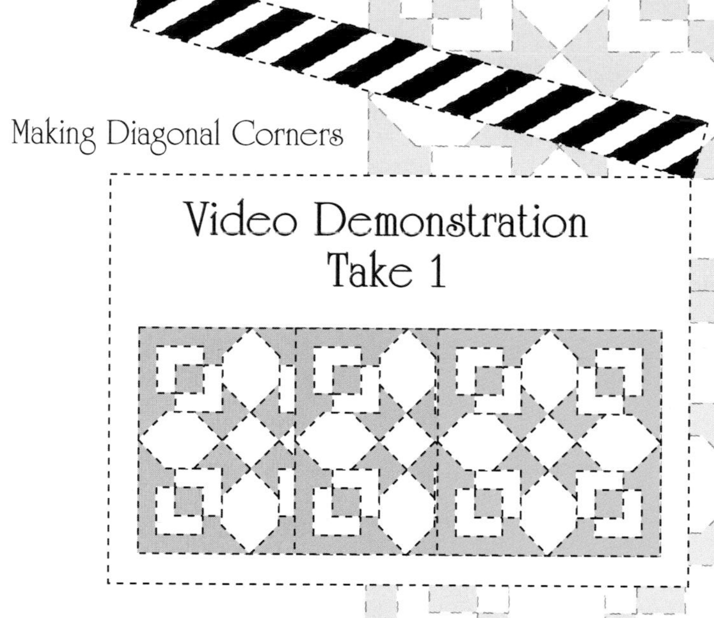

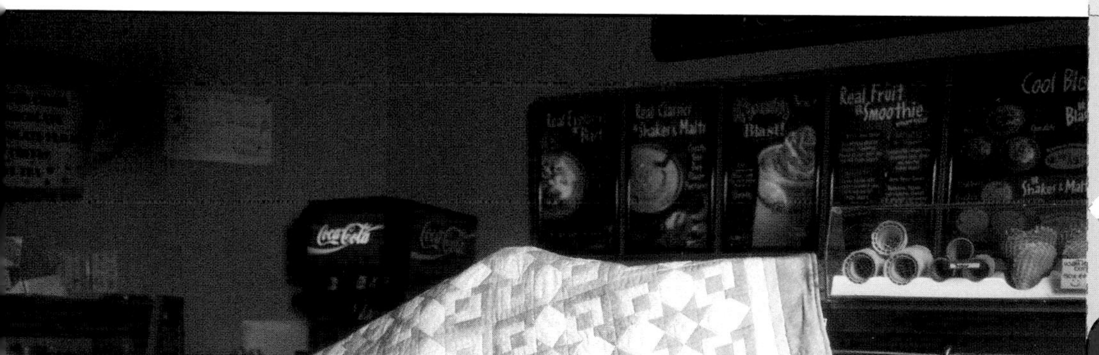

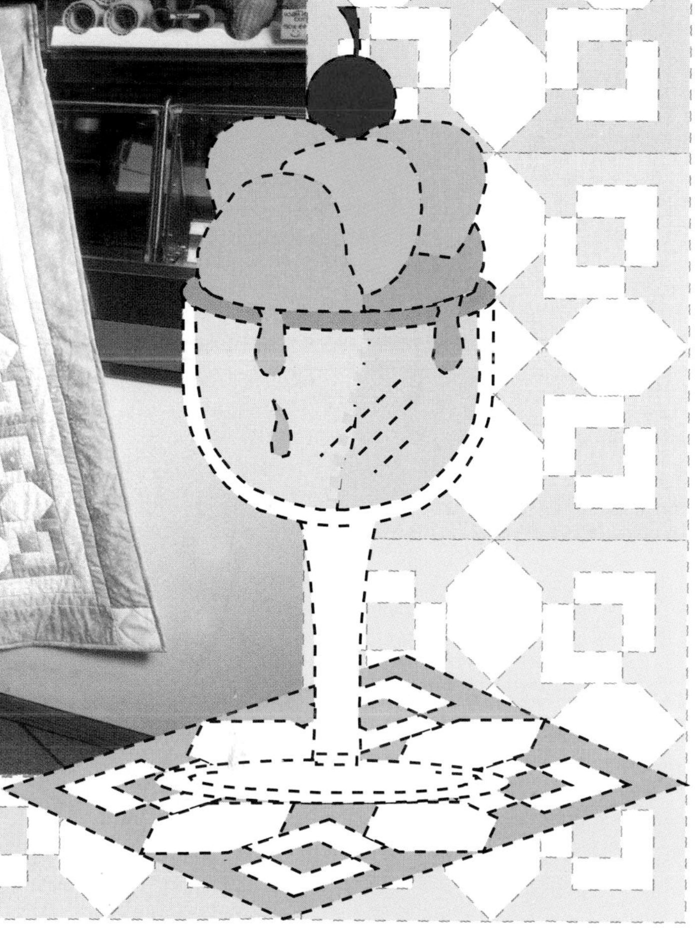

MATERIALS

- Fabric I 1 yard (need exactly 35") (light blue print)
- Fabric II 1 1/4 yards (need exactly 42") (white on white print)
- Fabric III 3/8 yard (need exactly 10 1/2") (light yellow print)
- Fabric IV 1 1/4 yards (need exactly 42") (ivory print)
- Fabric V 5/8 yard (need exactly 21") (light orange print)
- Fabric VI 2 yards (need exactly 68 1/2") (light green print)
- Fabric VII 1/2 yard (need exactly 17") (light violet print)
- Fabric VIII 1/2 yard (need exactly 13") (light pink print)
- Backing 5 yards

CUTTING

Cutting instructions shown in red indicate that the quantity of units are combined and cut in 2 or more different places to conserve fabric.

From Fabric I, cut: (light blue print)

- One 5" wide strip. From this, cut:
  - * Twenty-four - 1 1/2" x 5" (A6)
- One 4" wide strip. From this, cut:
  - * Twenty-four - 1 1/2" x 4" (A5)
- Seven 2" wide strips. From these, cut:
  - * 144 - 2" squares (A1, A7a, A8a)
- Eight 1 1/2" wide strips. From these, cut:
  - * Four - 1 1/2" x 38 1/2" (Border 4) Piece two together to = 76 1/2"
  - * Four - 1 1/2" x 25 1/2" (Border 3) Piece two together to = 50 1/2"
  - * Forty-eight - 1 1/2" squares (A4)

From Fabric II, cut: (white on white print)

- Eight 5" wide strips. From these, cut:
  - * Ninety-six - 3 1/2" x 5" (A7, B7, C7, D7, E7)
- One 2" wide strip. From this, cut:
  - * Sixteen - 2" squares (Border corners)

From Fabric III, cut: (light yellow print)

- Three 3 1/2" wide strips. From these, cut:
  - * Twenty-eight - 3 1/2" squares (A8, B8, C8, D8, E8, Border corners)

From Fabric IV, cut: (ivory print)

- Seven 3" wide strips. From these, cut:
  - * 192 - 1 1/2" x 3" (A3, B3, C3, D3, E3)
- Fourteen 1 1/2" wide strips. From these, cut:
  - * Four - 1 1/2" x 37 1/2" (Border 2) Piece two together to = 74 1/2"
  - * Four - 1 1/2" x 24 1/2" (Border 1) Piece two together to = 48 1/2"
  - * 192 - 1 1/2" x 2" (A2, B2, C2, D2, E2)

From Fabric V, cut: (light orange print)

- One 5" wide strip. From this, cut:
  - * Twenty - 1 1/2" x 5" (B6)
  - * Twenty-four - 1 1/2" squares (B4)
- One 4" wide strip. From this, cut:
  - * Twenty - 1 1/2" x 4" (B5)
  - * Sixteen - 1 1/2" squares (add to B4)
- Six 2" wide strips. From these, cut:
  - * 120 - 2" squares (B1, B7a, B8a)

From Fabric VI, cut: (light green print)

- One 5" wide strip. From this, cut:
  - * Twenty-four - 1 1/2" x 5" (C6)
- One 4" wide strip. From this, cut:
  - * Twenty-four - 1 1/2" x 4" (C5)
- Eight 3 1/2" wide strips. From these, cut:
  - * Four - 3 1/2" x 38 1/2" (Border 6) Piece two together to = 76 1/2"
  - * Four - 3 1/2" x 26 1/2" (Border 5) Piece two together to = 52 1/2"
  - * Forty-eight - 1 1/2" squares (C4)
- Seven 2 1/2" wide strips for straight-grain binding.
- Seven 2" wide strips. From these, cut:
  - * 144 - 2" squares (C1, C7a, C8a)

From Fabric VII, cut: (light violet print)

- One 5" wide strip. From this, cut:
  - * Sixteen - 1 1/2" x 5" (D6)
  - * Thirty-two - 1 1/2" squares (D4)
- One 4" wide strip. From this, cut:
  - * Sixteen - 1 1/2" x 4" (D5)
- Four 2" wide strips. From these, cut:
  - * Ninety-six - 2" squares (add to D1, D7a, D8a)

From Fabric VIII, cut: (light pink print)

- One 5" wide strip. From this, cut:
  - * Twelve - 1 1/2" x 5" (E6)
  - * Twelve - 1 1/2" x 4" (E5)
  - * Eight - 1 1/2" squares (E4)
- Four 2" wide strips. From these, cut:
  - * Seventy-two - 2" squares (E1, E7a, E8a)
  - * Sixteen - 1 1/2" squares (add to E4)

ASSEMBLY

BLOCK A

1. There are five different color variations of Block A, however all are made exactly the same way. Refer frequently to block illustrations for correct placement of color.
2. Use diagonal corner technique to make four each of Unit 7, one of Unit 8, and four of the quilt corner block.
3. The four corners of the block are made the same and turned

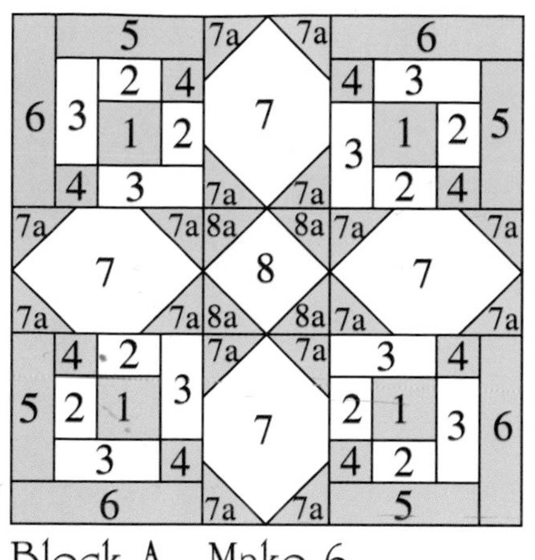

Block A. Make 6

Block B. Make 5

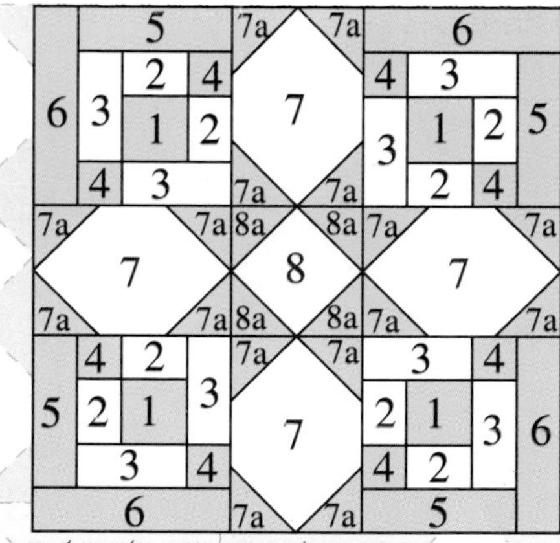

Block C. Make 6

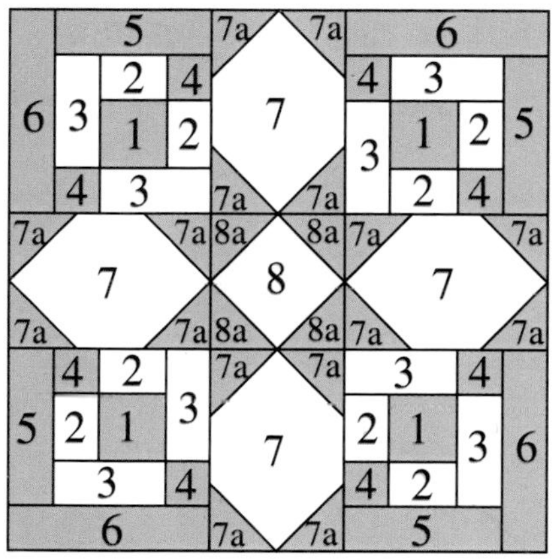

Block D. Make 4

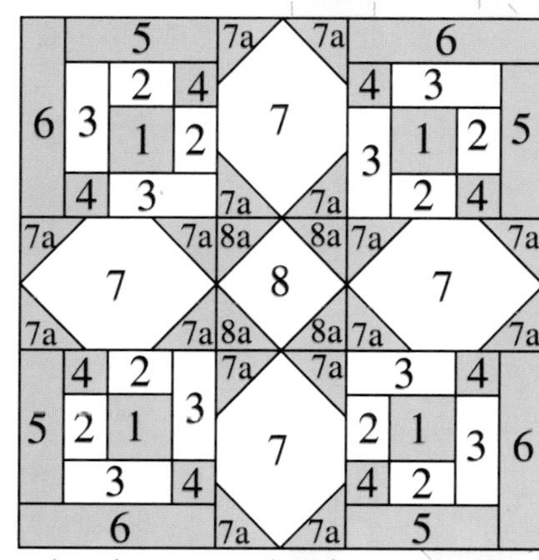

Block E. Make 3

when the block is sewn together.

4. Refer to top left corner of any block for these instructions. To piece block corner center, join units 1 and 2. Join units 2 and 4; then add them to the top of combined units 1-2. Join units 4 and 3 as shown; then add them to the bottom of the combined units. Join another 3-4 unit combination and add it to the left side of the previously combined units. Join Unit 5 to top of corner square; then add Unit 6 to left side to complete the block corner. Make 4 per block.

5. Assemble the block in rows, beginning in the top left corner. Join one corner block-Unit 7- and another corner block for Row 1. Make two of these rows.

6. For center row, refer to illustration and join units 7-8-and Unit 7 in a row.

7. Join the three rows together to complete the block. Make the required number of blocks in the color combinations shown above.

QUILT ASSEMBLY

1. Refer to quilt assembly diagram and begin by joining rows. There are six rows, consisting of four blocks per row. Join the rows together from left to right as follows:

Row 1: Block A-Block B-Block C-Block D.
Row 2: Block C-Block E-Block B-Block A
Row 3: Block B-Block A-Block D-Block C
Row 4: Block C-Block E-Block A-Block B
Row 5: Block A-Block B-Block D-Block C
Row 6: Block E-Block C-Block A-Block D

2. Join the six rows together, matching seams and points of Unit 7.

3. Join pieced Border 1 from Fabric IV to top and bottom of quilt. Join pieced Border 2 to opposite sides of quilt as shown

4. Using previously pieced strips of Fabric I, join Border 3 to top and bottom of quilt; then add pieced Border 4 to opposite sides.

5. Join pieced Border 5 from Fabric VI to top and bottom of quilt. Join quilt corners to opposite short ends of Border 6; then add this border to opposite sides of quilt.

QUILTING AND FINISHING

3. Quilt in the ditch around all patchwork. Make 295" of straight-grain, french fold binding and bind your quilt.

1a
1
5
3
6
4
2

Denim & Daisies

Finished size: 83 3/4" x 106 3/4

Flower blocks finished size: 16 1/2" square.

MATERIALS

Fabric I (navy denim) — 2 1/4 yards (need exactly 78 1/4")

Fabric II (white on white print) — 3/8 yard (need exactly 12")

Fabric III (ivory solid) — 2 1/8 yards (need exactly 73 3/4") * we used Ultra Suede

Fabric IV (soft yellow print) — 3 3/8 yards (need exactly 112 1/2")

Fusible pellon — 7 yards (18" wide)

Backing — 7 yards

Fabric V (solid light blue) — 3/4 yard (need exactly 24 1/2") * we used Ultra Suede

Fabric VI (blue print) — 2 yards (need exactly 68 1/2")

Fabric VII (solid medium green) — 3/8 yard (need exactly 11 1/2")

Fabric VIII (green print) — 3/4 yard (need exactly 26 1/8")

Tear-away pellon — 7 yards (18" wide)

CUTTING

From Fabric I, cut (navy denim)

- Three 17 3/8" x 42 3/8" wide strips. From these, cut:
  - * Five 17 3/8" squares cut in half diagonally to = 10 triangles for border Flowers B
- Cut remainder of last strip into one 12 1/2" wide strip,and three 1 5/8" wide strips. From these, cut:
  - * Two 12 1/2" squares cut in half diagonally to = 4 triangles for border corner Flowers C.
  - * Eleven 1 5/8" x 17" strips for frame on Flower A inner blocks.
- One 14 3/4" wide strip. From this, cut:
  - * Two - 14 3/4" squares for center block(s) back ground
- Seven 1 5/8" wide strips. From these, cut:
  - * One 1 5/8" x 17" strip. (add to 1 5/8" x 17" strips above for a total of twelve).
  - * Twelve 1 5/8" x 14 3/4" strips for frame on Flower A inner blocks.

From Fabric II, cut: (white on white print)

- Cut one 5 1/2" wide strip to accommodate the following cuts from templates.
  - * Six large X flower petals for Flower A (Template A6) on block. 5 1/4" square.
  - * Eight small flower petals for Flower A (Template A7) to be placed on center block. 1 1/2" x 3"
- Cut two 3 1/4" wide strips to accommodate the following cuts from templates.
  - * Fourteen border Flower B, and border corner Flower C large center petals. (Templates B4 and C1). 3 1/4" squares.

From Fabric III, cut: (ivory solid)

- Five 14 3/4" wide strips. From these, cut:
  - * Ten 14 3/4" squares for outer block, Flower A background
  - * Two large X flower petals for Flower A (Template A6) on center blocks. 5 1/4" sq.
  - * Eight buds for Flower A (A1 Template) to be placed in center and inner blocks. 2 1/4" squares.
  - * Twenty-four small flower petals for Flower A (Template A7) to be placed on inner blocks. 1 1/2" x 3"
  - * Ten center petals for Flower Block B (Template B5) for border flowers B. 2" x 3"
  - * Four center petals for border corner Flowers C (Template C3). 1 5/8" x 3 1/4"

From Fabric IV, cut: (soft yellow print)

- Four 14 3/4" wide strips. From these, cut:
  - * Six 14 3/4" squares for inner block Flower A background.
  - * Twenty-four 1 5/8" x 14 3/4" strips for frame on outer and center blocks.
  - * Twenty border Flower B small mirror image petals (Template B6). 2" x 2 1/4"
  - * Eight small border corner Flower C petals (Template C4). 1 1/2" x 3"
- One 17" wide strip. From this, cut:
  - * Twenty-four 1 5/8" x 17" strips for frame on outer and center blocks.
- * Ten 3 1/2" wide strips for inner quilt border
- One 1 1/2" wide strip. From this, cut:
  - * Eighteen centers for all Flower A's (Template A8). 1 1/2" squares.

From Fabric V, cut: (solid light blue)

- Two 5 1/2" wide strip. From this, cut:
  - * Ten large X flower petals for Flower A (Template A6) on outer blocks. 5 1/4" sq.
- Nine 1 1/2" wide strips for center quilt border.

From Fabric VI, cut: (blue print)

- Ten 3 1/4" wide strips for outer quilt border.
- Ten 3" wide strips for straight-grain french fold binding.
- Two 3" wide strips. From these and binding scrap, cut:
  - * Ten buds for Flower A (A1 Template) to be placed on inner blocks. 2 1/4" squares
  - * Forty small flower petals for Flower A (Template A7) to be placed on outer blocks. 1 1/2" x 3"

From Fabric VII, cut: (solid medium green)

- Three 3 3/8" wide strips to accommodate the following cuts from templates:
  - * Eighteen large leaves for all Flower A blocks (Unit A3) 2 5/8" x 3 3/8"
  - * Twenty leaves for border Flower B (Unit B2 right leaves, Unit B3 left leaves)

2 1/2" x 3 3/8"

* Twenty-four mirror image small leaves for Flower A (Unit A4) 1 3/8" x 2 1/4"

- One 1 3/8" wide strip. From this, cut:
  - * Twelve mirror image small leaves for Flower A (Unit A4) 1 3/8" x 2 1/4". Add to above.

From Fabric VIII, cut: (green print)

- Three 6 3/4" wide strips to accommodate the following cuts from templates:
  - * Eighteen long stems for all Flower A blocks (Template A2) 4" x 6 3/4".
  - * Four large stems for all border Flower B blocks (Template B1) 3 5/8" x 6 1/2"
- One 3 5/8" wide strip. From this, cut:
  - * Six more 3 5/8" x 6 1/2" pieces for (Template B1) to be added to pieces above.
  - * Four mirror image stems for all corner border Flower C blocks. (Template C2) 2 1/2" x 5"
  - * Seven 1 3/8" x 2 1/4" pieces for Flower A small leaves (Template A5)
- One 2 1/4" wide strip. From this, cut:
  - * Twenty-nine small leaves for Flower A (Template A5) 1 3/8" x 2 1/4". Add to above.

ASSEMBLY

BLOCK ASSEMBLY

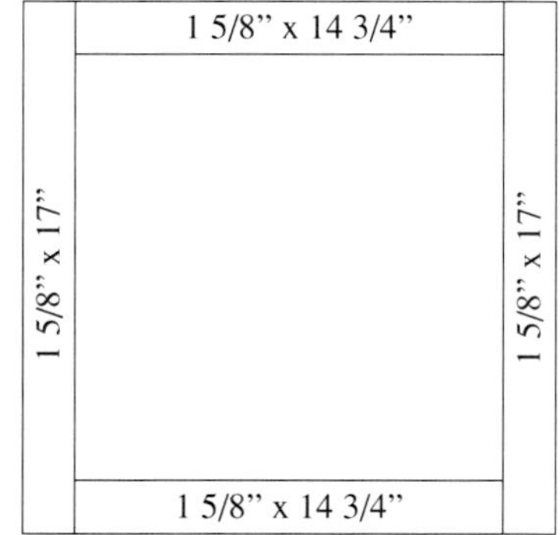

1. Refer to square block drawing and begin by joining 1 5/8" x 14 3/4" borders to blocks right sides together. Press borders out. Join Fabric I borders to the six Fabric IV squares. Join Fabric IV borders to all Fabric I and Fabric III squares. Join Fabric I borders to Fabric IV blocks.
2. Join all 1 5/8" x 17" borders to opposite ends of blocks as directed in Step 1. Press out.
3. For Fabric I triangular blocks, cut Fabric I squares in half diagonally as directed. Large triangle is for Flower B, and small triangle is for corner Flowers C. Refer to quilt diagram for correct placement of these flowers as they are mirror images.

Fusible Pellon Preparation

1. Draw all appliqué pieces onto smooth side of appliqué film. Begin with Fabric II templates. Turn templates on *wrong* side and trace around edges. We utilized as much of the appliqué film as possible, butting pieces up to each other. Cut out around pieces drawn together.
2. Place rough side of appliqué film with drawn shapes on *wrong* side of fabric. Press with hot, dry iron for 10 seconds. Move iron from one pressed place to another until all of the paper has been pressed down.
3. Cut all pieces out as drawn.
4. Continue this procedure for all fabrics that require appliqué's.
5. Place all like pieces in zip top plastic bags and mark flower letter and unit number on masking tape. Place tape on bags.
6. Trace each flower in its entirety onto a light weight, see-through paper or fabric to aid in correct placement on block. We like Do-Sew® as it is easy to pin and see through.

For Flower Block A

1. There are three color combinations for Flower Block A. Refer to flower drawings and quilt diagram for correct color combinations.
2. Turn each square block "on point." Place drawing of entire flower over the "on point" block and center it as shown in diagrams. Pin your drawing in place at the top so that it may be lifted up easily.
3. Begin with Unit 1. Peel paper off of appliqué piece, and place the appliqué down in proper position under placement pattern. Lift pattern and lay hot, dry iron on top of appliqué for 10 seconds. Appliqué should now be fused to the background block.
4. Continue adding units in numerical order; then press each one in place until flower is completed.

NOTE: If you are using Ultra Suede, a press cloth must be placed over Ultra Suede when pressing.

5. Repeat steps 1-4 for all Flower A blocks.

For Flower Block B

1. Center drawing of Flower B on large triangle of Fabric I as shown in quilt diagram. Flat stem edge of flower should be placed 1 1/4" up from long flat edge of triangle. Follow steps 1-4 above and prepare all Flower B blocks for appliqué.

For Flower Block C

1. Refer to quilt diagram for correct placement of corner flower C blocks. As these are mirror image blocks, you will make two of each. Center drawing of Flower C on small triangle of Fabric I as shown in quilt diagram. Flat stem edge of flower should be placed 1 1/4" up from short edge of triangle, according to placement of flower in corner. Follow steps 1-4 for Flower Block A to prepare all Flower C blocks for appliqué.

Flower A Top

7
Cut 40 Blue Print
Cut 24 Ivory Solid
Cut 8 White on White
Print
5
Cut 36 Green
Print
4
7
Cut 6 white
on white print.
Cut 10
blue solid
Cut 2
ivory solid
5
7
8
7
6
For #6, cut along solid
and dashed lines.
Dashed lines show
where #6 fits behind
petal #7
4
5
7
For correct position, and to draw stem pattern
accurately, tape Flower A bottom
along dashed line.
Cut 18 solid
green. Turn pattern
over and cut 18 more.
4
6 Template
example
Flower A2 - Blue solid/blue print.
Make 10. Place on Fabric III
block for Flower A.
Flower A1 - White/Ivory
Make 6. Place on Fabric IV
block for Flower A.

Flower A Bottom

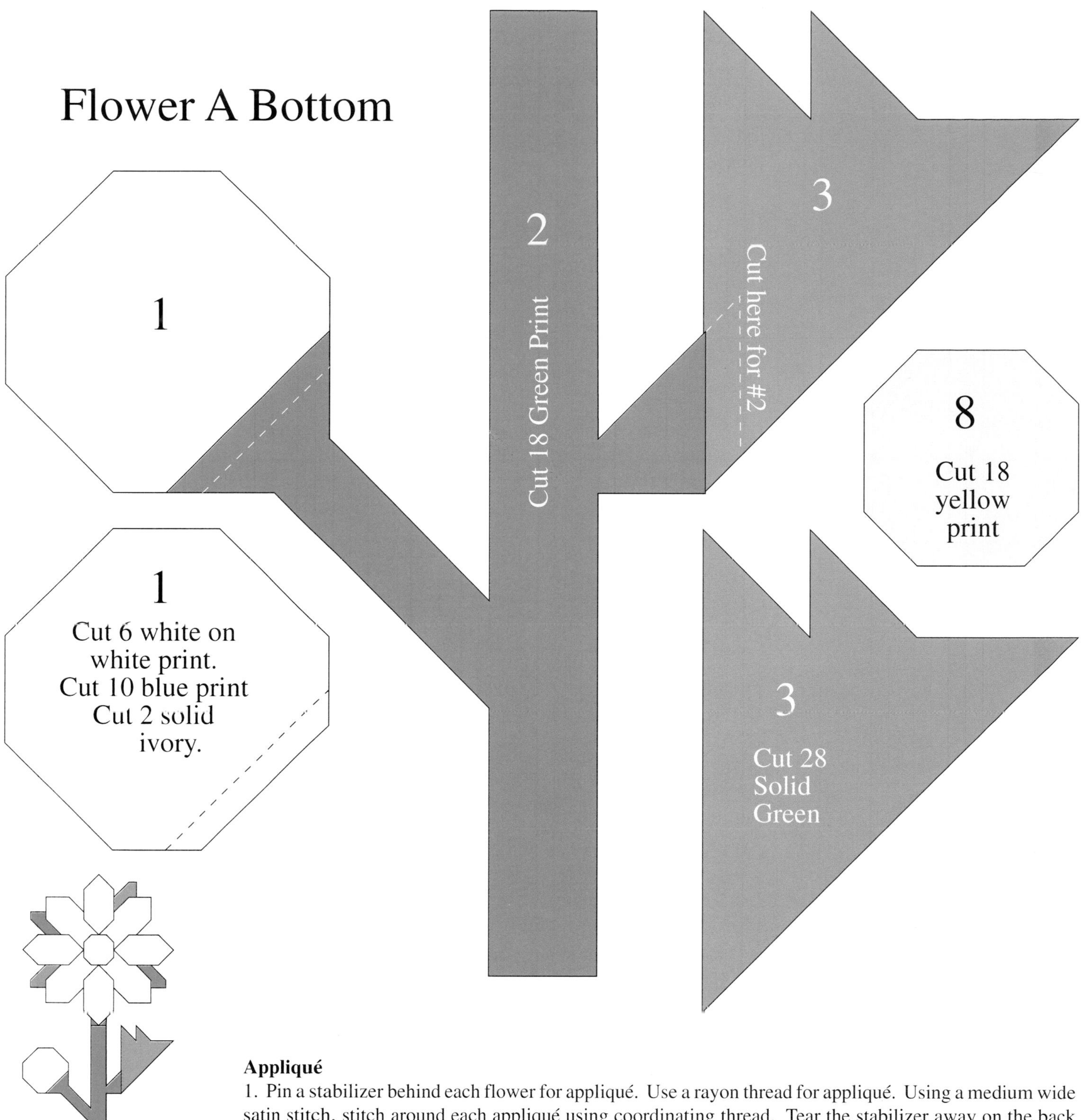

Flower A3 - Ivory/white
Make 2. Place on Fabric I block for Flower A.

Appliqué

1. Pin a stabilizer behind each flower for appliqué. Use a rayon thread for appliqué. Using a medium wide satin stitch, stitch around each appliqué using coordinating thread. Tear the stabilizer away on the back side when each appliqué is finished.

Quilt Assembly

1. Refer to quilt diagram, and join two B blocks to opposite sides of A block as shown (Row 2), positioning flowers correctly. Add Row 1 "C" corner block as shown. Continue joining blocks as shown in diagram for each row; then join rows together in numerical order.

2. For Border 1, top and bottom, join two 3 1/2" wide border strips of Fabric IV, and press center seam. For sides, join three 3 1/2" wide border strips of Fabric IV together, and press seams.

3. Pin short borders to top and bottom of quilt, matching centers. Stitch top and bottom borders to quilt. Trim excess and press borders out.

4. Pin side borders to quilt top sides, matching center of quilt top with center of borders. Join borders to quilt sides. Trim excess and press borders out.

5. Add Border 2 from Fabric V in same manner, and Border 3 from Fabric VI in same manner.

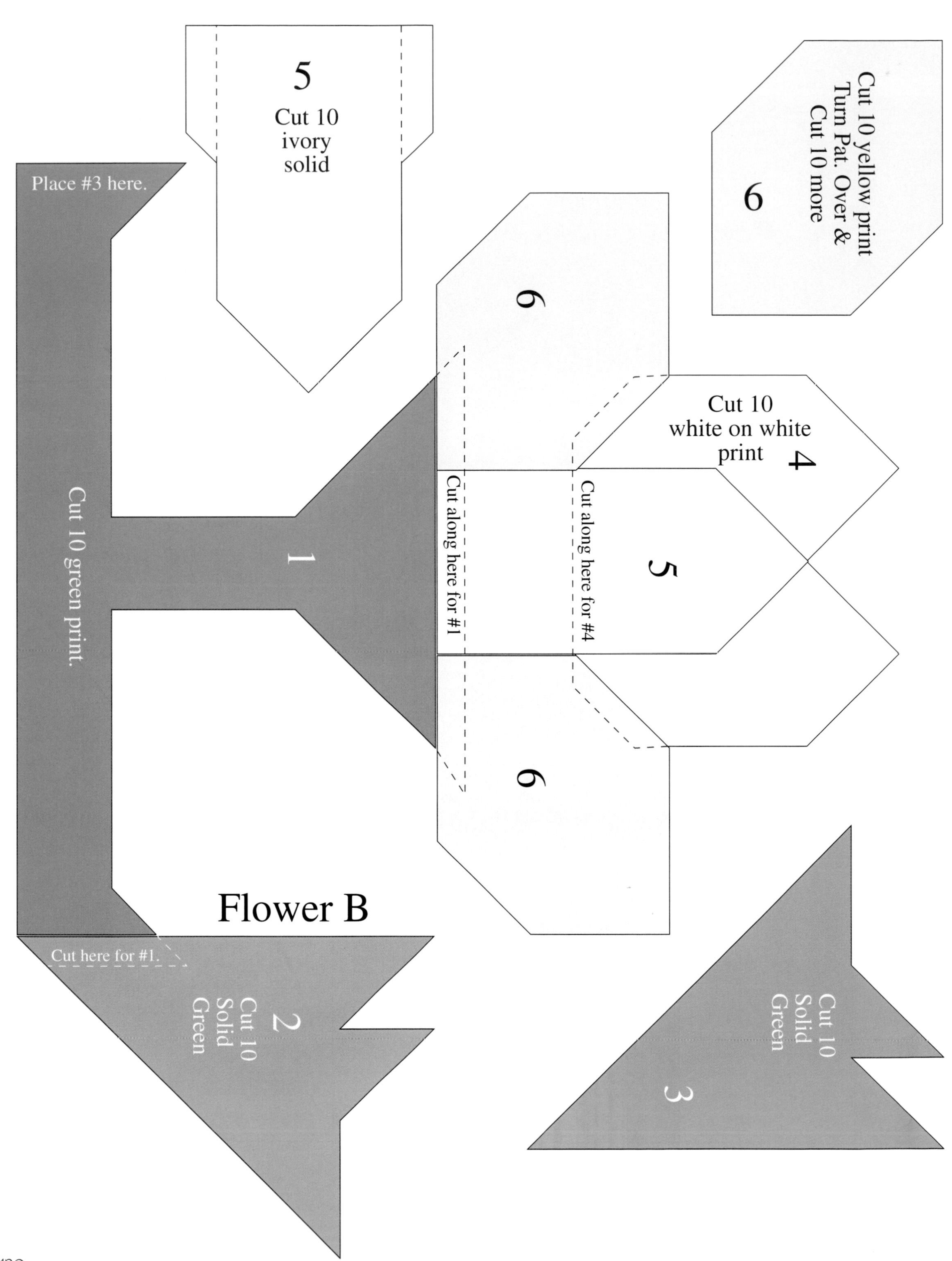
5
Cut 10
ivory
solid
Cut 10 yellow print
Turn Pat. Over &
Cut 10 more
6
Place #3 here.
6
Cut 10
white on white
print
4
Cut 10 green print.
1
Cut along here for #1
Cut along here for #4
5
6
Flower B
Cut here for #1.
2
Cut 10
Solid
Green
Cut 10
Solid
Green
3

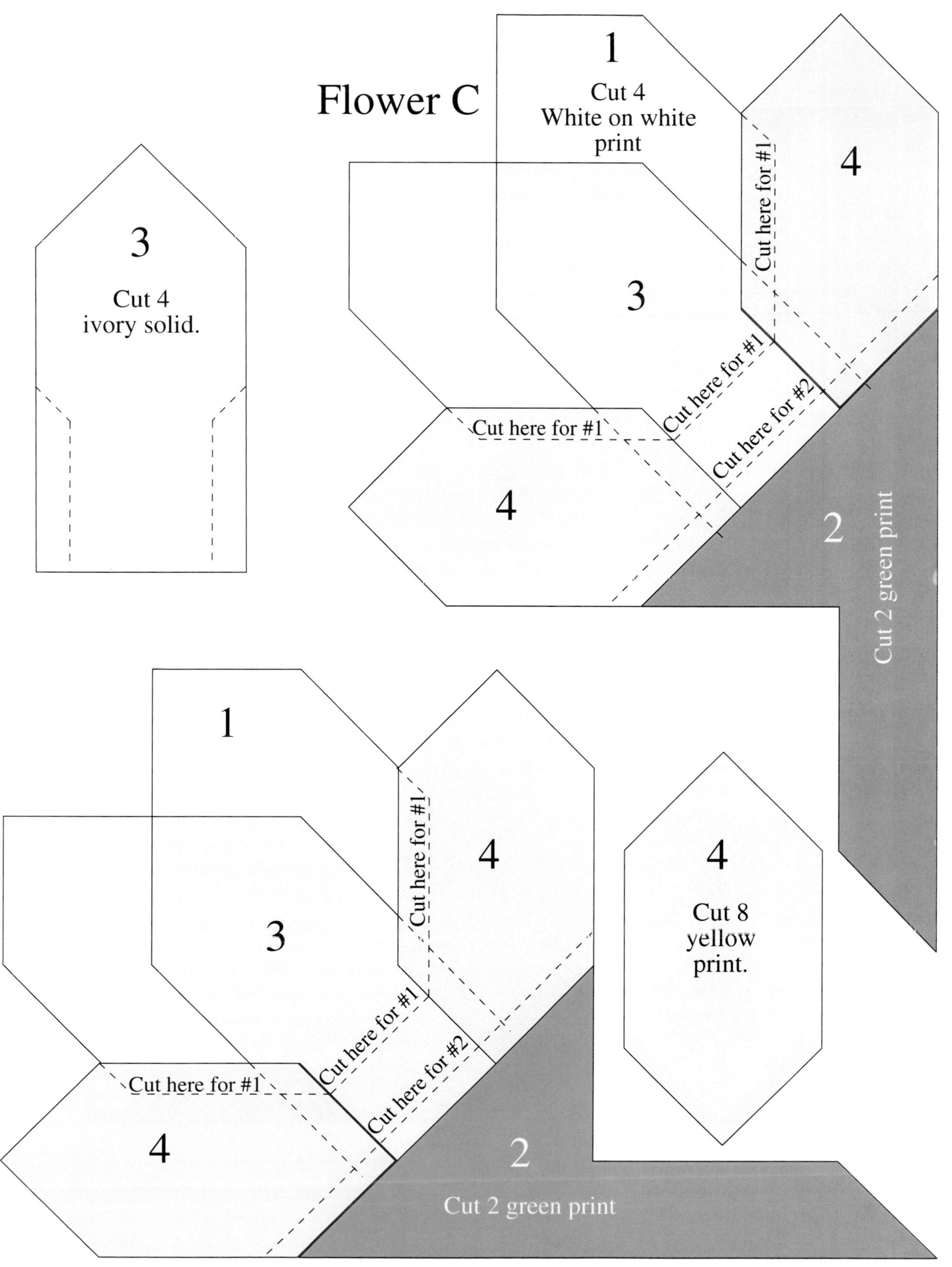
Flower C
1
Cut 4
White on white
print
3
Cut 4
ivory solid.
4
Cut here for #1
3
Cut here for #1
Cut here for #1
Cut here for #2
4
2
Cut 2 green print
1
Cut here for #1
4
3
Cut here for #1
Cut here for #1
Cut here for #2
4
2
Cut 2 green print
4
Cut 8
yellow
print.

Finishing

1. Piece quilt backing, (we used denim) and quilt as desired. We quilted around all of the appliqué's, and stitched in the ditch around the borders.
2. Make 390" of French Fold binding and apply to quilt.

Made for that denim and daisy girl:

My Quilting Friend

Celebrating the Gift of Friendship Through Quilting

Finished size: 63" square   Blocks A, B, C and D: 12" square

On A Personal Note:

There are some interesting techniques in the assembly of this quilt to speed things up, and we hope that you enjoy learning them, as well as putting them to use in future projects. Watch the demonstrations on our CD-ROM..

MATERIALS

- Fabric I — 2 1/2 yards (need exactly 88 1/4") (gray on black)
- Fabric II — 1/2 yard (need exactly 14") (dark green print)
- Fabric III — 1/4 yard (need exactly 6 1/4") (medium green print)
- Fabric IV — 7/8 yard (need exactly 32 3/4") (majenta print)
- Fabric V — 15/8 yards (need exactly 54 1/2") (gray/tan print)
- Fabric VI — 1/8 yard (need exactly 3 1/2") (solid pale yellow)
- Fabric VII — 1/2 yard (need exactly 15 1/2") (peach paisley print)
- Backing — 3 3/4 yards

A Special Thank You:
Thanks to our photographer, Chris Marona, from all quilting cat lovers. He had the patience to wait for this adorable calico to peek in the window.

Making Multi Diagonal Corners

Making Flying Geese Blocks

Making Diagonal Corners

Video Demonstration
Take 1

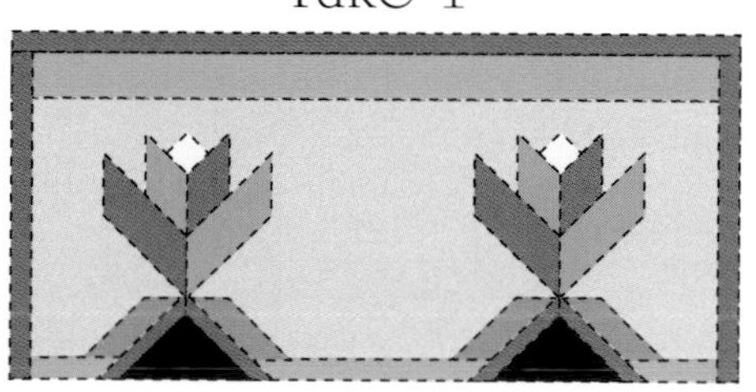

Making Diagonal Ends

Making Tulip Top

CUTTING

NOTE: All "Q" units in cutting instructions stand for "quilt top". These are units that are not incorporated into blocks. Cutting instructions shown in RED indicate that the quantity of units are combined and cut in 2 or more different places to conserve fabric.

From Fabric I, cut: (gray on black print)

- Two 12 1/2" x 42 1/4" wide strips. From these, cut:
  - * Four – 12 1/2" squares (Q1)
  - * Sixteen – 4 1/4" x 5" (A3, B3)
- Two 5" x 42 1/4" wide strips. From these, cut:
  - * Sixteen – 4 1/4" x 5" (add to A3, B3)
  - * Sixteen – 2" squares (A1a, B1a)
- Nine 3 1/2" wide strips. From these, cut:
  - * Thirty-two – 3 1/2" x 5 3/4" (A6, B6)
  - * Thirty –six – 3 1/2" squares (A4b, A5b, B4b, B5b, C1b)
  - * Sixteen – 2 3/4" x 3 1/2" (A2, B2)
  - * Seven – 2" squares (add to A1a, B1a)
- Five 2 3/4" wide strips. Four strips for Strip Set 3. From remaining strip, cut:
  - * Eight – 2 3/4" squares (B7c)
  - * Nine – 2" squares (add to A1a, B1a)
- Four 2" wide strips for Strip Sets 1 and 2.

From Fabric II, cut: (dark green print)

- Four 3 1/2" wide strips. From these, cut:
  - * Thirty-two – 3 1/2" x 5" (A7a, B7a)

From Fabric III, cut: (medium green print)

- Five – 1 1/4" wide strips for Strip Set 3. From remaining strip, cut:
  - * Four – 1 1/4" squares (Q1a)

From Fabric IV, cut: (magenta print)

- One 4 1/4" wide strip. From this, cut:
  - * Four – 4 1/4" squares (C1a)
  - * Six – 1 1/4" x 12 1/2" (D3)
- Five 3 1/2" wide strips. From these, cut:
  - * Sixteen – 3 1/2" x 5 3/4" (A4, B4)
  - * Thirty-two – 3 1/2" squares (A7b, B7b)
- Three 2" wide strips. Two for Strip Set 2. From remaining strips, cut:
  - * Sixteen – 2" squares (A1c, B1c)
- Four 1 1/4" strips. From these, cut:
  - * Two – 1 1/4" x 12 1/2" (add to D3)
  - * Eight – 1 1/4" x 11" (D2)

From Fabric V, cut: (gray print)

- One 12 1/2" wide strip. From this, cut:
  - * One – 12 1/2" square (C1)
  - * Two– 11" squares (D1)
  - * Eight – 2 3/4" squares (A7c)
- One 11" wide strip. From this, cut:
  - * Two – 11" squares (add to D1)
  - * Sixteen – 2 3/4" squares (add to A7c)
- Six 2 1/2" wide strips for straight-grain binding
- Eight 2" wide strips. From these, cut:
  - * Four – 2" x 32" (Q3 border) piece together to = two 2" x 63 1/2"
  - * Four – 2" x 30 1/2" (Q2 border) piece together to = two 2" x 60 1/2"

From Fabric VI, cut: (pale yellow solid)

- One 3 1/2" wide strip. From this, cut:
  - * Sixteen - 2" x 3 1/2" (A1, B1)

From Fabric VII, cut: (peach paisley print)

- Two 5 3/4" wide strips. From these, cut:
  - * Sixteen – 3 1/2" x 5 3/4" (A5, B5)
  - * Sixteen – 2" squares (A1b, B1b)
- Two 2" wide strips for Strip Set 1.

ASSEMBLY

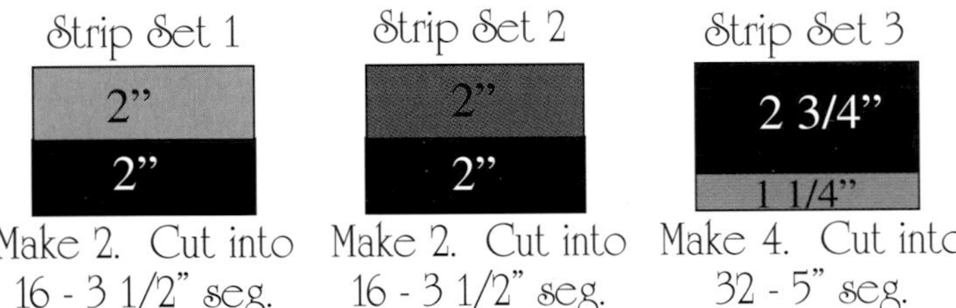

STRIP SETS

1. Refer to illustration below and make Strip Sets as shown. Cut into segments as directed. All three of these strip sets are used for Blocks A and B. Place your strip set segments into plastic bags as you have done for the units that you cut. Mark each bag and set strip set segments aside.

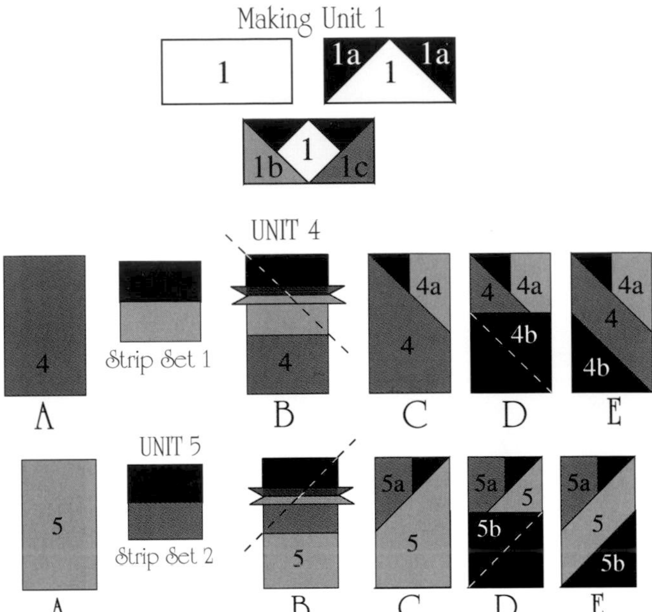

FLOWER BLOCKS A & B

1. To make the units for these two blocks, begin with Unit 1, shown at right. This is the basic Flying Geese block with *double* Flying Geese diagonal corners.
2. Use diagonal corner technique to complete the first Flying Geese part of this unit. Press corners out. Use diagonal corner technique once again, placing the diagonal corner units as shown above to complete the tulip top of the flower.
3. Join Unit 2 to tulip top; then add Unit 3 to opposite sides. Set this top section aside.
4. Units 4 and 5 are made the same way. They are, however mirror images and utilize different placement of color to give the striking effect the flower has.
5. To make Unit 4, you will use diagonal corner technique and a 3 1/2" Strip Set 1 segment. The strip set segment will be used as your diagonal corner. The illustration above shows the exact placement of the strip set on the main Unit 4 rectangle. Stitch your diagonal seam as shown and press out. Join diagonal corner 4b as shown to complete the unit.
6. Refer to the illustration above to assemble Unit 5. As you can see, it is a mirror image of Unit 4. Use 3 1/2" segment from Strip Set 2 and assemble as in Step 5.
7. To complete flower, refer to the block illustrations below and join units 4 and 5 as shown. Join Unit 6 to opposite sides of flower. Join tulip top section of the flower to main part of flower. Set aside.
8. Right and left leaf units A and B7 and A and B8 are made exactly the same way with the exception of diagonal corner 7c, which is a different color. To begin, refer to diagram of these units on next page and begin by using 5" segment of Strip Set 3. Use diagonal end technique as shown in illustration to join unit 7a. Trim seam and press out; then add diagonal corner 7b as shown. Refer to illustration frequently for correct placement of mirror image units and for correct color placement for Unit 7c, which is to be added next. Trim seam and press out.
9. Join the mirror image units together as shown in block diagrams; then join the completed leaf units to bottom of each flower to complete the A and B blocks.

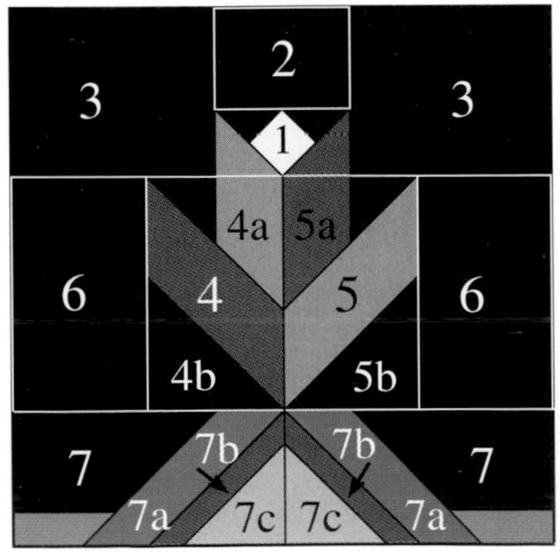

BLOCK A - Make 12

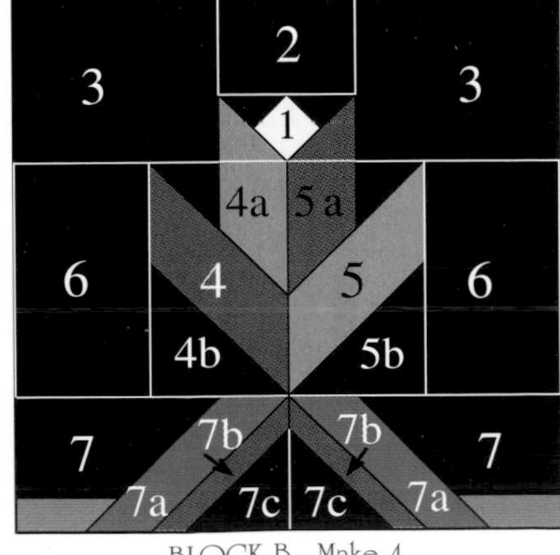

BLOCK B - Make 4

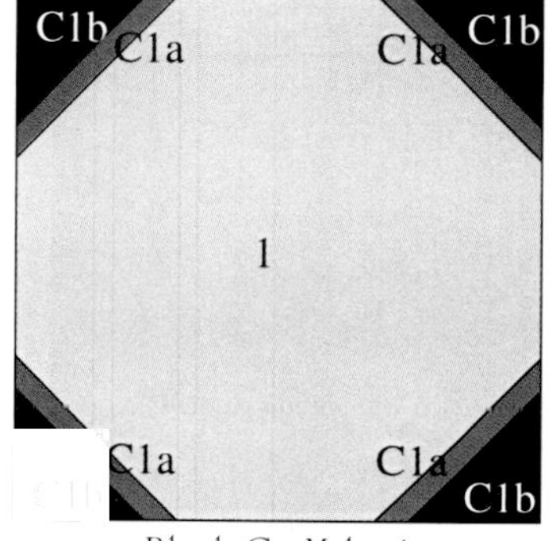

Block C - Make 1

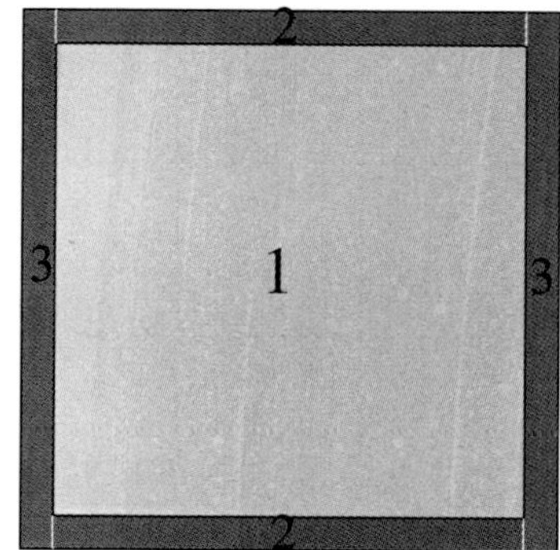

Block D - Make 4

CENTER BLOCK C AND SQUARE BLOCK D

1. Block C is made with multi diagonal corners. Join diagonal corner 1a first. Press out; then add diagonal corner 1b to complete the block.
2. For Block D, join units D2 to top and bottom of Unit 1; then add Unit D3 to opposite sides to complete block.

QUILT ASSEMBLY

1. Use diagonal corner technique to make four of Unit Q1.
2. To assemble quilt, begin with top row and join Unit Q1-Block A-Block B-Block A- and Unit Q1, turned to mirror image Unit Q1 on left. Make two of these rows.
3. For Row 2 of quilt, refer to diagram below for correct position of flower blocks. Join Block A-Block D-Block A-Block D and Block A in a row as shown with flowers facing the different directions as shown.
4. For Row 3, join Block B-Block A-Block C-Block A- and Block B as shown. Be as accurate as possible when joining all blocks, as matching seams is important.
5. For Row 4, repeat procedure in Step 3, referring to illustration with center flower Block A facing down, rather than up.
6. Join rows 1 and 2, carefully matching corner seams. Join center row to row 2. Pin carefully where center diagonal seams cross.
7. Join Row 4 to bottom row; then add to center row of quilt.
8. Join pieced Border Q2 to top and bottom of quilt as shown. Join pieced Border Q3 to opposite sides of quilt.

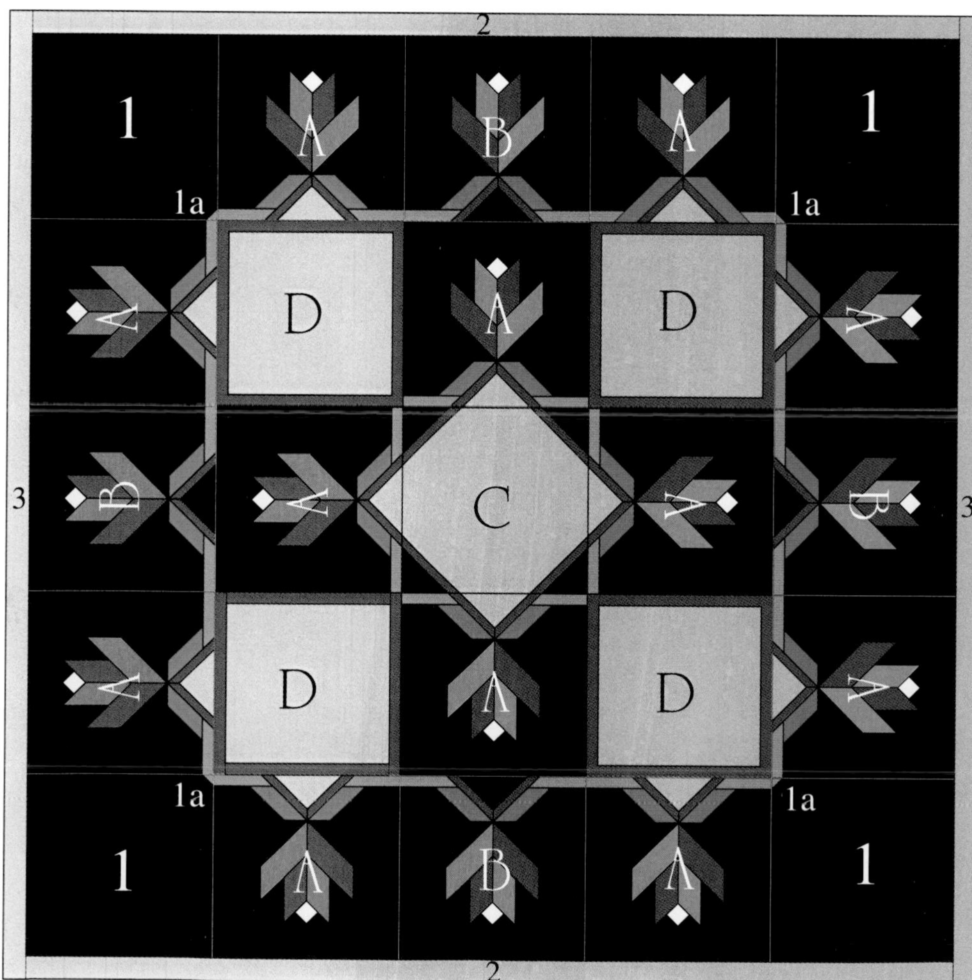

QUILTING & FINISHING

1. We quilted hearts in large, open blocks and Q1 corner blocks. Stitch in ditch around all patchwork.
2. Make 265" of straight-grain, french fold binding from Fabric V, and bind your quilt.

Quilting Friendships:

Pam
Robert
Chris
Pat
Karen
Mindy
Faye
Gigi
Jill
Sarah
Suzanne
Wanda
Calvin
Ryan
Dallas

My Heritage.....

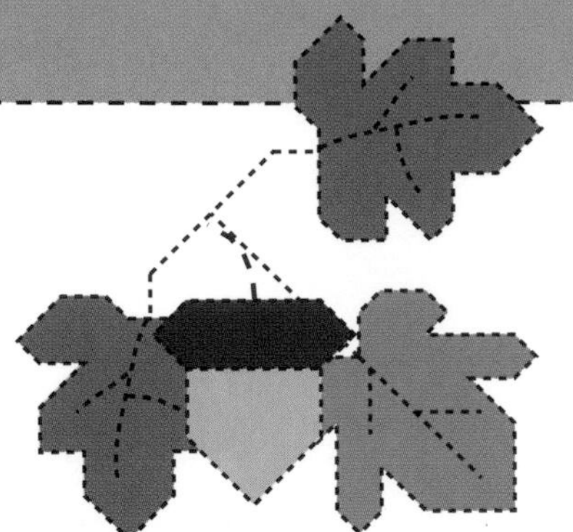

- Making Diagonal Ends
- Making Diagonal Corners

Video Demonstration Take 1

Finished size: 44 1/4" x 56 1/4"
Squirrel blocks A & B: 7 1/2" x 12 3/4"
Leaf blocks C, D, E, F, G, H, I, and J: 5 1/4" square
Acorn blocks: K, L, M, and N: 4 1/2" square
Large leaf blocks O and P: 6" square

MATERIALS

Fabric I 1/2 yard (need exactly 16 3/8")
(metallic gold print)
Fabric II 1/2 yard (need exactly 16 1/8"
(light olive print)
Fabric III 1/4 yard (need exactly 8 1/4")
(tan print)
Fabric IV 1 1/8 yards (need exactly 38 1/2")
(dark brown print)
Fabric V 1/4 yard (need exactly 5")
(dark brown check)
Backing 2 5/8 yards

Fabric VI 1/4 yard (need exactly 7")
(gold stripe)
Fabric VII 1/4 yard (need exactly 6 7/8")
(gold textured print)
Fabric VIII 5/8 yard (need exactly 21 3/4")
(medium olive print)
Fabric IX 1/4 yard (need exactly 4 3/4")
(dark olive check)
Fabric X 1/4 yard (need exactly 7 1/2")
(dark olive print)

CUTTING

Cutting instructions shown in red indicate that the quantity of units are combined and cut in 2 or more different places to conserve fabric. *NOTE: All "Q" units in cutting instructions stand for "quilt top". These are units that are not incorporated into blocks.*

From Fabric I, cut: (metallic gold print)
- One 3 1/8" wide strip. From this, cut:
  - Four – 3 1/8" x 9 1/2" (Q4)
- One 2 3/4" wide strip. From this, cut:
  - Four – 2 3/4" x 6 1/2" (Q39)
  - Four – 2 3/4" squares (A12a, B12a)
- Three 2" wide strips. From these and scrap, cut:
  - Four – 2" x 11" (Q3)
  - Four – 2" x 5" (A20, B20)
  - Eight – 2" x 2 3/4" (A2, A9, B2, B9)
  - Twenty – 2" squares (A4b, A17a, A19a, B4b, B17a, B19a)
- Two 1 5/8" wide strips. From these, cut:
  - Four – 1 5/8" x 13 5/8" (Q6)
  - Four – 1 1/4" x 3 1/2" (A16, B16)
  - **Two – 1 1/4" x 2" (A7, A14, B7, B14)**
- One 1 1/4" wide strip. From this, cut:
  - **Six – 1 1/4" x 2" (add to A7, A14, B7, B14)**
  - Twenty-four – 1 1/4" squares (A6a, A8b, A10a, A11a, A13a, B6a, B8b, B10a, B11a, B13a)

From Fabric II, cut: (light olive print)
- One 6 7/8" wide strip. From this, cut:
  - Two – 2 3/4" x 6 7/8" (Q24)
  - Two – 6 1/2" squares (Q32)
  - Two – 3 1/8" x 6 1/2" (Q31)
  - Two – 2" x 6 1/2" (Q2)
  - Two – 1 5/8" x 6 1/2" (Q5)
  - Four – 2" x 5 3/4" (Q12, Q25)
  - Two – 1 1/4" x 2" (E7, F7)

- One 2 3/4" wide strip. From this and scrap, cut:
  - * Four – 2 3/4" squares (A1, B1)
  - * Four – 1 1/4" x 2 3/4" (A15, B15)
  - * Forty-two – 1 1/4" squares (A3a, B3a, E1a, E3a, E4a, E5a, E6a, F1a, F3a, F4a, F5a, F6a, L3a, O1a)
- Two 2" wide strips. From these, cut:
  - * Two - 2" x 8" (Q1)
  - * Two – 2" x 5" (Q30)
  - * Twenty-two – 2" squares (A4a, B4a, E2, F2, E3b, F3b, L1a, N1a)
  - * Two – 1 5/8" x 3 1/2" (Q23)
  - * Two – 1 1/4" x 3 1/2" (A5, B5, L2, N2, Q22)
- Two 1 1/4" wide strips. From these, cut:
  - * Two – 1 1/4" x 5 3/4" (Q11)
  - * Two – 1 1/4" x 5" (Q10)
  - * Sixteen – 1 1/4" x 3 1/2" (add to A5, B5, L2, N2, Q22)

From Fabric III, cut: (tan print)

- One 3 1/2" wide strip. From this, cut:
  - * Six – 3 1/2" squares (K1)
  - * Four – 1 1/4" x 3 1/2" (A13, B13)
  - * Four – 2" x 2 3/4" (A6, B6)
  - * Four – 2" squares (A8, B8)
- One 2 3/4" wide strip. From this, cut:
  - * Four – 2 3/4" x 6 1/2" (A12, B12)
  - * Eight – 1 1/4" x 2 3/4" (A10, A11, B10, B11)
  - * One – 2" x 5" (A18, B18)
- One 2" wide strip. From this, cut:
  - * Three – 2" x 5" (add to A18, B18)
  - * Four – 1 1/4" x 4 1/4" (A16a, B16a)

From Fabric IV, cut: (dark brown print)

- One 6 1/2" wide strip. From this, cut:
  - * Four – 3 1/8" x 6 1/2" (Q36)
  - * Two – 2 3/4" x 6 1/2" (Q37)
  - * Six – 2" x 6 1/2" (Q35)
  - * Four – 1 5/8" x 6 1/2" (Q38)
  - * Four – 1 1/4" x 5" (Q34)
- One 5 3/4" wide strip. From this, cut:
  - * Sixteen – 7/8" x 5 3/4" (Q33)
  - * Eleven – 2" x 5" (L3, M3, N3)
  - * Four – 1 1/4" x 5" (add to Q34)
- Eight 2 1/2" wide strips. Five strips for straight-grain binding. From remainder, cut:
  - * Four – 2" x 4 1/4" (A3, B3)
  - * Thirty-six – 2" squares (C2, C3b, D2, D3b, K1a)
  - * Two– 1 1/4" x 5" (add to Q34)
  - * Four – 1 1/4" x 3 1/2" (K2)
  - * Eight – 1 1/4" x 2" (C7, D7)
- Five 1 1/4" wide strips. From these, cut:
  - * Two– 1 1/4" x 5" (add to Q34)
  - * Eight – 1 1/4" x 3 1/2" (add to K2)
  - * 104 – 1 1/4" squares (A7a, A8a, B7a, B8a, C1a, C3a, C4a, C5a, C6a, D1a, D3a, D4a, D5a, D6a, K3a)

From Fabric V, cut: (dark brown check)

- One 5" wide strip. From this, cut:
  - * Four – 3 1/2" x 5" (A17, B17)
  - * Four – 2" x 5" (A19, B19)
  - * Eight – 2" squares (A18a, B18a)

From Fabric VI, cut: (gold stripe)

- Two 3 1/2" wide strips. From these, cut:
  - * Fifteen – 3 1/2" squares (A4, B4, L1, M1, N1)

From Fabric VII, cut: (gold textured print)

- One 6 7/8" wide strip. From this, cut:
  - * Two – 5 3/4" x 6 7/8" (Q14)
  - * One – 5 3/4" x 6 1/2" (Q26)
  - * One – 1 1/4" x 6 1/2" (Q13)
  - * Six – 2" x 5" (K3)
  - * Two – 2" squares (P4a)
  - * Four – 1 1/4" x 2" (P2, P6)
  - * Six – 1 1/4" squares (P1a, P4b)

From Fabric VIII, cut: (medium olive print)

- One 7 1/4" wide strip. From this, cut:
  - * Two – 2" x 7 1/4" (Q19)
  - * Two – 1 1/4" x 7 1/4" (Q18)
  - * One – 5 3/4" x 6 1/2" (Q8)
  - * One – 1 1/4" x 6 1/2" (Q21)
  - * Two – 2 3/8" x 5 3/4" (Q27)
  - * Ten – 2" x 5 3/4" (Q29, C3, D3)
  - * Two – 1 5/8" x 5 3/4" (Q9)
- One 2 3/4" wide strip. From this, cut:
  - * Eight – 2 3/4" squares (C4, D4)
  - * Four – 1 5/8" x 5" (Q17)
- Four 2" wide strips. From these, cut:
  - * Eighteen – 2" x 2 3/4" (C1, C5, D1, D5, O6)
  - * Forty-four – 2" squares (C6, D6, G2, G3b, H2, H3b, I2, I3b, J2, J3b, M1a, O4a, O5a, P5a, P7)
  - * Two – 1 5/8" x 2" (Q15)
  - * Eight – 1 1/4" x 2" (G7, H7, I7, J7, O2, Q16)
  - * Four – 1 1/4" x 5" (Q20, Q28)
  - * Two – 1 1/4" x 3 1/2" (M2)
- Three 1 1/4" wide strips. From these, cut:
  - * Eight – 1 1/4" x 3 1/2" (add to M2)
  - * Seventy – 1 1/4" squares (G1a, G3a, G4a, G5a, G6a, H1a, H3a, H4a, H5a, H6a, I1a, I3a, I4a, I5a, I6a, J1a, J3a, J4a, J5a, J6a, O1a, O4b, M3a, N3a)

From Fabric IX, cut: (dark olive check)

- One 2 3/4" wide strip. From this, cut:
  - * Two – 2 3/4" x 3 1/2" (O3, O5)
  - * Four – 2 3/4" squares (E4, F4, I4, J4)
  - * Twelve – 2" x 2 3/4" (E1, E5, F1, F5, I1, I5, J1, J5, O1, O4)
- One 2" wide strip. From this, cut:
  - * Four – 2" x 5 3/4" (E3, F3, I3, J3)
  - * Four – 2" squares (E6, F6, I6, J6)

From Fabric X, cut: (dark olive print)

- Two 2 3/4" wide strips. From these, cut:
  - * Two – 2 3/4" x 32 3/4" (Q7)
  - * Two – 2 3/4" x 3 1/2" (P3, P5)
  - * Two – 2 3/4" squares (G4, H4)
- One 2" wide strip. From this, cut:
  - * Two – 2" x 5 3/4" (G3, H3)
  - * Eight – 2" x 2 3/4" (G1, G5, H1, H5, P1, P4)
  - * Two – 2" squares (G6, H6)

ASSEMBLY

SQUIRREL BLOCKS A & B

1. Blocks A and B are constructed in exactly the same way, however they are mirror images. Please refer to illustrations often for correct placement of mirror image units.
2. Use diagonal corner technique to make one each of units 3, 4, 6, 7, 8, 10, 11, 12, 13, 17, 18, and 19.
3. Use diagonal end technique to make one of unit 16.
4. To assemble blocks, begin by joining units 1 and 2; then add Unit 3 to bottom of combined units.

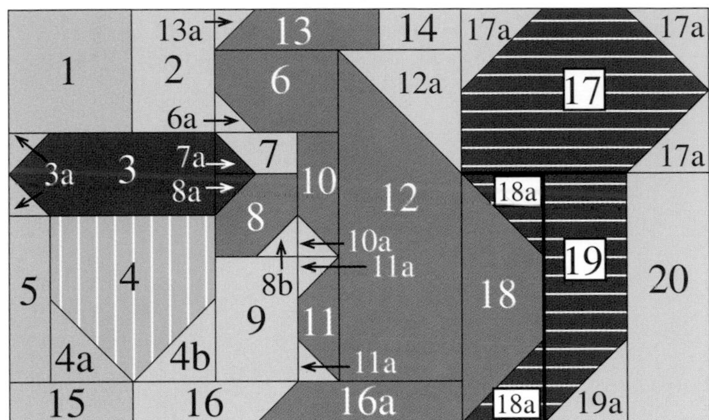

Block A - Make 2.

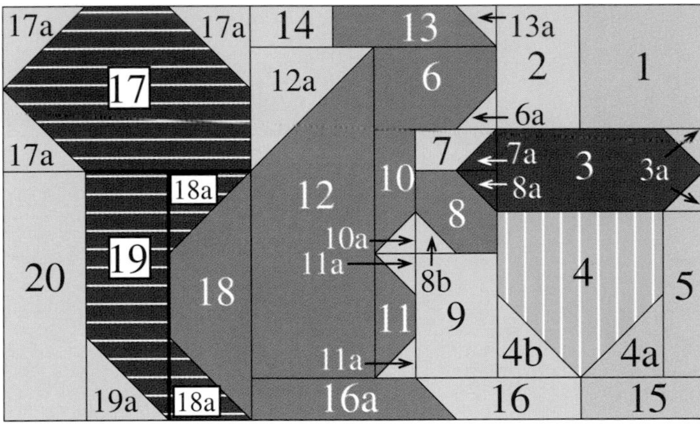

Block B - Make 2.

5. Join units 4-5. Add to combined units 1-3. Join units 7-8-and 9 in a vertical row. Join units 10 and 11; then add combined units 10-11 to combined units 7-9 as shown. Join Unit 6 to top of units 7-11; then add Unit 12 to side. Join units 13 and 14 and join to top of squirrel front units.
6. Join acorn and squirrel front units together. Join units 15 and 16; then add to squirrel bottom. Join units 18-19, and 20 in a row as shown; then add Unit 17 to top of combined tail units. Join tail to squirrel front to complete block. Make 2 of each block.

LEAF BLOCKS C, D, E, F, G, H, I, AND J

1. All leaf blocks are constructed in the same way, although there are mirror images of each. Refer often to illustrations for correct placement of mirror image units. Colors vary also depending upon the blocks. Be careful to check correct colors as well.
2. Use diagonal corner technique to make on each of units 1, 3, 4, 5, and 6.
3. To assemble block, join Unit 2 to opposite sides of Unit 1; then add Unit 3 to bottom of combined units. Join units 4 and 5, matching diagonal corner seams. Join units 6 and 7; then join combined units 4-5 and 6-7. Add these combined units to bottom of Unit 3 to complete block.

Block C - Make 4

2 1a 1 2 1a 3b 3 3a 4a 6 5 4 6a 6a 7 5a 4a

Block D - Make 4

4. Refer to illustrations for correct colors and mirror image units. Make the number of blocks as instructed below each illustration.

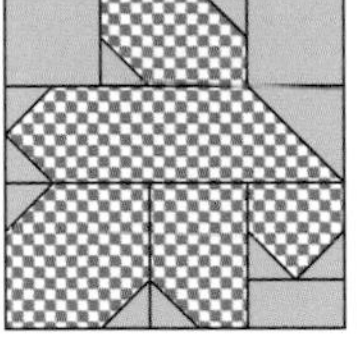

Block E - Make 1

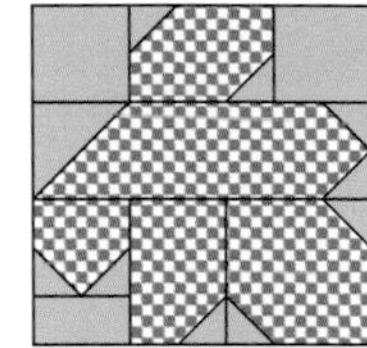

Block F - Make 1

ACORN BLOCKS K, L, M, AND N.

1. Refer to illustrations below and make required number of each block. Check colors carefully for correct placement.
2. Use diagonal corner technique to make one each of units 1 and 3.
3. To assemble, join Unit 2 to opposite sides of Unit 1; then add Unit

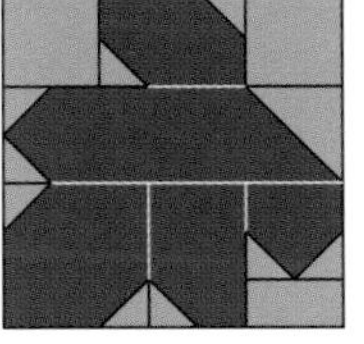

Block G - Make 1

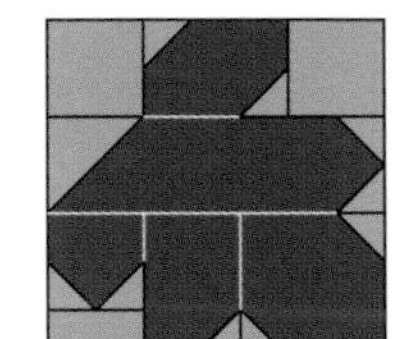

Block H - Make 1

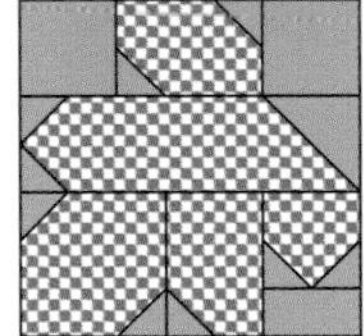

Block I - Make 1

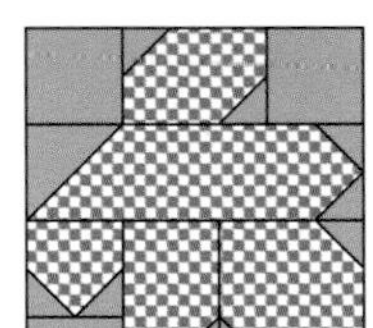

Block J - Make 1

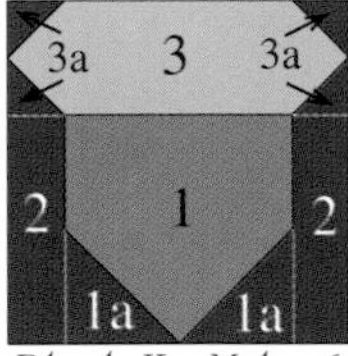

Block K - Make 6

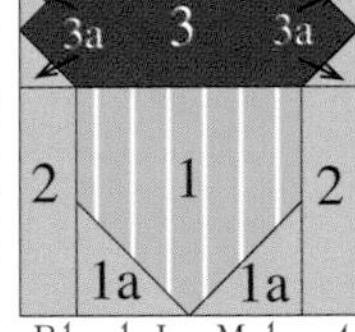

Block L - Make 4

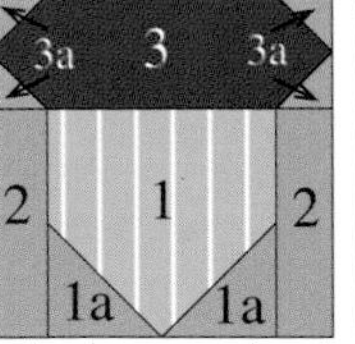

Block M - Make 5

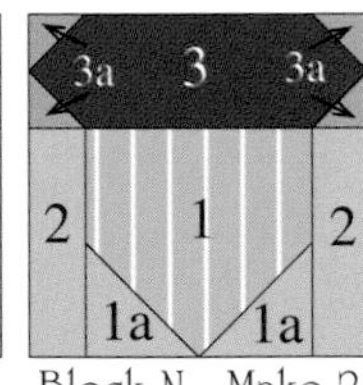

Block N - Make 2

LEAF BLOCKS O AND P

1. For both blocks, use diagonal corner technique to make two each of mirror image units 1 and 4. Use diagonal corner technique to make one of Unit 5.
2. To assemble Block O, join mirror image Units 1 as shown; then add Unit 2 to opposite short ends. Join Unit 4 to opposite sides of Unit 3; then join the two rows of combined units together.

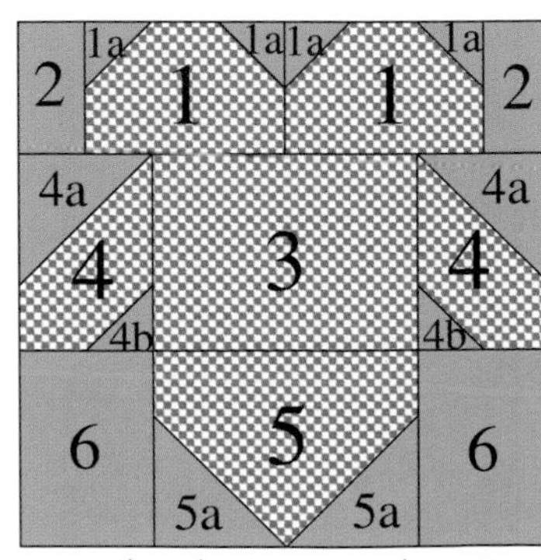

Block O - Make 1

4. Join unit 6 to opposite sides of Unit 5; then add this row to bottom of leaf to complete Block O.

5. The first two rows of Block P are made the same way. For the last row, join units 6 and 7; then add to opposite sides of Unit 5. Join this row to leaf bottom as shown.

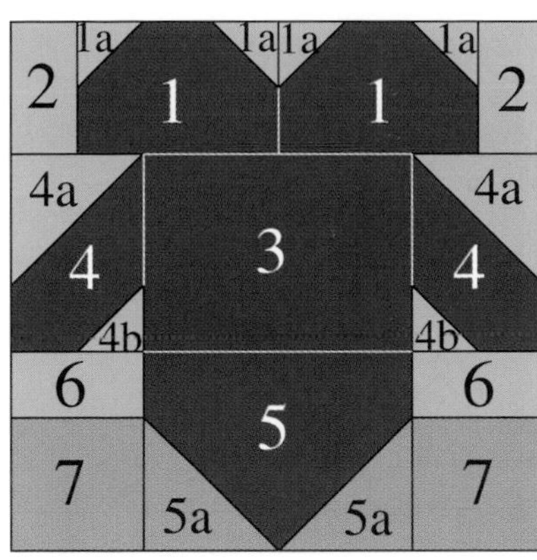

Block P - Make 1

QUILT ASSEMBLY

1. Beginning at top of quilt, join squirrel blocks A and B to opposite sides of Unit Q1. Join units Q3-Q2-Q3 in a horizontal row as shown. Add these combined units to top of squirrels; then join Unit Q4 to opposite sides as shown. Join units Q6-Q5-And Q6 in a horizontal row and add this row to the bottom of the squirrel section. Make two of these sections. Join Unit Q7 to top of one section and to bottom of remaining section. Set the two sections aside.
2. Refer to quilt illustration and join blocks I and J to opposite sides of Unit Q8. Join units Q9 and Q11 and add to opposite sides of leaf blocks I and J. Join Unit Q10 to top of Block L; then join Unit Q12 to sides of Block L as shown. Join the Block L combination to opposite sides of Unit Q11 as shown to complete row. Join this row to bottom of one squirrel section. Refer to illustration for correct placement. Unit Q7 will be at the top of this squirrel section. Be careful to match all seams.
3. Refer to quilt assembly diagram for correct placement of units for next large leaf section. Begin this section by joining Unit Q13 to top of Block P. Join Unit Q20 to opposite sides of Block M; then add Unit Q21 to top of Acorn M. Join the acorn to the bottom of Block P as shown.
4. Join units Q15 and Q23 as shown. Join units Q16 and Q22 in a vertical row as shown. Make 2 of each. Refer to illustration for placement of mirror image units and join the combined units Q15-Q23 and Q16-Q22 to opposite sides of Block N; then add Unit Q24 to bottom as shown. Join these acorn sections to bottom of Unit Q14. Join combined unit Acorn Block N to opposite sides of Leaf/Acorn blocks P and M.
5. To complete this section, join Unit Q17 to top and bottom of Block M. Join Unit Q18 to one side and Unit Q19 to the other as shown, reversing the units for mirror image placement. Join Unit Q25 to right side of leaf Block F. Join another unit Q25 to left side of leaf Block E. Join Acorn Block M to top of leaf blocks E and F a shown so that Unit Q19 is on top of Unit Q25, matching seams. Add this acorn/leaf combination to opposite sides of center section. Join this completed center section to bottom of leaf/acorn row as shown.
6. To assemble the next row, join Unit Q28 to top of Acorn Block M as shown. Join Unit Q27 to one side of Acorn M and Unit Q29 to other side, referring to illustration for correct placement of mirror image units.
7. Join leaf blocks G and H to opposite sides of Unit Q26 as shown; then add Acorn Block M to opposite ends of row, checking placement of Unit Q29. Join this completed row to bottom of quilt top.
8. For remaining row, join Unit Q31 to opposite sides of Block O. Join Unit Q30 to top of Acorn Block L as shown. Add the acorn blocks to opposite sides of Unit Q31; then add Unit Q32 to row ends. Join this row to top of remaining squirrel section matching seams. Join this section to bottom of quilt as shown.
9. For side borders, join Unit Q34 to opposite sides of Acorn Block K. Make six. Join Unit Q33 to opposite sides of Leaf Blocks C and D as shown. Make eight.
10. For left vertical border, begin with Unit Q39, joining it to Unit Q35. Join the remainder in the following order: Block C-Unit Q36-Block K-Unit Q38-Block D-Unit Q36-Block K-Unit Q38-Block D-Unit Q36-Block K-Unit Q35-Block C-Unit Q37-Block K-Unit Q38-Block D-Unit Q35-and Unit Q39.
11. For right vertical border, join units and blocks in same numerical order, reversing the leaf blocks by beginning with Leaf Block D rather than C as shown.
12. Join vertical borders to opposite sides of quilt top.

QUILTING AND FINISHING

1. We incorporated the names of everyone who worked on our book and CD-ROM into the acorn blocks on the quilt. The names were first printed with a fine felt tipped marker, then satin stitched by machine with dark brown thread. The quilt is meant to be a family tree so that you may record your heritage with names from your family.
2. You may record the names with a fabric pen or satin stitch as we did. Should you choose to satin stitch, place tear-away pellon or the stabilizer of your choice behind the area to be stitched. Tear it away upon completion of stitching.
3. Veins in leaves and acorn tops were also satin stitched, along with a few vines.
4. We marked leaf designs for quilting in the empty blocks, and stitched in the ditch around all of the patchwork.
5. Make 215" of straight-grain, french fold binding from 2 1/2" wide strips of Fabric IV and bind your quilt.

Quilt Assembly Diagram

MATERIALS FOR PILLOWS

Finished size: 11 1/4" x 15 3/4"

- Fabric I — 3/8 yard (need exactly 11") (metallic gold print)
- Fabric II — 1/8 yard (need exactly 2 3/4") (light olive print)
- Fabric III — 1/8 yard (need exactly 4") (tan print)
- Fabric IV — 3/4 yard (need exactly 23 1/2") (dark brown print)
- Fabric V — 1/8 yard (need exactly 7 1/4") (dark brown check)
- Fabric VI — Scrap (need exactly 3 1/2" x 7") (gold stripe)

CUTTING

From Fabric I, cut: (metallic gold print)

- One 11" wide strip. From this, cut:
  - * Four – 1 5/8" x 11" (pillow top 2 and 4)
  - * Two – 1 1/4" x 10 1/4" (pillow top 6)
  - * Two – 2" x 5" (A20)
  - * Two – 1 1/4" x 3 1/2" (A16)
  - * Two – 2 3/4" squares (A12a)
  - * Four – 2" x 2 3/4" (A2, A9)
  - * Ten – 2" squares (A4b, A17a, A19a)
  - * Four – 1 1/4" x 2" (A7, A14)
  - * Twelve – 1 1/4" squares (A6a, A8b, A10a, A11a, A13a)

From Fabric II, cut: (light olive print)

- One 2 3/4" wide strip. From this, cut:
  - * Two – 2 3/4" squares (A1)
  - * Four – 1 5/8" x 2 3/4" (pillow top 1 and 3)
  - * Two – 1 1/4" x 2 3/4" (A15)
  - * Two – 2" squares (A4a)
  - * Two – 1 1/4" x 10 1/4" (pillow top 5)
  - * Two – 1 1/4" x 3 1/2" (A5)
  - * Four – 1 1/4" squares (A3a)

From Fabric III, cut: (tan print)

- One 2 3/4" wide strip. From this, cut:
  - * Two – 2 3/4" x 6 1/2" (A12)
  - * Two – 2" x 2 3/4" (A6)
  - * Four – 1 1/4" x 2 3/4" (A10, A11)
  - * Two – 2" x 5" (A18)
  - * Two – 2" squares (A8)
  - * Two – 1 1/4" x 4 1/4" (A16a)
- One 1 1/4" wide strip. From this, cut:
  - * Two – 1 1/4" x 3 1/2" (A13)

From Fabric IV, cut: (dark brown print)

- Two 11 3/4" wide strips. From these, cut:
  - * Two – 11 3/4" x 13 1/2" (long pillow backs)
  - * Two – 7 1/2" x 11 3/4" (short pillow backs)
  - * Two – 2" x 4 1/4" (A3)
  - * Four – 1 1/4" squares (A7a, A8a)

From Fabric V, cut: (dark brown check)

- One 3 1/2" wide strip. From this, cut:
  - * Two – 3 1/2" x 5" (A17)
  - * Two – 2" x 5" (A19)
  - * Four – 2" squares (A18a)
- Three 1 1/4" wide strips. From these, cut:
  - * Four – 1 1/4" x 14 3/4" (pillow top 7)
  - * Four – 1 1/4" x 11 3/4" (pillow top 8)

From Fabric VI, cut: (gold stripe)

- One 3 1/2" x 7" piece. From this, cut:
  - * Two – 3 1/2" squares (A4)

MY HERITAGE PILLOWS

1. Cut all pieces from the cutting list for pillows and assemble blocks A & B as instructed for quilt.
2. To complete pillow tops, join pillow top units 1 and 2. Join to bottom of squirrel blocks. Join pillow top units 3 and 4; then add to top of squirrel blocks.
3. Refer to illustrations for mirror image placement, and join pillow top units 5 and 6 to opposite sides of pillow top. Join borders 7 to top and bottom of pillow top; then add borders 8 to opposite sides.
4. For pillow backs, press under 1/4" on each 11 3/4" side of pillow backs; then press under another 1/4". Top stitch hem in place. Pin pillow backs right sides facing on top of pillow top. Backs will overlap. Use 1/4" seam and stitch around outside of pillow.
5. Turn pillow right side out and press. Top stitch in the ditch around the borders, forming a small flange.
6. Make pillow forms 1" larger all the way around than the finished pillow size.

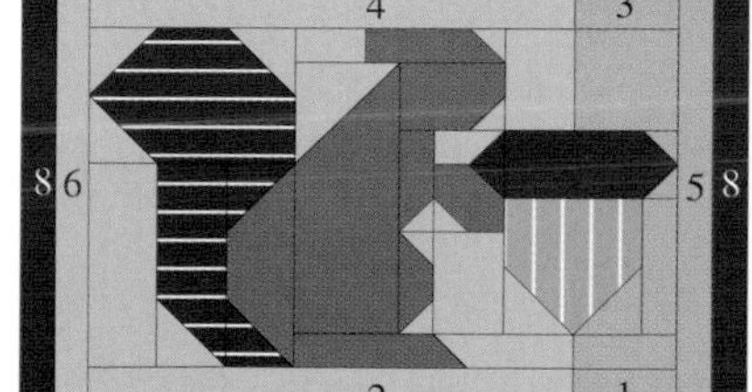

My Heritage
Date:

The
New
Century
Grandmother

Colorado Wedding

Finished Size: 88" x 103"

On A Personal Note:

I know so many quilter's (including me) who have always wanted to make this beautiful, traditional quilt, but have been intimidated by the curved piecing and time consuming job. Robert designed this "quick pieced" version, and the two of us cut and pieced the top in 5 days. I selected a simple palette of only six fabrics to make the fabric selection a breeze. So take heart! Now you can do it too! Additional color choices are on our CD-ROM.

MATERIALS

Fabric I (light blue batik)	1 1/4 yards (need exactly 44")
Fabric II (medium blue print)	1 7/8 yards (need exactly 67")
Fabric III (light green batik)	1 3/8 yards (need exactly 48")
Fabric IV (med/dark green print)	1 3/4 yards (need exactly 61")
Fabric V (unbleached muslin)	5 5/8 yards (need exactly 198")
Fabric VI (navy batik)	2 1/4 yards (need exactly 79")
Backing:	7 3/4 yards

CUTTING

From Fabric I, cut: (light blue batik)
- Cut ten 2 1/2" strips for Strip Sets 1 & 3.

From Fabric II, cut: (medium blue print)
- Three 4 1/2" wide strips. From these, cut:
  - * Forty-eight – 2 1/2" x 4 1/2" (C1, D1)
- One 2 7/8" wide strip. From this, cut:
  - * Twelve – 2 7/8" sq. Cut 10 in half diagonally (E1b, F1-triangle-square, F1b, G1 triangle-square, G1b)
- Cut strip to 2 1/2" width. From this, cut:
  - * Three – 2 1/2" squares (E1a, I1a)
- Cut twenty 2 1/2" wide strips. Ten for Strip Sets 1 & 3.

From remainder, cut:
  - * 153 – 2 1/2" squares (E1a, I1a)
  - * Two – 2 1/2" x 4 1/2" (C1, D1)

From Fabric III, cut: (light green batik)
- Cut nineteen 2 1/2" wide strips for Strip Sets 1, 2, & 3.

From Fabric IV, cut: (med./dark green print)
- Fifteen 3 3/8" strips for Strip Set 2.
- Four 2 1/2" strips for Strip Set 3.

From Fabric V, cut: (unbleached muslin)
- Eight 12 1/2" wide strips. From these, cut:
  - * Seventy-one – 4 1/2" x 12 1/2" (H1, I1)
- Three 8 1/2" wide strips. From these, cut:
  - * Twenty-seven – 4 1/2" x 8 1/2" (A1)
- From scrap, cut:
  - * Three – 4 1/2" x 8 1/2" (A1)
  - * Twelve – 4 1/2" squares (A3)
  - * Six – 2 1/2" x 4 1/2" (A4)
- Sixteen 4 1/2" wide strips. From these, cut:
  - * Three – 4 1/2" x 8 1/2" (A1)
  - * 108 – 4 1/2" squares (A3)
  - * Fifty-four – 2 1/2" x 4 1/2" (A4)

From Fabric VI, cut: (navy batik)
- Use 1 yard for 2 1/2" wide bias binding.
- One 2 7/8" wide strip. From this, cut:
  - * Fourteen – 2 7/8" squares. Cut 12 in half diagonally (D1b, F1 triangle-squares, F1a, G1 triangle-squares, F1a)
- Sixteen 2 1/2" wide strips. From these, cut:
  - * Eight – 2 1/2" x 4 1/2" (E1)
  - * 244 – 2 1/2" squares (C1a, D1a, H1a)

ASSEMBLY

STRIP SETS

1. Refer to illustrations below and begin by making Strip Set 1 as shown. Cut segments as directed. Repeat this procedure for all three strip sets.

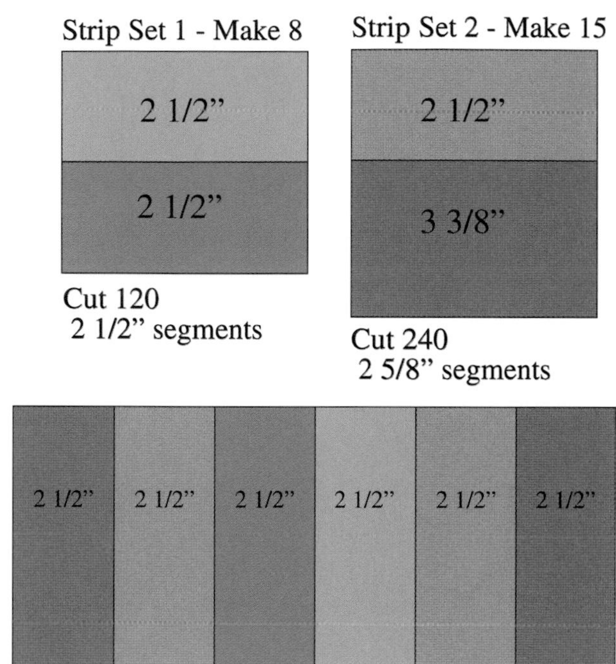

Strip Set 3 - Make 2. Cut 22 - 2 1/2" segments.

BLOCK A, UNIT 3 CORNERS

1. Using segments cut from Strip Set 2, refer to illustration below and cut diagonals as shown. You will cut 120 "righties", and 120 "lefties."

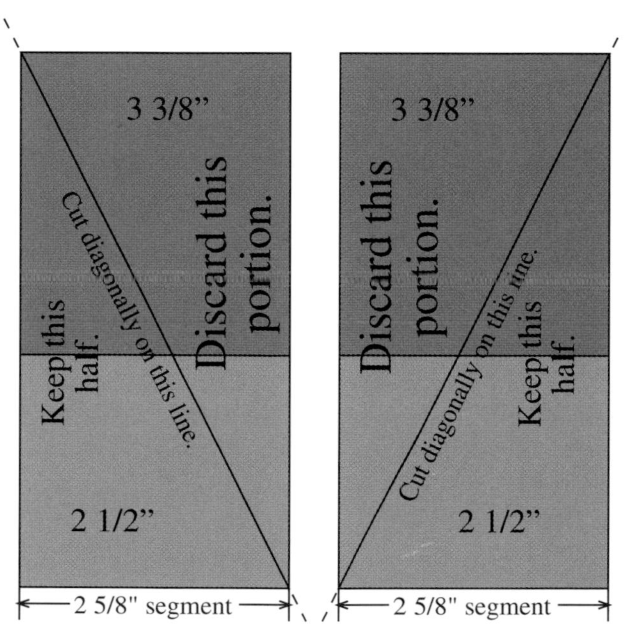

Cut 120 of each for Block A, Unit 3

2. Using template pattern, cut a template from plastic making sure that your template is accurately cut according to the pattern given.,

3. Follow the steps given below to complete Block A, Unit 3 corner. Make 120 corners.

Step 1

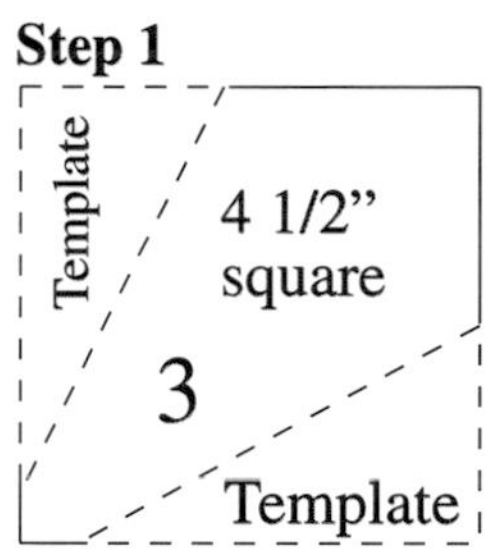

Lay plastic template on 4 1/2" square represented by dashed line. Draw diagonal lines as shown above.

Step 2

Point of strip set segment extends 1/4".

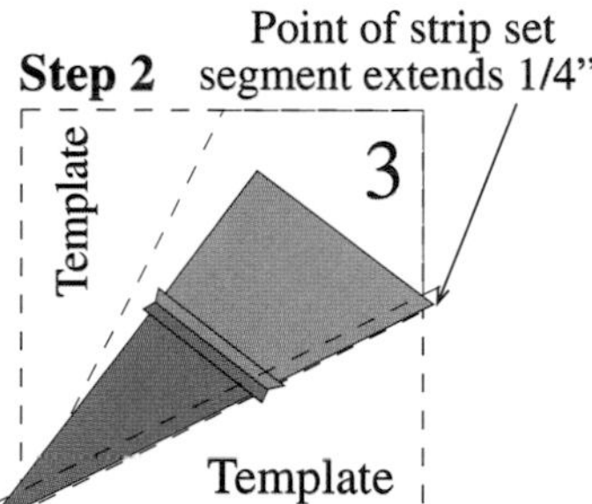

Place cut Strip Set 2 segment along diagonal line drawn, with 1/4" of point extending as shown. Stitch in place using 1/4" seam.

Step 3

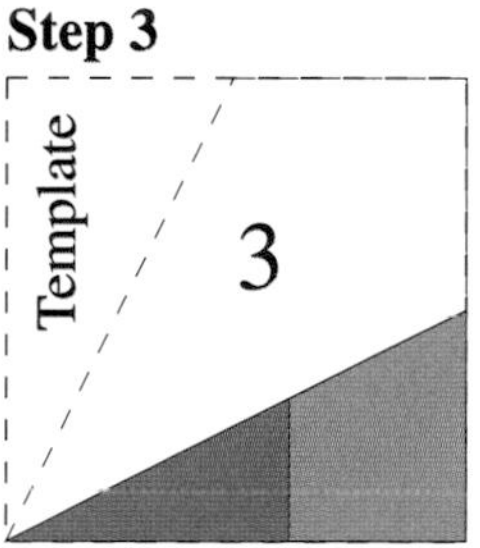

Press sewn segment in place.

Step 4

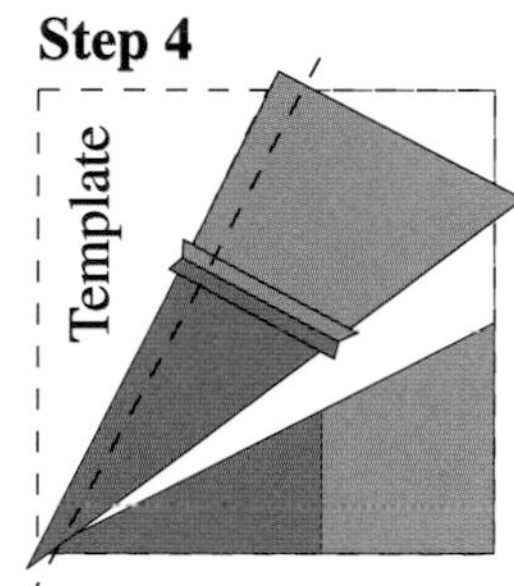

Place the other cut segment that is slanted in the opposite direction along remaining diagonal line with 1/4" of point extending. Stitch in place with 1/4" seam.

Step 5

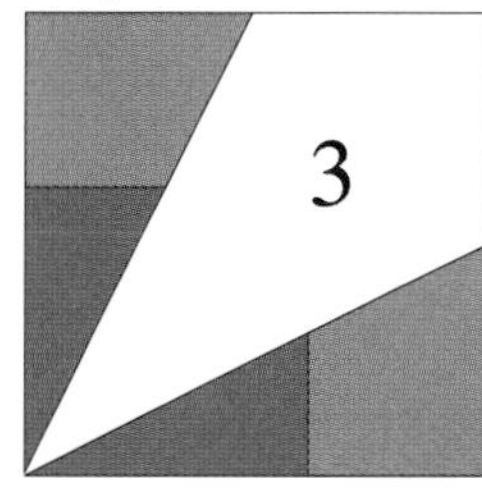

Press second sewn segment in place to complete corner.

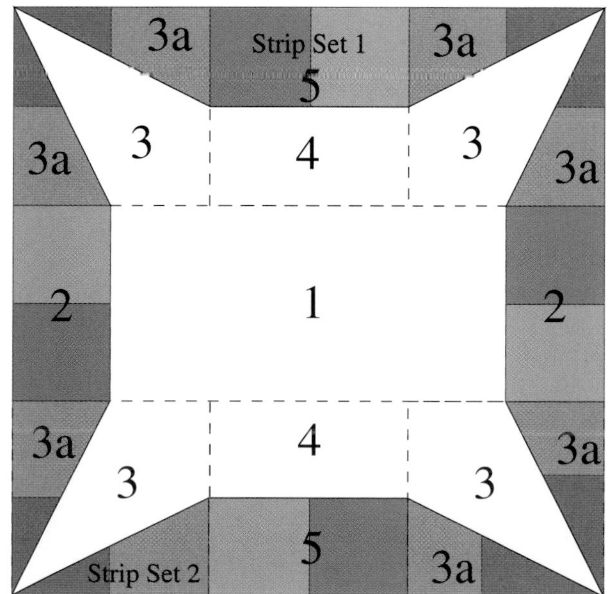

Block A - Make 30

Completing Block A.

1. Join cut segments of Strip Set 1 to Unit 4 as shown in block illustration. Make two for each block.
2. Join cut segments of Strip Set 1 to opposite sides of center Unit 1 as illustrated. Make sure that your strip set segments are placed as shown in illustration.
3. To assemble block, begin by joining Unit 3 corners to opposite sides of combined units 4 and 5. Make two. Join the three sections now completed to opposite long sides of combined units 1 and 2 to complete the block. Make 30 blocks.

Block B.

1. Block B is the outside scalloped edge of the quilt. It is also Strip Set 3 cut into the segments as instructed. To complete this block, trim off corners on a diagonal as shown.

Cut 1 from template plastic

This line even with square

This line even with square

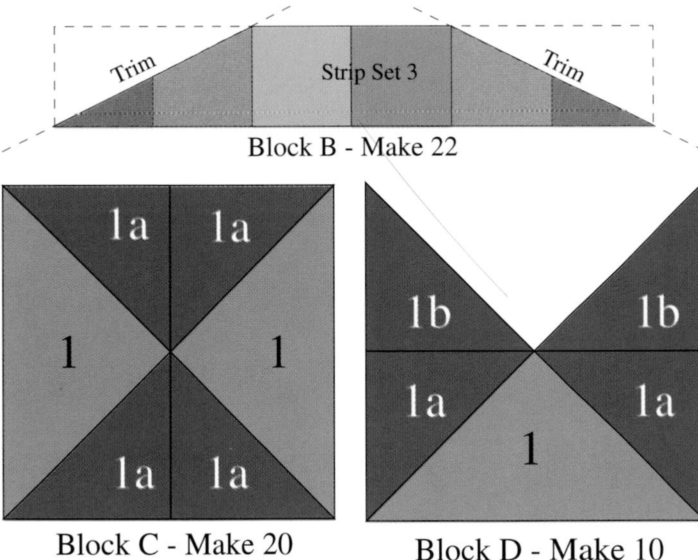

Block B - Make 22

Block C - Make 20

Block D - Make 10

Block C

1. Block C is two combined Flying Geese blocks. Use diagonal corner technique to make forty of Unit 1; then join the two sections together as shown, matching seams.

Block D

1. Use diagonal corner technique to make ten Flying Geese blocks for Unit 1. Join the 45° triangles of Fabric VI to the top of the block as shown, one at a time and press outwards.

Block E

1. Follow the step for making Block D to make Block E. The only difference is that Fabrics II and VI are reversed.

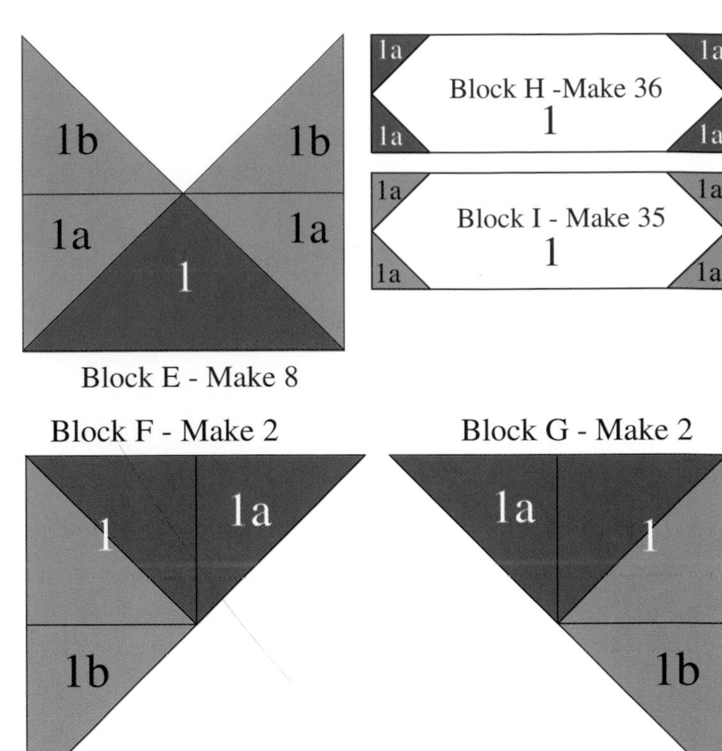

Block H -Make 36

Block I - Make 35

Block E - Make 8

Block F - Make 2

Block G - Make 2

Blocks F and G

1. Place 2 7/8" squares of fabrics II and VI right sides together, and using The Angler 2™, make one half square triangle for each block. Remember, when the half square triangles are completed and cut apart, one sewn square = two half square triangles.
2. Join your remaining triangles of Fabrics II and VI to each triangle-square as shown, making sure to position your half square triangles and triangles correctly as the blocks are mirror images.
3. These blocks are for quilt corners. Make two of each.

Blocks H and I

1. Use diagonal corner technique to make 36 of Block H and 35 of Block I.

Quilt Assembly

1. The quilt is assembled in simple rows and goes quickly. Begin with Row 1 and join four E blocks, and five I blocks as shown. Join an F block to left corner and a G block to right corner. Complete the row by adding the B blocks to the top of each I block. Make two of these rows, the second being for Row 13.
2. Row 2 is made by joining five A blocks and six H blocks. To complete the row, join B blocks to opposite short ends. Make six of these rows for rows 2, 4, 6, 8, 10, and 12.
3. Row 3 is made by joining five I blocks with four C blocks as shown. Join D blocks to opposite short ends of the row. Make five of these rows for rows 3, 5, 7, 9, and 11.
4. Refer to the quilt assembly diagram and join all rows together beginning with Row 1 as shown.

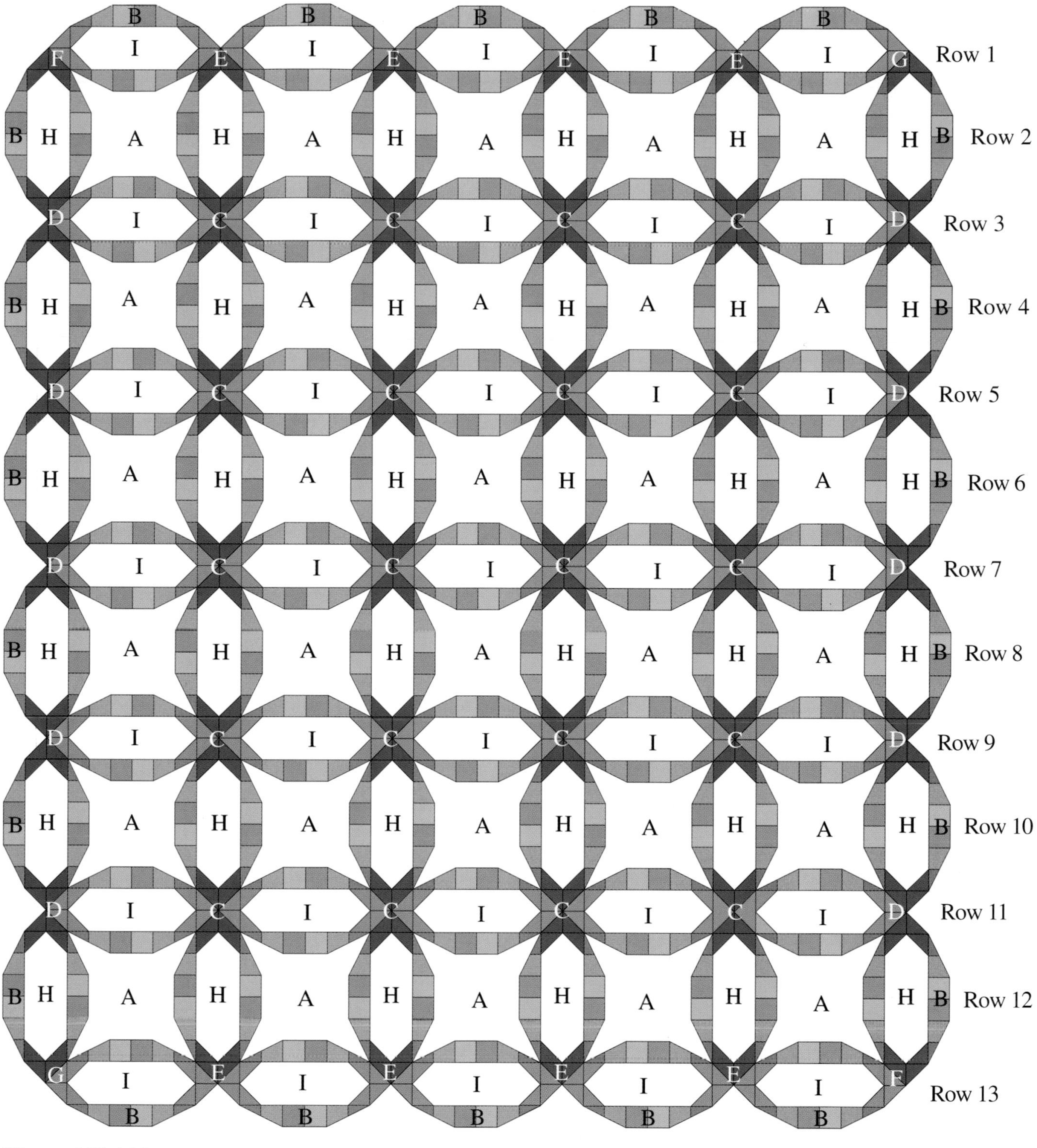

B B B B B
F I E I E I E I E I G Row 1
B H A H A H A H A H A H B Row 2
D I C I C I C I C I D Row 3
B H A H A H A H A H A H B Row 4
D I C I C I C I C I D Row 5
B H A H A H A H A H A H B Row 6
D I C I C I C I C I D Row 7
B H A H A H A H A H A H B Row 8
D I C I C I C I C I D Row 9
B H A H A H A H A H A H B Row 10
D I C I C I C I C I D Row 11
B H A H A H A H A H A H B Row 12
G I E I E I E I E I F Row 13
B B B B B

Quilting and Finishing

1. We used June Tailor "Mix 'n Match" Templates for Quilter's. For the motif in Block A center, we used circles A, E and F, flower template C, and leaf templates A and C.
2. For the motif in Blocks H and I, we used flower template D, leaf templates A and C, and circle template A.
3. Quilt "in the ditch" around all patchwork and make 400" of 2 1/2" wide bias binding and bind your quilt.

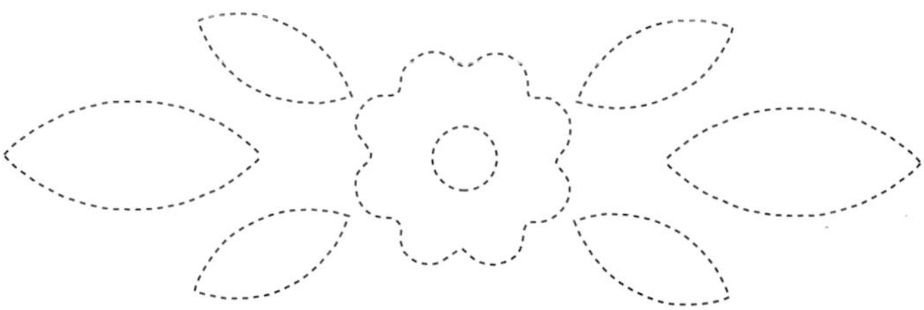

Grandma's Wonderful Quilts: